Praise for

Sabotaged by Emotions

This is truly an inspirational work. Stacey describes her journey through depression by being founded in her faith in conjunction with Dialectical Behavior Therapy (DBT) techniques to bring healing. This book would be a valuable resource and a story of hope for anyone suffering from depression.

Robert (Licensed Professional Counselor, L.P.C.)

Stacey has given all who have gone through the 'tunnel of darkness' insights that few have had the words or images (or courage) to share. Having walked and prayed with her through this journey, I am pleased to see where God has led her. May this story with her insights be a source of hope to all who read this book.

Mike (Pastor of Community & Global Ministries, Depression Survivor)

Stacey's clarity in writing is amazing. I am so impressed with how God is speaking to her and working through her in the midst of all of this depression. She is definitely an example of the "abiding" life.

Christy (Wife, Mother, and Cancer Survivor)

OMG, Girl!!! This is great! You're right, it reads like a devotional. I enjoyed it very much. It is very soothing and comforting with the scripture being perfect! It's eloquent.

Julie (Teacher and Water Aerobics Instructor)

This was awesome! It blew me away. I love what I read. It was so spot on about depression and what she went through and how she combats it. I especially liked the characteristics that she pointed out about how she feels about herself.

Betty (Mother and Depression Survivor)

I have worked with people who struggled with depression for over thirty years. I have never heard anyone express themselves so eloquently about the actual process depressed individuals experience. She has given a voice and a face to this mysterious disorder through her soul searching quiet times. I am so glad God gave her the talent of pouring out her heart when she is hurting. Many will be blessed by her endeavor. I really believe that this book will minister to family, friends, and significant others of those going through depression.

Mary Lou (MS, CPS, CRC and Cancer Survivor)

Sabotaged by EMotioNs...

My Journey toward Inner Healing

By Stacey W. Smith

Sabotaged by Emotions
My Journey towards Inner Healing
by Stacey W Smith

Printed in the United States of America

ISBN 9781622304714

Unless otherwise indicated, Bible quotations are taken from The HOLY BIBLE, NEW INTERNATIONAL VERSION, NIV. Copyright © 1973, 1978, 1984 by International Bible Society..

Email: sowingseedsforeternity@gmail.com

www.xulonpress.com

Prayer

"God, it has been very difficult this last ten years, especially the last two years. I am suffering from severe depression and possibly Borderline Personality Disorder. God, even though I am mentally ill, I can still hear Your still small voice in my spirit. My spirit is alive and well! You have blessed my intimate time and devotional times. My heart reaches out to You in worship. I focus on my Bible verses and listen as You speak in my spirit. I am learning how to discern what You are telling me so I can capture it on paper. My memory is impaired so I have difficulty remembering what You speak my heart. Writing has become an excellent tool so I can capture all the encouragement directly from You, Lord. Your work in my life has been written down so I won't forget. When I read the chapters at a later time, the words encourage me to keep on applying the lessons that You taught me. My hope is that this book will encourage others who suffer from emotional issues. Lord, I also hope that this book will be an encouragement to families and support personnel" (Stacey W. Smith).

"WAIT QUIETLY IN MY PRESENCE while My thoughts form silently in the depths of your being. Do not try to rush this process, because hurry keeps your heart earthbound. I am the Creator of the entire universe, yet I choose to make My humble home in your heart. It is there where I speak to you in holy whispers. Ask My Spirit to quiet your mind so that you can hear *My still, small voice* within you. I am speaking to you continually: words of Life...Peace...Love. Tune your heart to receive these messages of abundant blessing. Lay your requests before Me and wait in expectation" (Young, 2004, p. 276).

Insight

Sabotaged by Emotions is a three year journal covering Stacey's intense struggle with depression. She starts out with her history then she focuses on the last ten years of her life. The chapters were written while she was experiencing severe depression and some chapters while in a crisis.

Stacey poured her heart into writing because it was helping her to really internalize and apply the concepts from her counseling sessions. Due to her memory challenges she repeats concepts to help her remember them. Many chapters repeat the ideas of God's peace and unconditional love because it took so much work to really embrace these positive qualities. She also repeats what she has accomplished in her life out of desperation to feel valuable. She is slowly learning that her value is not based on what she has done, but on who she is.

Dedication

This book was written for four reasons. First, I wrote it to help me remember the therapy and what the Lord spoke in my heart while I was applying Dialectical Behavior Therapy (DBT) and having electroconvulsive therapy (ECT). Second, I wrote this book for my family. I didn't want them to see this as a "sick" time, but actually as a time of great inner healing. I wanted my husband, Roger, to know what is going on in my inner life so he can have an opportunity to help me make wise decisions. I wanted to give my three married daughters, Angela, Kristen, and Cheri a glimpse of my inner life to help them process the immense changes in my personal life as well as family life. I want to give my two younger daughters, Rachel and Helen, the history of my life to help them understand why my moods were so erratic, and how God is restoring me back to inner peace. Third, I wrote this book for my psychiatrists, my counselors, my pastors, and others who were guiding me in the process of inner healing. Lastly, I wrote this book for others who struggle with emotional instability and suicide ideation. My hope is that as the Lord brings comfort to me during the intense depression, that my story would bring comfort to others who struggle with their own emotional issues.

Disclaimer:

My story is not meant to give answers or solutions to depression and emotional instability. I am simply communicating my story about my struggles and frustrations with severe depression. I would like to share the skills and insights that I am learning to help others who deal with their own mood disorder. My desire is to share what I have been through to let those who also struggle with emotional issues and suicide ideation know they are not alone and that there is hope for healing.

Table of Contents

Part 3: *Treating the Whole Body* 137

Part 4: *Combating Severe Depression* 157

Part 5: *Recovery Is Possible* 233

Part 1

History Gives Insight

Chapter 1

My Childhood Years

Living in God's Living Room in the Mountains

The Northwest portion of the United States is a beautiful place to grow up. I was born in Spokane, Washington. My family moved to Great Falls in the plains of Montana where wheat fields covered the horizon. A couple of years later we moved to the mountainous region of western Montana called Missoula, where I spent the rest of my childhood with my two sisters, one older and one younger. We also had a highly trained German shepherd name Cajun. She was a Seeing Eye dog that had some minor health issues. Mom and Dad brought her home, and mom continued to train her. We also had hours and hours of fun camping, backpacking, and snow skiing. The outdoors was my salvation.

Many good things took place in my childhood. My parents loved to go camping, but we did not camp in the state campgrounds—no way. We drove up into the high mountains on forest service roads and then on old rutted logging roads to camp along the shores of the remotest lakes in Montana, Idaho, and Washington. The scenery was breathtaking. We saw swans with the reflection of snowcapped mountains behind them in the water. We saw deer, elk, bear, and moose. One time a moose walked right through our campsite, waded along the lake shore, swam across the middle of the lake, and climbed up over a ridge on the far side of a lake! I have many more memories of zillions of mosquitoes, a creek toad we named Rockefella, frogs, tadpoles, and a snipe hunt that my dad sent us on. By the way, my sisters and I wandered around the woods looking for a snipe. We realized that dad had tricked us so we decided to trick him back. We put a rock in the bag and came back to camp, moving the bag to make it look like a live animal. Much to our delight, my parents were afraid of what we had caught in the bag until we dumped out our rock. Ha! Ha! By the way, my parents drank beer while camping but I didn't care because I was playing in *God's living room*. That's what dad called the wilderness. Camping was part of my emotional salvation to keep my mind off the painful home life. I put down all my defenses and opened my arms wide to embrace the beauty of creation.

> "How precious are My children who are awed by nature's beauty; this opens them up to My holy Presence. Even before you knew Me personally, you responded to My creation with wonder." (Young, 2004, p.221).

We backpacked several times but one time I remember was in the Bitterroot Mountains. It was in July and hot in Missoula. We hiked along Bass Creek up into the mountain to a lake where we planned to set up camp. We had to cross the creek several times to stay on the trail. Sometimes we waded through the creek which was very cold, and other times we walked on slippery logs crossing over the creek. We walked the trail through the trees with Cajun running the trail up for maybe a mile and then ran down the trail behind us. She never seemed to tire. Every once in a while we would hear her barking through the trees and figured that she had found a deer to chase. We really did hope she wouldn't find a porcupine. They were bad news for her.

As we walked the trail into the high mountains the summer temperature cooled down significantly. When we finally reached the lake, much to our surprise there was a full-fledged blizzard! It was so beautiful but freezing cold! We hiked back down the mountain a ways to set up camp in a clearing full of wild flowers. One thing I remember on that backpacking trip was that when we got thirsty we would have one of our sisters take our cup off the backpack, and we would dip it in the creek to get some of that wonderful fresh cold water. It tasted like mountain spring water! I don't know how smart we were, but we never suffered for it.

Skiing in the Mountains of Montana

My parents were experienced downhill skiers and taught all three of us girls how to ski. We spent many weekends skiing at Snowbowl, just outside Missoula. Sometimes we went up north to Kalispell to ski at Whitefish. The scenery was breath taking. Snow covered trees lined the slope, and the view from the top of the ski slope into the mountain range was beautiful. The snow covered mountains are breathtaking.

I was a hellion on skis. Look out world, here Stacey's coming down the slope! You better get out of the way or else! My mom used to lecture me about safety all the time. My dad frequently took me to the advanced slope. (I think he thought I was his son since I was so athletic.) I couldn't ski those slopes! In fact, one time I just flipped over on my back and slid all the way down the slope, head first. The ski patrol checked on me to make sure I was alright. I was safer on my back than skiing! Once again being in the great outdoors helped me to forget about the pain of rejection that I was beginning to feel while in middle school. I just pushed that pain way deep down inside me and forgot about it.

Creativity Abounds

I remember the creativity my parents possessed. My mother was an artist. She mainly painted water color pictures and oil paintings. She was very talented. I remember one picture she painted was in the mountains in the winter. My uncle started a fire to burn an old snag. There was snow everywhere but the snag burned amazingly bright. The top of the snag was consumed with a fire ball! Dad took pictures then mom painted the scene with oil paint. She also painted old barns from the Missoula valley with water color. I am blessed to have two of her pictures hanging on a wall in my living room. My father was an entrepreneur which requires tremendous creativity. For a while he ran gas stations and repaired cars. The amazing thing is that he taught himself electronics to become a ham radio operator and CB repairman. He was always expanding his mind. I was so proud of mom's creativity and dad's entrepreneurship.

Difficult Memories

These were the fond childhood memories of my family life but that is where it stops. Even though I grew up in paradise, that's what I considered Montana; my home life was difficult. When I was ten years old I began to realize that my mother drank too much. When she drank she used to speak so negatively about my father. I was really confused and hurt. Dad wasn't that bad; he gave me lots of hugs. I loved him. Mom's drinking really bothered me and I told my best friend who lived in the house just behind our house about mom's drinking. Her own mother was very upset with me because I had talked badly about my own mother, so she wouldn't let her daughter play with me anymore. I was devastated. This was the first rejection that I had ever felt. Mom was very upset with me too. She said I had revealed a family secret. This was the beginning of mom's rejection of me. I didn't know what to do with the painful feelings so I suppressed them and didn't tell anyone. I now know as an adult that my mother was in total denial about the drinking problem. In fact, anyone that even hinted that she had a problem, she totally rejected.

I was the middle daughter of three girls. My older sister was four years older, and as an adult I learned that she suffered from schizophrenia. When I was a kid I didn't know she was my half-sister. The fact that her hair was brown and my little sister and I had light blond hair didn't raise any questions in my mind. We seemed to get along, but she ignored me most of the time because I was just her annoying little sister. I now know that is typical teenager behavior. Most of the time, she acted strangely but I didn't know that something was wrong with her. I loved her. We are adults now and get along fine. Currently she is happily married. At some time in her young adult life, she became a Christian.

My younger sister, who was two years younger, was very social so I saw very little of her. When we were together my social skills were lacking. I just didn't treat her very well and if she had a chance, she would tell you that she didn't like me. I know this now because she told me so in my adult life. We get along fine as adults, because I apologized for treating her badly. She is married and has three children. Her life has been difficult which lead her to call out to the Lord for help. She is now a Christian.

Creative Play

As a child, I remember playing alone with troll dolls for hours. I made clothes out of felt for all eleven of them. My greatest creation was a heaped up blanket on the floor for a mountain so the trolls could ski! I made skis out of Popsicle sticks with felt boots glued to them. I made elaborate scouts (the old four wheel drive vehicles) out of Lego's. My dolls also went camping in the wilderness of the bushes in my backyard. I played dolls for many years, but I was somewhat self-conscious that I stilled played dolls into my junior high school years and my early high school years. None of my friends played dolls anymore. I never told anyone my secret. I lived in a make believe world. I remember my dad commenting that there were people that entered the County Fair with their troll doll creations. What fun! I thought about entering the fair, but I was pretty insecure in my creations.

Teenage Life

Dad worked hard all the time to make a living; he was a good provider. Early on he was part owner of a gas station and later bought a truck stop. He wasn't home much but I knew he loved me. One way he showed his love was to give me hugs.

When I was a teenager, Dad studied on his own to be a ham radio operator. He had a world map hanging on the wall of his radio shop Dad put colorful pins in the places of the world where he had talked to someone on the radio. He was also a CB radio repairman. He built a shop in the basement at the bottom of the stairs where he ran a business. I was proud of him.

Mom was a type of person that showed very little affection. She sat in her favorite kitchen chair and played solitaire for hours on end. Every other night she drank until she was drunk. Mom used to get really mad at my dad and throw things down stairs which hit the door of his radio shop then crashed to the floor. I used to hide in my bedroom feeling very upset but expressed nothing. I remember mom attempting suicide with a gun several times. This really scared me. I didn't cry because I had to be strong for my little sister. We held each other tightly while listening to the conflict between mom and dad in their bedroom, and then the explosion of a gun! O my God!

I struggled with my thoughts and feelings during my Junior High School years. One day, while in school, I wrote a poem to express the confusion I was feeling.

> *"I seek throughout my heart for love and peace,*
> *but if it comes I will not live nor die.*
> *I live a life of loneliness and war,*
> *the fight between my conscience and my soul."*

By Stacey W Smith, 1970

When I was in my high school years my dad bought a truck stop. Dad and mom worked at the truck stop during day and drank with truckers every night. We stopped camping, backpacking, and skiing – no more of *God's living room* experience. There was no way to release the inner tension inside me. My parents were sleeping when I got up for school and when I came home after I took care of my necessities. I fixed all my own boring meals: boiled egg and toast every morning and hamburger patties and canned green beans every evening. Once in a while I made goulash which mom had taught me how to make. I ate my midday meal at the school cafeteria. I went to bed. I never saw Mom and Dad. I guess since they believed that I was so strong emotionally and successful in every-thing. I did well at school and acted so mature, that they thought I didn't need them. I had successfully suppressed all my negative emotions so deep inside that everyone thought I was strong. My grandmother used to tell me that she was amazed at how well I was handling the difficulties at home. She seemed to understand how difficult life was for me.

During my junior year in high school, I started having a very hard time which led to what I guess must have been an emotional breakdown. I'm not sure what happening. I cried uncontrollably for hours. I was begin-ning to hate mom and wrote my feelings on paper. I remember writing how much I missed camping. I hid this paper in my drawer. Mom decided to stop working and came back home to take care of me. She found my writing in my drawer and screamed at me. She tore up my journal papers, and threw them in the garbage. I was crushed and felt more rejected. I cried and cried so very hard. Later, I attended Alanon one time. That plan backfired as soon as mom found out. She hated me for calling her an alcoholic. Our relationship was a total disaster from that point on. She told me she loved me only because she was my mother but she didn't like me at all. That was an emotional bomb for me, the ultimate rejection. I hated mom.

Since I was neglected and rejected during my life as a teenager, I had a couple directions to go with my life:

1. drugs and sex or
2. do something constructive so I could be proud of myself.

I chose the latter. I was subconsciously trying to win my parent's affec-tion. (I don't know why, because it was futile.) I did very well in school. School was my only life. I was an A-B student and was especially strong in science. Much to my surprise, I received several science awards at school. I don't think I ever told my parents. To this day I'm surprised that I received a science award since I didn't really try very hard. I guess that science was a gift from the God I didn't know.

My effort went into music and sports. I joined the band in elementary school. My band director thought I had natural talent so he picked out oboe as my instrument. By the time I reached high school I was playing awful. I was so embarrassed when I played those little solos in the band music so I contemplated whether I should either quit playing oboe or take lessons. I decided to take lessons from the oboe professor at the University of Montana. Thank God! I improved by leaps and bounds and made first chair my sophomore, junior, and senior years in both the high school band and the orchestra. I really loved music. I learned how to successfully make oboe reeds. This helped my playing. Strangely, several times my oboe instructor commented about the tremendous amount of tension in my shoulders. I could feel it, but I just assumed it was just the result of gymnastics. I know now that the tension in my shoulders was the result of pent up anger towards my mother. I pushed that comment aside and continued to work hard in music. The Solo and Ensemble Festival was a wonderful place to show off my playing! I played solos, flute – oboe duets, oboe – bassoon duets, and in woodwind quintets (flute, oboe, clarinet, bassoon, and french horn). I received superior ratings in everything that I played in. By the time I was a senior I not only made first chair All State Band, but I made first chair in All Northwest Band. I played the Handle Oboe Concerto in G Minor with the orchestra as my high school senior solo and received a standing ovation! Guess what? My parents attended this concert! I went to Shakees Pizza Parlor with the orchestra members after the concert, and then went home to discover my mother crying. I asked her if she was okay. She told me that she had no idea that I could play oboe so well. I was deeply touched by her response.

Playing in sports was a wonderful outlet for my stress filled body. I joined track my freshman year and competed in high jump. I was pretty good at it. Later I joined cross country, but running wasn't my thing. I think, however, that the running was good for me. My sport of choice was gymnastics. I didn't know what gymnastics was until I took it in PE class my freshman year. I loved it so much that I joined the school gymnastics team! I stopped track and cross country; I was too busy. I had some limitation in gymnastics. I couldn't do floor exercise and beam because I wasn't flexible enough. Dad didn't want me to do vault because he thought it was too dangerous. So I did uneven parallel bars. I was good at this apparatus. I was strong and daring. (Little did dad know, the uneven parallel bars was probably more dangerous than vault.) I had some pretty bad falls. One time I hurt my back and another time I tried to dislocate my knee. My parents never knew about either of these falls because I believed they would never have done anything to help me. During my senior year I did many great exhibitions on bars at the high school home basketball games. I gained the admiration of my classmates and that felt great! I had the potential of getting first place in uneven parallel bars in the state gymnastics meet in Kalispell. I was ready to dazzle the world! At the pinnacle of my gymnastics experience, I went up to perform my routine and guess what, I fell. I still received a decent score. I just know if I hadn't fallen, I would have won state on the uneven parallel bars. FYI, my dad attended a few gymnastics meets and Mom never did see me compete.

College Years

Soaring into the Wonderful World of Music

After high school I attended the University of Montana and doubled as a music major in teaching and performance. I dropped the sports for lack of time. I received a music scholarship to play in the traveling wood-wind quintet, and was first chair in the band and orchestra my freshman year. I played in the pit orchestra for the operetta "Die Fledermaus" by Johann Strauss. It was so much fun. I loved music! I was receiving straight A's except for Piano in Class and Sight Singing class. I had never sang or played piano before. One of the voice students in my Sight Singing class told me I sounded like a frog when I sang. How humiliating! When I practiced piano, I could read and play the treble clef and bass clef separately but putting my two hands together was very challenging to say the least! I had my work cut out for me!

At the end of the winter quarter, I began crying in the middle of my classes, so I left to cry in the restroom. I went to the infirmary many times for help. I attended group therapy on campus several times, but I couldn't tell my story, or express my emotions. I seemed to be stuck. However, the emotions got so out of control in school, I couldn't even go to some of my classes without crying uncontrollably and exiting the classroom. During middle of one band concert, I cried while sitting on the front row of the stage during the performance and had to leave stage to camp out in the restroom to cry uncontrollably. My music teachers were very supportive which helped me limp along for the rest of the quarter. My oboe instructor shared the Love Chapter from 1 Corinthians 13. This passage ministered to me greatly. I made a poster using calligraphy on parchment paper of this verse and read it often. My oboe instructor took me, along with several other musicians, into the snow covered mountains around Missoula to cross country ski. The mountains were beautiful all covered with the deep snow. One time when we stopped to rest, I took off my skis to do front flips into the deep snow. It was exhilarating!

After this magnificent outing it was time for finals. I had to withdraw from Math, Piano in Class, and Sight Singing. I received a "B" in Music Theory which was a miracle. My professor told me I received a "C" on the final even after missing half the classes. He told me that I was really gifted in music theory! I had to psych myself up to play my jury. A jury is when you play your musical solo before several university music professors for your final grade. It is an unnerving event in normal circumstances, but I was an emotional wreck. I had to get a grip on my emotions so I ran around the music building until I was totally exhausted, then I went in the band room and played for the music teachers. I remember nothing except that I received an "A" for my oboe playing. Right after playing I went back to the infirmary, and then the doctor arranged for me to be admitted to the psychiatric floor of the hospital in downtown Missoula. He put a medical block on spring quarter at the University of Montana. This means I would not be permitted to attend school next quarter. Everything had come to a stop in my life. My dreams and aspirations as a musician had come to a halt.

The Psychiatric Hospital Experience

My life was ruined. I hated life, especially my mother, and now I hated music. I laid in bed for hours with the same music stuck in my mind playing over and over hauntingly. I couldn't stop it so I got really mad and threw a book across the hospital room. It landed flat against the wall and made a very loud noise! I was scared that maybe I had done something wrong on a psych floor. A nurse came by to make sure I was okay. I told her what happened and that seemed to be all right. I cried a lot as I worked on a jigsaw puzzle with a picture of a sail boat washed up against the shore of a lake. That is how I felt. I had nothing—no future and no direction for my life. All the wind was out of my sail. Life as I knew it had ended.

The doctor prescribed an antidepressant to help me. He talked to me every day and suggested that I have shock therapy. That scared the living daylights out of me and I said, "No way!" While lamenting in my depression, I tried to encourage another patient that was very depressed. I think she was more depressed then I was. I don't think my words helped her very much.

Near the end of the week, I asked the doctor if I could leave the hospital on Sunday to visit the Episcopal Church a couple blocks away. This is the church where my grandmother took me to visit when she came to visit us. I told the doctor I would come right back. I knew that was an impossible request but worth a try. Much to my surprise the doctor said, "Yes!"

Off I trotted down the sidewalk in my tee-shirt and blue jeans to a church full of people with ladies who wore fancy hats. I shook the minister's hand as I walked in then sat on a pew near the front of the sanctuary. I don't remember much about the service except kneeling during prayer. I cried so hard the whole time. One moment in the middle of the service, I thought I heard a voice say,

"One day your joy will return, just not all at once."

Suddenly I was crying tears of joy! What was happening to me? I felt this strange feeling called joy! When it was time to leave church, I shook the minister's hand while crying because of depression or was it tears of joy? I remember trotting right back to the hospital.

I don't remember anything about the second week on the psych ward of the hospital, except that I asked the doctor if I could go back to church again the next Sunday. Much to my surprise he said, "Yes" again. Off I trotted back to the church full of people with ladies who wore fancy hats. Once again, I shook the minister's hand and sat down near the front of the church and cried as I kneeled in prayer. I don't even remember anything again except I thought I heard that voice tell me again,

"One day your joy will return, just not all at once."

I was immediately overcome with tears of joy again. How could this happen? This time the whole experience caught my attention. Could this be the voice of God? I never had given the concept of God much thought even though both my grandparents had taken me to church when they visited. I took a Bible History class in the public school where I failed the pretest. At the end of the class I won the Most Improved Award. I had learned some Bible stories but still didn't know anything about a real God. However, could this voice I was hearing be a real God? The message was the only encouraging thing I had heard since getting depressed. Was this God? I decided to choose to believe it was God's voice and that I would believe in Him from now on. I told God that I would believe that Jesus was His Son if the Bible taught it. I was still crying for joy and realized that I felt happy!

I remember nothing about the hospital stay after that Sunday except that I had to find a place to stay. I refused to go back home and live with my parents. The hospital personnel lined up a retirement home for me to live. Since I had no money the owner wanted me to help clean. I remember sitting on the floor in front of a toilet holding some cleaning supplies just crying and crying. I couldn't seem to do anything yet, so I was kicked out onto the street. I was wearing my tee-shirt and blue jeans to find somewhere else to find a place to stay. I went to the University of Montana campus and asked an acquaintance I had met in the infirmary if I could stay with her. She had a basement apartment a block away from the music building. She kindly opened up her home to me for free and I was grateful to have a place to stay.

Back to College

For some reason the doctor at the campus infirmary forgot to put the medical block put on me at school so I registered for band, orchestra, and private oboe lessons during this spring quarter. I don't remember much except I spent many hours hanging out in the filthy apartment where I was living. There were dirty dishes piled up in the sink and clothes laying everywhere. It is strange that I don't remember where I ate. I had no money. On Sundays I walked to the Episcopal Church which was around a mile away and began to make friends.

In my Christian infancy, I read a scripture that said, "Honor your mother and father." I had a serious problem; I hated my mother with a passion. I knew I was wrong. After many weeks of meditating on this verse, I gathered up enough nerve to try to reconcile with mom. I went home to apologize for my teenage rebellion. I talked to her while she was in bed in her bedroom. The curtains were closed and darkness seemed to permeate the room. She listened to me for a moment then, without looking at me said, "I don't accept your apology." Immediately I was shocked and deeply hurt. For the first time in my life I realized that mom was sicker then I was. Alcohol was controlling her life. God somehow took away my hatred and I felt sorry for her for the first time. I realized that I should probably try to avoid seeing her any more then I had to. It was too painful.

During the summer I went to occupational therapy. We did all kinds of crafts and pet therapy. This was fun. I went off my psychiatric medication with no ill effects. It was time to go on with my life. I worked as a live-in babysitter for a lady. I was well enough to take care her son and do light house work. In the fall, I went back to the university so I searched for a new place to stay. I found the Wesley House, and I was honored to be given the opportunity to move in it. I was so excited to be living with Christians who believed like me. They sang together with a guitar accompaniment in the living room of the house! You mean Christians can have church in a house!

An interesting thing happened to my dad while I was living in the Wesley House. My dad attended a Catholic Cursillo and gave his life to the Lord. He came to the Wesley House to pick me up for a drive. We talked for hours that night and connected for the first time in my life. It was wonderful! I asked him if he was going to attend church. He responded with no. He thought that would create too much conflict with mom. I grieved deeply in my heart for him. Dad wanted me to attend a Cursillo too, so I did. It was an amazing retreat and I felt deeply loved by God and God's people. God was slowly revealing Himself to me during the various church activities and functions. I was feeling His love and my joy *was* returning.

I continued to take classes at the University of Montana. I took several science classes, a math class, ROTC, as well as the music classes electives. When spring quarter came I took the Piano in Class and Sight Singing classes so I would have completed a full year of credits towards the music degree. After finishing my second year of college, I had one of two choices to make:

1) continue music school for the next three years or
2) start something totally different like join the Army.

ROTC had an effect on me. Could it be that I could join the service and move away? My dad served in the Air Force. Maybe this could be a fresh start.

Chapter 2

Military Life

A New Beginning

*e*fore the end of spring quarter of college, I decided to enlist in the Army so I could have a new life. I believed that I needed to start over at some other location for a new beginning. I took the Army exam, even though it was hard for me emotionally; I guess I still was not fully recovered from depression. The great news was that I qualified for microwave electronics! A new start in something different! I was looking forward to the change. As I was waiting to go active duty and head for basic training at Fort McClelland, Alabama, I decided to just try out for the Army band. I went to Fort Lewis, Washington and played my best for a Sargent who played in the band. The tryout involved sight reading this crazy music that didn't make any musical sense. The Sargent was amazed at my playing and thought I played it perfectly with no mistakes! I thought that I had probably made some mistakes. The music was so crazy that no one would be able to tell if I messed up even a little. He immediately contacted the special bands: the D.C. Band along with other special bands. The Forces Command Band needed an oboe player. Bingo, I was heading for a new home in Deep South, the *Gone with the Wind* country known as Atlanta.

Finishing up College before I Went Active Duty

At the end of the spring quarter of my second year of college life, I was beginning to hang out with boys. I felt pretty awkward and distrustful of them, but it was fun anyway. I met this one guy named Jim that was majoring as a hydrologist in Forestry. He was pretty cool. We used to eat at the cafeteria together with his forestry friends. One of his Canadian forestry friends was afraid of mountains; she felt like she would fall off the mountain! That seemed odd to me.

As time passed, Jim decided to do something fun that I hadn't done in years. We went camping with my sister, Lynn. I remember that I was pretty stressed from school so this camping trip was great to help my mind relax. As we hiked on this trail to a lake, I stopped often to gaze upon all the wild flowers. I was caught up in the beauty along the trail. The stress of school floated away, and I was beginning to relax. We set up camp and then canoed along the shore of the mountain lake. It was so peaceful—I was in *God's living room* again. That spring quarter Jim and I started getting serious, and were thinking about our future together. He wanted to marry me! We had a problem. I was going in the Army for three years and he still had to finish getting his college degree. We decided to get pre-engaged. That way we had some commitment but had a door out if the three years apart proved to be too difficult.

Basic Training

Could I Make it Emotionally?

Basic training at Fort McClelland, Alabama proved to be miserably hot and humid. Welcome to the South you Northerner! I had joined the Army under the Stripes for Skills Program so I was given the rank of E-3. This proved to be interesting in basic since everyone else was an E-1. The drill sergeant saw me with that E-3 rank on my shoulder and immediately designated me as platoon leader. O brother, I knew nothing about the army and basic training, but boy did I learn fast! I was supposed to teach everyone else in the platoon how to polish boots, iron uniforms, line up our clothes perfectly in our locker and foot locker, make our bunks so tight that a quarter would bounce on it, clean the showers with tooth-brushes, and run the floor buffer without ramming the machine into furniture or people.

I had many jobs like leading the platoon in physical training which was no problem since I was an athlete. Pushups were easy for me so I taught many of the girls how to do pushups. We did sit ups which many of girls couldn't do either. Because of gymnastics in High School, sit ups were no problem. We ran a mile every day and did the obstacle course. I had to march the platoon around base and into the mess hall which was no problem as either since I had learned to march in the band. There were some differences between marching in the band and marching in the Army but no big deal to learn.

We learned many army skills like firing the M-16 rifle. For some reason I was good at the M-16 and received the sharp shooter award. We also had night fire. I had no idea if I ever hit the target, even when watching the tracer bullets. Another weapon we fired was the M-60 machine gun. We fired M-60 machine guns at a shed down the range. This weapon was a disaster for me to manage since we had to lie in the prone position with our left arm outstretched to hold the strap at the end of the gun to keep the tip down with the right hand on the trigger. I wasn't strong enough to hold down the gun during the kick, so I just watched all the tracer bullets fly above the shed! And now I had to throw these hand grenades. I couldn't throw balls and now these scary hand grenades. My throwing arm was pitiful and my drill sergeant yelled at me and told me that I would have killed myself if the grenade had been live! Then there was the tear gas chamber! Much to my relief the gas mask worked great until we had to take it off. That tear gas was wicked on the eyes, nose, and throat – yuck! I stated my social security number very quickly when I exited the gas chamber and staggered well away from that gas chamber to regain my composure. We had to crawl flat on our tummy in the red clay and get our face filthy dirty. If our faces weren't dirty enough we had to crawl on the course again.

The company bivouac was difficult. My buddy and I pitched our tent for perimeter defense. That was easy because of all the camping I did, but we had to pull guard duty all night even though I didn't get any sleep the night before during night fire on the firing range. Our goal was to keep the enemy, which were the drill sergeants, from breaking through our perimeter. In the middle of the night, when our company commander walked up to me, I was so tired that I forgot what I was supposed to say to him. I stumbled over my words so bad that he told me to go to bed!

The amazing thing about basic training to me was that I handled it emotionally very well. Not everyone did. In fact, I had only one emotional problem! I had a meltdown one evening that appeared to be over nothing to do with the military. I had been thinking about home for a short moment then cried very hard. Later when I called home, I found out that there had been a major fight at that exact same time I had the melt down. I knew that I had to disconnect myself emotionally from home even more.

I graduated from basic training and headed to Montana to visit my family. That proved quite a disaster. While all the family was in the kitchen

I told all about Basic Training. However, I made the mistake when I said I missed the mountains. World War III immediately broke out. Mom thought I missed the mountains more than her. I didn't know what to say. Of course, that wasn't true. It was just an innocent statement. Dad supported me and tried to get mom settled down. Even as I write this I still get upset. I remember nothing else of the visit.

The Army/Navy School of Music

Back into the Music I Once Loved

The Army/Navy School of Music in Norfolk, Virginia proved to be great fun. I had six months to learn as much as I could. I had oboe lessons but I already knew how to play oboe and make oboe reeds. I was first chair in the student band and second chair to my oboe instructor in the faculty band. I mastered all the music theory with ease. My oboe instructor invited me to play in the Virginia Beach Pop Orchestra. This was quite an honor and lots of fun! I found out that I was only going to be at the school of music for just three months since the Forces Command Band in Atlanta really needed my oboe playing.

Church Hopping

While at the school of music I had a really nice Christian roommate that played clarinet. She introduced me to several other Christian musicians. I remember one of the guys played euphonium (baritone) and had played in the Salvation Army Band. He not only could play his instrument well but he knew about the Church and Jesus Christ. We all went church hopping while we were at the School of Music. There was no point in making any one church our home since we weren't going to be in the area very long. We attended a Baptist church, an Episcopal church for my sake, a Charismatic church, and several other churches. I remember being a little spooked at the Charismatic church, especially when I was told that one guy had a demon cast out of him. My favorite memory was when we went to Virginia Beach to have church. We had a Bible study right there on the sandy beach where we were sitting on driftwood, not on a pew in a church building or in a chair in a living room. We were in *God's living room* having church! It was wonderful! I had never had church outside! I didn't even know that was possible. I was learning about Jesus from these humble saints and loved it!

Army Forces Command Band

Playing Music in the Northern City of the South, Atlanta

At the three month point in school, I decided that I wanted to learn how to play saxophone for marching band. That idea never jelled because the Army sent me to the Forces Command Band in Atlanta, Georgia. They needed me right away, I guess. Off I went to *Gone with the Wind* country. Atlanta was huge, and nothing like Missoula, Montana. The southern accent was hard for me to understand. I had never seen so many African Americans before. All we had in Montana were white people and American Indians living on reservations. This was a new experience. Once these people found out I was from Montana they told me that I wasn't prejudice. I guess not. I didn't even know what prejudice behavior was like, except what I had read in my history books about the KKK. In my ignorance, I thought that that kind of hatred was long gone. I probably should have known better. One evening I went to the day room in the women's quarters to watch TV. I entered the room and sat down, then shockingly observed the whole room of African/American women slide away from me as far as they could to the other side of the room. I could tell that I was not wanted in the room and guessed that this must have been an example of reverse discrimination, so I left.

The Forces Command Band was a sixty member band on the army base called Fort McPherson in a small suburb just south of Atlanta. It was a very good band, full of talented musicians! Some of the players were ex-band directors that loved to play their instrument. There were more guys then gals in the band but fortunately a rumor followed me from the school of music that I wanted to be a Catholic nun. I liked that rumor! I was also pre-engaged to the guy at the University of Montana. These rumors kept the guys away from me. No one made advances.

I played second oboe to a guy who out ranked me. Roger was an E-6 and I was still an E-3. Shortly after arriving, I was given the rank of E-5. This was great, except for one thing; I played better oboe then Roger and was quite snobbish about it. (I'm not proud of my attitude.) Roger's main instrument was alto saxophone, and he loved playing in the jazz band. One of his favorite instruments to play was the bari sax in the Nine Piece Jazz Band. Oboe was Roger's doubled and he played oboe quite well.

Roger was from Great Falls, Montana! There aren't very many Montanans living in Georgia. We decided to hang out together since we had so much in common. I was quite surprised he wanted to hang out with me because of my snobbish attitude early on. We both lived on base. He lived in the band quarters and I lived in the woman's quarters. We hung out in the day room at the band. We ate at the local restaurants since neither one of us liked the food at the mess hall. Shortly after arriving at the band, I was given the first chair position.

The Forces Command Band was a traveling band so we traveled all over the Southeast. However, at first most of the performances were the Bicentennial Show Band. This was the band's opportunity to celebrate the 200th birthday of the United States. The show band performed a multimedia show titled "200 Years of Readiness." The show consisted of several singers, a twenty piece show band, and a multimedia presentation using three screens with slide projectors and motion picture. It was a magnificent bicentennial show but I wasn't in it. I just hung out at the band quarters while the band traveled. Later I joined the tech crew and helped run the slide projectors.

During my early years at Fort McPherson, I went to the infirmary for counseling to help me cut the emotional apron strings to my mom. I knew it wasn't healthy relationship and I needed healing in this area.

The typical responsibilities I had in the band consisted of concert band practices and woodwind quintet practices. We sight read most of our music which was easy for me. I was also learning alto saxophone so I could march in parades around the Atlanta area and the once a month retirement parade on base. I played sax in the pouch band for small gigs around town such as Boy Scout jamborees and other small gatherings of people. Most of the time, I practiced my instruments. The non-musical things we did included physical training which seemed to be a joke and police call (picking up cigarette butts.) I cleaned the latrines many times. A guy that was over me in the band told me that all girls were good for is cleaning the latrine. That statement made me really mad and I slapped him across the face! I knew I was going to get an Article 13 for my behavior. I had one thing going for me, and that was that the Commanding Officer was also a female. I didn't get in trouble but I never did that again.

Preparing for the Future

I thought often about what I might do after serving my time in the Army. One possibility was to attend nursing school somewhere in the Atlanta area since I had been so strong in science. Another possibility was to go back into music, possibly to Georgia State University. If I went back into school in music, then I needed to work on my oboe, piano, and singing skills so I took oboe, piano, and voice lessons. Since I didn't have a car, my instructors came to the army base and taught me in the practice room at the band quarters.

My oboe instructor played in the Atlanta Chamber Orchestra. He was a very expressive musician and I wanted to learn to play expressively from him. After while he lined me up for an audition to play a solo with the Atlanta Chamber Orchestra! I played the Oboe Concerto by Cimarosa by memory. I loved the music so much that I could put my whole heart in it. When I played in the audition I did really good but had only one problem; I had a memory lapse right at the beginning of the second movement but recovered quickly. That was the only goof. I found out later that if I hadn't had that memory lapse then I would have won the competition! Instead, a harp player won. What a disappointment!

My oboe teacher also taught me piano. I began gaining the coordination to play both hands together on the piano. This was very hard for me and I practiced many hours to master this skill. I learned to sing from a really good voice teacher who sang in the Atlanta Civic Opera. Boy was she good! I found out that she had sung in professional operas in New York City as well. I used to sing for hours in the practice room. I joined the chapel on base and sang a solo during a church service! No frog voice any more. I thought I was going to die: no instrument to hold for security and no music stand to hide behind. I went to the bathroom fifteen times (no joke!) before performing "Little Lamb, Who Made Thee?" by William Blake. It was a success, I didn't die! Later my voice teacher worked with me to help my sight singing. This proved to be very difficult for me except when I held my hands like I was playing oboe. The pitches came to me easily then—what a mystery. I spent many hours practicing oboe, piano, and voice. I was a deeply satisfied musician. However, I remember as I was practicing, I felt like I just couldn't play outside the box. For some reason my music seemed to lack the real expression of my heart.

Atlanta had many community musical groups. I played in the Cobb Symphony and the Emory Woodwind Ensemble. I had only one problem and that was the Army gigs took precedence over the community groups. This put the community groups in a bind from time to time.

God Reached Out to Me at a New Church

One Sunday a trombone player from the band invited me to a small fledgling church just south of Hartsfield Airport called Atlanta Christian Center. They were meeting in an ugly old refurbished car shop. The music was terrible; a honky-tonk upright piano with untrained singers pained my ears. However the teaching was very good and the people passionately loved Jesus. I knew that I was severely lacking in Biblical education so I decided to go back to the church. I was very shy at first and just sat in a chair near the back of the church. I felt uncomfortable there but I was so hungry to get to know God better. This church reminded me of the Charismatic church I had visited in Norfolk, Virginia. The main thought that crossed my mind was just because the people worshipped differently than I was comfortable with, it didn't mean it wasn't God's church. After visiting for several months I decided to join the church.

The people at Atlanta Christian Center passionately loved the Lord, and slowly I began to make friends. Later, I was water baptized by emersion and shortly after that I received the Baptism in the Holy Spirit. Wow! My spiritual life started growing by leaps and bounds. I joined the Bible College that was meeting in the evenings at the church and soaked up the teaching. I loved learning God's Word!

Later, an amazing thing happened. The pastor's father-in-law moved from Anchorage, Alaska and joined the church. He was a fantastic musician! He could play piano and tenor sax like no one else. He formed an instrumental orchestra at the church. Wow, this retired Air Force colonel could write amazing arrangements for the orchestra. He didn't even use a score to help him write; he just wrote the parts on music paper while transposing the music in his head! The pastor's wife, who played sax, and I joined the group as well as several other instrumentalists in the church. I began inviting my army buddies to church. The other oboe player was one of the first ones to join. He played sax in the orchestra. Later a drummer came and then several others. We were having a blast playing God's music together! The talent of the army musicians helped this fledgling group sound pretty good.

A Season of Romance

Roger and I were hanging out. We spent many hours making oboe reeds and talking about anything that crossed our minds. We were both from Montana and had fathers who were entrepreneurs. We had so much in common. We ate out every day and enjoyed being around each other. He drove me to Atlanta Christian Center for church. After several months of visiting, Roger decided to join the church. Even though we were hanging out a lot, I was still pre-engaged to another guy from the University of Montana. He eventually graduated from college with a degree in Forestry specializing in Hydrology. His first job was in Fairbanks, Alaska. I don't think we could have lived further away from each other. We talked on the telephone a few times but didn't visit each other, but I was still committed to him.

Life in the army was moving right along. I received a request to teach oboe at the Army/Navy School of Music in Norfolk, Virginia! This was quite an honor. I thought about it for several days and thought about my career as a musician. I couldn't turn down such a great opportunity, so I wrote up a resume proudly listing all my credentials. Was this my God promoting me to this prestigious position? I supposed that I not only would become first oboe in the faculty band, I might be honored to play first oboe in the Virginia Beach Pop Orchestra. I couldn't wait!

One day I started feeling pretty sick and my right side was hurting. I thought it was gas, but I was running a fever. I could hear my dad's voice in my head asking me if my right side hurt. If it does, it might be your appendix. I decided to not go to work and go to the infirmary on the army base to get it checked out. All I remember the nurse saying was, "It's not your appendix because that is on your left side. If you don't get better then you should go to the hospital." I went back to my apartment pretty mad because I was sure my appendix was on my right side.

Several hours later I was feeling worse, so I asked Roger to take me to the hospital. He took me to the emergency room. After many hours of waiting and examinations by several doctors, it was determined that I had appendicitis. Roger stayed with me the whole time in the emergency room up until I had surgery. He even visited me frequently in the hospital room. Roger knew I wasn't available to date because of my boyfriend in Alaska, but he was a super friend to me anyway.

After I recovered from the appendicitis, I couldn't stop thinking about how nice Roger was to me. I could tell that not only was he a friend, but he might be the nicest guy I had ever met. My heart was drawn to him, and was drifting away from my college friend. I had a couple problems. There was still the possibility that I was moving to Virginia to teach at the Army/Navy School of Music, and how was I going to break up with this guy when he lived so far away? I didn't want to just tell him over the phone. My life had become very complicated so God was going to have to sort this out.

Can God Move Mountains?

Life got back to normal with the army band and going to church. Roger and I were still hanging out together, and I was wondering how God was going to handle such huge issues if Roger might be the one. I received my Army's orders to teach at the Army/Navy School of Music. As far as I knew the Army had made their decision and once the orders were cut, it was set in stone. Nothing could change it. What did God want me to do? Now was my chance to find out if I was going to Virginia or staying in Atlanta to pursue my relationship with Roger. I put in my request to stay in Atlanta to my superiors, and suggested another good oboe player for the position. Guess what? The Army honored my request and I tore up my orders. This was one huge mountain out of the way! Was I was free to pursue my new lover?

The next huge mountain was breaking up with my college sweetheart in Alaska. God was not through performing miracles. I heard a rumor that the band was going to go on tour to Alaska! I couldn't believe it, not a band from Atlanta! Why not one closer to Alaska? Roger had been to Alaska several years earlier when he was in the Ft. Lewis band in Washington State. Why not the Ft. Lewis band this time? At any rate the rumor was true and the Forces Command Band was going to Alaska! I really wondered if this was a divine act of God so I could break up with my college friend in Alaska and marry Roger.

In the beginning of October the band flew to Sitka, Anchorage, and Fairbanks Alaska. It was the most beautiful scenery I had ever looked at! Sitka was situated at the base of glacial mountains right next to the shore of the Pacific Ocean. There were sail boats galore in the bay next to the mountains. We then went to Anchorage. It was a bigger city but the scenery was just as beautiful! We walked on glaciers and visited North Pole, Alaska. The band flew over the Alaska Range in a C-130 airplane to Fairbanks. The band members sat strapped in web seating that was for parachute jumpers. The cargo, which included all the band instruments and supplies, was tied down in a big pile in the middle of the plane. We were invited to look at the Alaska Range from the cockpit of the plane. I had seen and lived in the Rocky Mountains, but had never seen a range of mountains so wide. Fairbanks was a beautiful city.

I had arranged to take leave from work in Fairbanks after the tour was over. The band left and there I was in the wild country of Alaska preparing my heart to break up with my college sweetheart. Of course one of life's diversions was the tour to Denali National Park where I saw Mt. McKinley.

I stared at that huge mountain while we drove to the park. There was just as much mountain above the clouds and there was below the clouds! While we traveled through the park, I was amazed at the tundra and lack of trees. The few trees I saw were deformed from the permafrost. The ground is frozen all year round so the roots can't get established. I saw several mountain sheep and at least a dozen blond grizzly bears. Alaska is so beautiful!

When my college sweetheart, Jim, and I were back in Fairbanks I had to come up with a good reason to breakup with him. I really didn't want to hurt him since he really was a pretty neat guy. When he was at work, I read my Bible and sought God for wisdom. Jim was attending a Baptist Church which had a haunted house for the kids. I was a bit disturbed since I believed that Christians should not celebrate Halloween. I talked to him about my faith and believed that we were unequally yoked. He was Baptist and I was Charismatic and believed in the Baptism in the Holy Spirit. After visiting Fairbanks Christian Center, which was a church like the one I was attending in Atlanta, we decided to end our relationship. Just for the record, later my college sweetheart received the Baptism in the Holy Spirit, joined Fairbanks Christian Center, got married, and became the Christian School principal.

I was free now to pursue my relationship with Roger. In a very short time we decided to get married. The first thing that needed to happen was before we got engaged, Roger had to ask my Father for my hand in marriage. He wrote a wonderful letter to my dad but as fate may have it, the letter never arrived in Missoula. It got lost in the mail! So my Roger wrote another letter and my father responded with his permission for him to marry me.

We didn't let the cat out of the bag until we went to Reno, Nevada at Christmas to announce our engagement to Roger's parents. It was an insightful experience to meet his parents. I had been trying to figure out why Roger was so calm. I knew I had emotional baggage from my child-hood, but he appeared to be extremely stable. I knew there must be some hidden childhood baggage, but as I got to know his family, I decided that what I saw in my fiancé was his true self with no trauma from his childhood. His parents had raised him in the church and they were very stable. I really liked Roger's parents and thoroughly enjoyed my visit. They seemed to like me and were very happy for their son.

After arriving back in Atlanta, we announced our engagement to the army band and the church. Everyone was so happy for us even though they could see us getting married way before we even considered it. We planned to get married on March 1st at Atlanta Christian Center.

I wanted my younger sister to be my maid of honor, so I bought her a plane ticket to fly from Missoula, Montana to Atlanta. We were pretty poor since we were both living on enlisted salaries so we needed a simple wedding. Our pastor at Atlanta Christian Center was going to marry us. My oboe/piano teacher played classical piano while my voice teacher sang a solo. He then played Jesu, Joy of Man's Desiring on oboe for our processional with another musician friend from ACC, playing the accompaniment on piano. He then played Christian music for the closing of the wedding. Many people at church helped us with the wedding by supplying the candelabras and flowers, making the cake, doing the makeup and hair for the ladies in the wedding party, planning and implementing the reception, as well as everything else in the wedding. Our wedding was the biggest event that Atlanta Christian Center had up to this point. The church had around fifty members and the band had sixty members and they all came to our wedding!

We went to FDR State Park to stay in the honeymoon cabin for a couple days. Believe it or not, it snowed the afternoon of our wedding! This was rare to get snow at this time in the spring in Georgia. The cabin was very drafty so we built a fire in the fire place and snuggled to keep warm. Right after that the band went on tour to Louisiana and of course Roger and I got to room together! This seemed like an extension to our honeymoon.

I moved into Roger's apartment and shortly after that we rented a tiny house in East Point from one of the band members. Life got back to normal at the band and at church. Both Roger's and my time in the service were coming to an end. I had decided to attend nursing school at Georgia Baptist School of Nursing and my husband had decided to study computers at Control Data Institute. My last gig with the Army Band was the Fourth of July concert at Stone Mountain, Georgia. I remember playing the 1812 Overture with the canons going off in the music.

Chapter 3

Early Years of Married Life

❧❦

Finding Our Place in the Real World

e were two love birds living in a tiny two bedroom house that we loved. We planted a very large garden and grew many different kinds of vegetables. Our favorite vegetable was the silver queen corn. Wow, was that corn sweet! We grew tomatoes, onions, lettuce, spinach, broccoli, potatoes, as well as other vegetables. We loved to invite people over from church to the house for dinner and serve them freshly cooked home grown vegetables.

One of our favorite events was inviting singles from church to our house for Christmas dinner and games. We celebrated our first Christmas alone then decided that we would not celebrate Christmas alone ever again. We were too far away and too poor to travel to Reno to see Roger's dad or Missoula to visit my family. Plus there was always a risk to travel to those places in the winter. Our church members became our family, especially the singles. We were married but didn't have children so we didn't really fit in with the married crowd so we continued to hang out with the singles. We had a blast setting up our tiny house for ten guests or more. We feasted and fellowshipped to our hearts content. This was a tradition that we engaged in for many years.

As soon as I got out of the Army I went to the Georgia Baptist School of Nursing in downtown Atlanta. Fortunately the Army paid for the schooling. I didn't have a car so I rode Marta to school and home. I remember cracking the books while riding on the bus. Nursing school was very hard for me. My memory isn't the greatest so I had to study a lot. Of course, I took the basic courses such as Biology, Chemistry, Psychology, and the Nursing courses. Some of the classes were exempted like Math and English because I took them at the University of Montana. The good news is that I made the Dean's List at school and was highly respected as a good nursing student.

After finishing the first year of school, I was exhausted. I was reconsidering whether I really wanted to work so hard. I had very little time with Roger, and I was getting unhappy. I had to work so hard in my studies to master the material because my memory wasn't the greatest. After thinking it over I decided to quit nursing school and work at the Christian School at Atlanta Christian Center. I remember my fellow nursing students were shocked that I would put my husband above school, and my teachers were very disappointed. Much to my amazement, rumors spread all the way to Clayton State University Nursing School about my desire to quit school to be with Roger. No one seemed to understand. I really loved my husband and wanted to be with him.

I remember beginning my job as a teacher at the Atlanta Christian Center Christian School. I was so nervous to be in front of all the students. I wanted to crawl under the desk and hide. I was not used to public speaking. We used the ACE curriculum and I taught around eight fourth through sixth grade students. I remember completing several English paces in my spare time to brush up on my English skills. I was pretty weak in English. Math and science were my subjects. As I gained experience teaching the students, I became more comfortable and enjoyed teaching.

As soon as Roger got out of the Army he attended Control Data Institute, CDI. This is a technical school which teaches computer programming. He did very well in school and after nine months graduated at the top of his class! He was then blessed to get his first job as a programmer developing software for Control Data, a company that does payroll processing. We were amazed and very grateful to the Lord. Just for the record, Control Data has changed names over the years and Roger is still blessed to have a job with the same company thirty years later!

After teaching kids for a couple years, I began to get more creative in my approach. I loved teaching the kids and connecting with them. One of my mottos was study hard and play hard. During recess I used to catch frogs and chase the girls around campus! We had fun! Eventually I became principal for the elementary and middle school. My ability to organize grew by leaps and bounds. Teaching and leading became one of my strong areas. I was good at it. However, at the end of this school year the church decided to close the school.

Now just for some miscellaneous information, let me tell you about Snow Jam '83 in Atlanta. One late morning in March, while everyone was in school and working, the heavens opened up and dumped a foot of snow starting from the south side of Atlanta going to the north side! This was very unusual and caught everyone by surprise! Everyone was stuck at school and in work. The problem was that no one knew how to drive in that much snow! All the teachers and students at the school where I worked walked several miles through the snow over to the pastor's home. There were cars spinning their tires and sliding all over the roads! It looked like a mess! I watched the news while keeping warm at the pastor's house. The interstates all around Atlanta looked like parking lots. No one was going anywhere. In fact, many people were abandoning their cars on the interstate to stay in hotels downtown! Roger worked on the north side of Atlanta and was trying to get home—not on the interstate! Many hours later Roger called me from home. It took him five hours to get home going the back roads! The good news is that he had learned how to drive in the snow while growing up in Montana. He eventually picked me up from the pastor's house and we went back to our house. We were blessed to have a church friend stay with us because he couldn't get home. Many people were dislocated that day and hopefully all of Atlanta learned a lesson to stay home even if there is a threat of snow.

Early in our marriage we were very involved serving at Atlanta Christian Center. We both served in the sound ministry. We had received experience while serving in the Army Band that helped us really run a tight ship. Roger ran the sound system for the church services. He also ran the sound for special events like school plays and weddings. My involvement was mainly focused on the tape ministry. I took orders and made copies of the sermons on cassette tapes. Shortly after getting involved in the sound system, Roger was put in charge of the sound system. He did this for fifteen years. I was so proud of him. He was really good!

Even though I was involved in the tape ministry, I served in the nursery. I wanted to get pregnant and have my own baby, but it seemed that I couldn't get pregnant. I visited an infertility specialist and had an infertility workup – not fun. He determined that I had a hormone imbalance and proceeded to help me get pregnant. This took years so in the mean time I dutifully attended many baby showers to bless those young mothers. It was hard for me and I shed many tears.

The church started a Bible College so my husband and I decided to attend the evening classes. We took Old Testament Survey, New Testament Survey, Church History, and many other classes. Eventually I received a Bachelors' Degree in Christian Education.

Family Life: From Infertility to Five Daughters

Now I was still trying to get pregnant. I had served in the nursery for six years and was getting quite skilled at taking care of infants. I rubbed shoulders with many mothers who were having their babies at home. I was very interested in home birth as well. Many mothers were teaching their children at home. I felt confident that I could do this too, but God had to open my womb.

Now I was beginning to really struggle with the fact that I was infertile. I went to the Bible and did an in depth study on barrenness. God opened many wombs in the Bible and gave these women sons. This is what I wanted God to do for me. I prayed a lot and rode the emotional rollercoaster every month of hoping to get pregnant. Going to baby showers to bless other mothers became more and more difficult for me. Waiting with patience was getting harder and harder. I was still getting help from my gynecologist and taking hormones.

Finally after one month I wondered if I was finally pregnant. After not believing the store bought pregnancy test, I went to my gynecologist to get blood work done. I was pregnant and my doctor referred to this child as a blue ribbon special. I was really excited! The fulfillment of a dream finally was taking place! Now I wanted homebirth so I contacted the midwife. She agreed to be my midwife. Wow! Now I had to face the challenge of finding a doctor backup for homebirth. I didn't know if anyone would take a chance since I had been infertile. I started by asking my own gynecologist who did the infertility workup. He delivered babies at South Fulton Hospital. Maybe he would back me up? I got brave and finally asked. He responded with, "That's a great idea!" I was shocked! He was originally from South America where all the mothers had homebirth. He was very familiar with the whole concept and wanted to support me. I was truly blessed!

The whole church was super excited for me and had a huge baby shower. Every woman in the church attended and I received many gifts and blessings. This was truly a very exciting time in my life! After carrying the baby for nine months, I went into labor and had her at home. Roger cut the umbilical cord. My blue ribbon special was an eight pounds four ounce baby girl. She was as healthy as could be with an Apgar of 10. We named her Angela. With all the help from my midwife, pastor's wives, and experienced mothers I learned how to nurse her right away. Roger stayed home from work and took great care of me. He fixed me breakfasts and the church provided dinners for a couple weeks. We had one big challenge. Angela was very colicky. After taking dairy out of my diet she got happier and so did I!

Just a year and a half later I got pregnant with my second child. I still had to take hormones but everything went well. The only frustrating part was the progesterone that I had to take was making me have terrible morning sickness. It was so bad that my Angela was hanging over the toilet pretending to throw up! Sigh... After nine months I had my second daughter at home. She was very healthy with an Apgar of 10. Roger cut her cord and I immediately breast fed her. We named her Kristen. At the birth I had a good friend of mine be with Angela so she could watch the birth of her sister. It went great! The church once again provided meals for a couple weeks. We had a wonderful bonding time together and everything went well. However, Kristen was colicky and I couldn't figure out what I was eating that was causing the problem. After I cut out all the colicky foods, milk, cheese, onions, and everything else out she got better and I wasn't eating enough. I added the foods back in and kept breast feeding her. We just had to endure the colic which was very difficult.

After some time went past an amazing thing happened. The church asked me to teach a parenting class. Apparently with all the wonderful training I had from the church mothers, I was becoming a model mother. I was honored to be able to speak in other women's lives. Shortly after teaching the parenting classes the pastor asked me if I would be interested in taking on the position of Home School Coordinator at Atlanta Christian Center. I had to think about that for a while. Even though I wanted to home school, my children were still too young. I did have the Christian school experience so maybe I could help the moms while I learned about home schooling. I agreed to take the position. There were maybe fifteen home school families in the church. This was a big responsibility.

Life was going along when I found out I was pregnant with my third child. I was quite busy overseeing the home school program and raising my two daughters. My husband and I attended marriage seminars and were doing great! After nine months our third daughter, Cheri, was born at home. She was very healthy with an Apgar of 10. She breast fed like a trouper but proved to be a clingy baby. She wanted me all the time and wouldn't let anyone else hold her. Needless to say, I was very tired. I remember overseeing a home school American history presentation with Cheri riding my hip. Sigh... I was very frustrated and tired. The history presentation was a tremendous success.

Now life was moving right along and I got pregnant with our fourth child. I was now home schooling my own children and teaching the girl's program at the church on Wednesday evening church service. I resigned from the home school program and focused on teaching my own children. I passionately loved the Lord and began writing a curriculum for the girl's program. I wanted the girls to really know God and with the skills I learned about hands on teaching through home schooling I wanted to reach their hearts with Jesus' love. Several women joined me to teach the girls. We had an intense time as the girls were having a revival in the classes. I started a dance team and had my daughter, Angela, and another lady in the church choreographed a jazz dance called, "7 Ways to Praise" by Carmen. The girls loved the dance. After nine months my fourth daughter was born. She was healthy with an Apgar of 10 too. We named her Rachel. She was a great breast feeder and turned out to be my easiest baby. I was thankful since I now had four daughters and was overseeing the girl's program at church.

Now life still didn't slow down. I was very busy home schooling my girls and writing my book. An amazing thing happened, the children's ministry director asked me to work at the children's camp. I said "Yes," and ended up leading a boys' team. Imagine that! My military background helped, especially Basic Training.

After a little less than four years I got pregnant with my fifth baby. I was still home schooling and working with the girl's on Wednesday evening. After nine months my fifth daughter Helen was born at home. She was healthy with an Apgar of 10 and a great at nursing. Once again the church provided us with two weeks of meals. I had one problem—I was forty-one and exhausted. I told my husband that I couldn't get pregnant again and continue to home school. My pregnancy days were over for good. My Helen was a very sensitive baby and we had to be very careful to not over stimulate her. She did not like the infant nursery and cried the whole time she was in there. When I dropped her off, I would just tell the nursery worker that when they got tired of taking care of her page me. I would relieve them and take her to the nursing baby's room. The good news is that when she moved up to the toddler room, she was very happy. She had the nickname Rembrandt. She was very good at coloring inside the lines of the coloring book at the young age of two.

Home schooling five daughters proved to be an exhausting job. I wanted to do it right since I seemed to have very bright girls. I started a co-op with some other home school mothers. I taught science classes at my home two hours a day, three days a week for the first half of year. I had a friend would teach history for the second half of year. We offered writing classes and art classes at our homes. The Lord provided history mothers who wanted to co-op for many years. I could take a break during the history part of school and focus on my attention on the younger children.

When my first daughter, Angela, finished eighth grade, Roger and I decided to put her in a Christian school. Angela did very well in school making almost straight A's. I did have to help her with her homework since she wasn't used to the heavy work load. We figured that when Kristen reached high school we would put her in school.

God's Gift for our 20th Wedding Anniversary

Our twentieth wedding anniversary was quickly approaching and we wanted to make this celebration meaningful. After all, the first twenty years of our marriage was consumed with work, work, and work. We went from Army life to corporate work. We went from no children to home schooling five daughters. It was time for us to play!

A wonderful couple offered to give us free buddy passes to Europe. They were well traveled in Europe and could give us great instructions where we should go and experience the cost cutting life and the simplicity of European life. She was a native German and he could speak many European languages. We considered this offer pretty seriously.

One of our considerations was that this was a one-time vacation, even though it would be tremendously meaningful. But if we were going to spend that much money, could we make an investment in a concept that could result in many vacations? Roger suggested we buy a pop-up trailer and go camping. Wow, was I excited. This was a great idea. It was a step back into one of the most meaningful times in my life, camping in *God's living room* when I was a child.

We shopped with our large family in mind. We needed a pop-up that could sleep at least the seven of us and possibly add a couple friends. We wanted the pop-up equipped with the equipment for camping in the hot muggy south as well as travel over two thousand miles across the United States to Montana. We decided that an air conditioner for camping in the south would be nice. We wanted the equipment necessary for primitive camping in the national parks and the cold weather of Glacier National Park and Yellowstone National Park. I remembered camping as a child and crawling out of my sleeping bag in the morning putting on my coat and anything else that would keep me warm in the cold air. I always looked forward to warming my hands while sitting around the campfire with dad every morning. We decided to get a gas heater and buy a portable electric heater. We wanted hot and cold running water. We bought a pop-up that sleeps nine. How exciting!

Our first camping trip was at Vogel State Park in North Georgia. We had been invited by one of Roger's coworkers to go along with his church, Grace Church to go camping. We had our minivan equipped with a hitch and all the equipment necessary to pull this pop-up across country, and packed it for the three days of camping. We then drove to the camper store and picked up the trailer. We drove up to Vogel State Park and set up the campsite. We had a marvelous time.

Early on in our camping years, we decided to travel to Missoula, Montana to visit my family. This may be the only way for our family of seven to even get to see my parents and sisters. Flying was too expensive. We did some serious planning for this 2000 mile trip. First of all, when was the best time to travel with five young daughters? Which route should we take? We wanted to camp at the National Parks along the way. We had to decide how long this trip would take since Roger had to take off work.

We decided to take a week to get to Montana. First we left in the evening and drove all night as we took the southern route on Interstate 20 out of Atlanta to Texas where we camped at a KOA campground the next night. A serious storm was coming so we quickly opened up the pop-up before the heavens opened. This was the heaviest rainfall we had ever experienced! The campground was flooded. All the tents were flattened and people were drying their sleeping bags in the dryer! We were high and dry. After spending the night, we headed to Arizona to visit the Petrified Forest and camped at the Grand Canyon. We applied our primitive camping skill successfully. When we headed north, we visited Roger's dad in Reno, Nevada and saw his brother, Allen. We then visited the Hoover Dam. After traveling north to Utah, we camped at Zion National Park, Bryce Canyon National Park, and stayed at a KOA along Salt Lake. We continued traveling north into Idaho and visited the Craters of the Moon then went on to Missoula, Montana.

We saw my extremely happy parents, older sister, my little sister, her husband along with her three children. We set up the pop-up in my parent's backyard. Lynn's family lived in my parent's basement so with our seven we had a huge crowd. My parents weren't used to so many people so we took the girls away from the house every day to Rattlesnake Park and up to the picnic area in Patty Canyon. My sister's kids and my girls played in Rattlesnake Creek for many hours. The girls had never seen a cold clear mountain creek water before.

After several busy days of visiting Roger and I decided to go up to Glacier National Park for a few days to give my parents a break. The park was beautiful except that we all got the stomach flu. Even though it was summer, Glacier Park was cold. We spent many hours hanging out in the van to get warm. After getting well we drove on the Going to the Sun Highway up to Logan Pass. We hiked on the snow covered trail to Hidden Lake. We saw many ugly mountain goats. Their winter coat was half off! The girls loved hiking and playing in the snow! After camping in Glacier we headed back to Missoula to visit the family some more. We spent a week in Montana then decided to head back to Atlanta.

We took a different route home. First we headed to eastern Montana and Wyoming to Yellowstone National Park to camp. I was amazed at how green Yellowstone looked since several years earlier most of the park was up in flames from the worst forest fire it had ever had. We saw many of Yellowstone's black bears and buffalo. We headed south through Grand Teton National Park on to Colorado to Rocky Mountain National Park where we camped. We drove on the highest road in the US and saw many deer, several moose, and bears. We then headed east to St. Louis and through many acres of corn fields over to Mammoth Cave National Park in Kentucky We were pretty tired as we drove south to Atlanta. All in all, our trip took us three weeks.

It has been ten years since we bought the pop-up and we have camped with our church at Vogel State Park just about every year, except during the volleyball season when we were at volleyball tournaments with Cheri. We have camped with church friends at several other Georgia state campgrounds. We are grateful for the experience our friends have had camping in Georgia; they gave us tips to help us discover the best camping in Georgia and in the South. We have camped at campgrounds all over Georgia and several campgrounds in Florida. We camped on the beach on the Florida Panhandle at Fort Pickins. That campground doesn't exist anymore because of a hurricane. We were excited when we would camp at the campground at Disney World.

One of our favorite Georgia campsites is George L. Smith State Park, just two-and-a-half hours south of Atlanta towards Savanna. This campground is unusual since it is located on a lake that is full of Cypress trees. There are canoe trails in the lake which provides hours of entertainment for teenagers and adults! The scenery is breath taking and atmosphere is peaceful. We decided to make it a tradition to camp there every year at Thanksgiving. When our children were young, we always served the full Thanksgiving spread on Thursdays. At first we fried the turkey for a couple years, and then we used a roaster oven for many years. Now are son-in-law smokes the turkey! We have sweet potatoes with marshmallows, corn bread, green bean casserole, dressing, and the condiments such as olives, pickles, and cranberries.

Through the years our family has grown and we have had to switch the Thursday celebration to Wednesday to accommodate our married children. This year two of my daughters and son-in-laws are married and are still coming to camp with us. A year ago a handsome young man asked my husband for Kristen's hand in marriage. He revealed his plan to propose to her right here at George L. Smith State Campground. He invited his parents from St. Louis to join us for Thanksgiving. We have grown from a family of seven to a family of ten along with in-laws! I am so grateful to have such a wonderful Thanksgiving tradition that even my adult children want to continue to participate. I am looking forward to many more years of Thanksgiving with even a bigger family! Rachel and Helen are still at home and my older girls haven't had children yet.

Another one of my favorite camp grounds is in The Great Smoky Mountain National Park. We set up camp in the Smokemont Campground on the south side of the park close to Cherokee, NC. Since this is a national campground, it is primitive camping with no hookups to electricity and water. Camping at Smokemont reminds me of camping in Montana when we tent camped and never had hookups. Smokemont had great entertainment for the children. They went tubing down the river at the campground. We hiked the six mile Smokemont Loop Trail; even our youngest daughter hiked at three years old!

One of my favorite places is Clingman's Dome in the top of the Smoky Mountains. The forest consists of spruce and fir trees and smells just like Montana! One time my older two daughters and I hiked eight miles on the Appalachian Trail from Newfound Gap to Clingman's Dome. The trail was rocky and all uphill. I had hoped to see some wildlife but my girls teased each other all the way up the trail. O well, there goes my time of tranquility, but the laughter of my girls brought me great joy. I remember feeling like I was a child as I reached out with both hands to feel the tall grass on both sides of the trail. The smell, the scenery, and the company still make it one of my most memorable experiences at the Smokies. I have hung onto that memory through some really tough times.

Chapter 4

Life Gets Tough

My Father-in-Law Gets Cancer

*L*fe has difficult times and now it is our turn. Responsibilities continue even during life's trials. I was home schooling my young children, teaching them to read and write as well as all the other subjects. The first challenge we faced was when my father-in-law had radiation treatment for colon cancer at the Atlanta VA Hospital. He had a VA hospital in Reno where he lived but there was no one there to care for him while in treatment so we invited him to stay with us. We had to do some gyrations to get him to the VA and back home every day. I had three children at that time and Roger was working on the north side of Atlanta. We worked as a team to get Grandpa taken care of. Roger dropped him off at the hospital on his way to work. When Grandpa was done with his treatment he called me and I drove up through Atlanta with the kids to pick him up. There was only one problem; our two-year-old daughter cried all the way to the VA hospital every day. The other kids and I were severely stressed by the time we picked up Grandpa. There is good news: our daughter slept all the way home! The treatments were a success and Grandpa went back to Reno. We survived!

Hitting a Horse!

One time during the summer our middle daughter came down with the chickenpox and gave it to Grandpa. We felt bad for Grandpa but it turned out that he got over it. The chickenpox wasn't over in our family though. All her sisters came down with chickenpox at once. They were miserable. On Wednesday night I had a speaking engagement at church.

Now that my middle daughter was over the chickenpox, we went to church. My husband was staying home with three sick girls. We proceeded to load up for church and my daughter sat next to me in the middle seat while I drove. We headed up the road and I put on the brakes so my neighbor could turn left into his driveway. We proceeded to go forward when a horse ran in front of us and I hit it! The horse landed on the hood of the car, then crushed the top of the car down in the middle and landed behind us on the road. The car was totaled but we were fine. It was a miracle! To this day we comment on how our daughter had a horse land on her head and lived through it! We went home to the chicken pox household extremely shaken.

Living with a Border

We decided to open up our home to a single girl from our church to live with us. It turned out that she lived with us a couple years. Life was not easy with a border, but we loved her deeply and wanted to help her get on her feet again. She didn't always make the best decisions so we lovingly tried to speak into her life. Of course there was turbulence, but our love for each other helped calm the experience.

One of the benefits of having her stay with us was that she encouraged Roger and me to go on a date nights regularly. Of course, during that season of time we had four young children. We didn't know anyone who would babysit four children and of course we couldn't afford to pay for a sitter either. She knew my husband and I needed a break, and she was very willing to help us out. Roger and I had relaxing times on these date nights which was unusual for parents of young children.

Another fond memory is when our border and the girls and I went to visit the gardens. One of the memories I have about this trip is that some people noticed we were a white family and our border was black. We deeply loved her, but we began to realize that having a black girl live with us was not acceptable by some people. Our border felt blessed to be living with us and loved us even more because we were white and she was black.

We loved having a border live with us but there were many challenges along the way. One of the comments she makes is that we loved each other even though we knew the good, the bad, and the ugly about each other. These statements are true. Life was a challenge with her living with us, but it was a time of deep love for each other. She is now married to a wonderful husband and has two children. Throughout the many changes that have taken place in both our lives and families our bond continues to be strong.

Grandpa Moves In

We were not through with having borders live with us. My father-in-law visited us several times a year. Since he had asthma, our smoke free environment was inviting to him. We had many grandchildren still at home. His health was deteriorating and my husband and I were concerned about him living alone. I knew he wouldn't move in with us because he didn't want to be a burden. He wanted to be the provider. I prayed about this hurdle and felt inspired to tell him that we needed him to move in with us to help financially. Of course we didn't need this money but I wanted him to feel like he was helping us out and not a burden. It worked! He agreed to move in.

Grandpa Passes Away

Life was going well when my father-in-law moved in with us. He struggled with asthma and once in a while got pneumonia which was serious. We were thankful for the VA hospital. He lived with us for two wonderful years before passing on to be with the Lord. We had a memorial ceremony near home then went to Reno to bury him next to his wife. I deeply grieved. After being with Roger's brothers in Reno for the funeral, we all visited the Casinos. They played to dollar slots while we played the nickel slots! As we were walking around the Casino I wondered if I was pregnant. When we arrived back in Atlanta, I found out I most certainly was pregnant. Nine months later I had my fifth and last daughter.

Church Split

The church which we attended for over twenty years split. This proved to be an extremely painful event. At the beginning of the turbulence I was still the director of the Girl's Program at church. I was teaching a class using the curriculum I wrote. It was so successful that we had a revival in the class. I was somewhat aware of what was going on causing the church split, but my focus was on teaching these girls about the Lord. Many of my closest friends starting leaving the church and eventually we left too. We not only attended the church but we were deeply involved in serving in the church the whole time. The breaking off of relationships proved to be very painful.

My Father Passes Away from Cancer

While pregnant with my fifth daughter I found out that my father had lung cancer in both lungs. He decided to not going to go through treatment, but he wanted to stay at home. I flew from Georgia to Montana to visit my bedridden father when my last child was six weeks old. I wanted him to have the opportunity to see his youngest granddaughter. My Mom and Dad were so happy to see her that they wanted to be alone with her. I was nervous about it, but I went with my sister to enjoy my niece's choir concert. Later, I came home to find Helen sleeping next to my father tucked under his arm. I will always remember that picture in my mind. After leaving Montana I learned x-rays were taken, and they discovered that Dad had bone cancer throughout his body. He died shortly after that. I grieved deeply.

Trials Yield Inner Strength

One thing about experiencing trials in life is that they can make me strong on the inside. I have to trust Jesus to guide me in the difficult decisions and trust that He was in complete control. The whole process is very hard for me. When life gets tough, I get mad at God. I am one of His children so I expect the best of life. I now believe that this belief is a western mentality. What I need to consider is that God's best is an expression of His grace in my life during the trial. This is His gift to me. God loves me and will never forsake me.

Chapter 5

Emotional Landslide!

Physical, Emotional, and Spiritual Breakdown

*M*y life was going great, or so I thought. On the surface I was performing perfectly, but physically and emotionally things were beginning to deteriorate. However, I was a professional at suppressing my emotions and ignoring my physical and emotional health. After all, I had a large family to care for: my husband and five lovely daughters.

The first sign of the landslide was when I had a sinus infection, and after many rounds of antibiotics I healed up just to find out I lost my voice for a total of three months. This was a physical breakdown. The next sign of the landslide was when I started feeling really stressed. I knew I was heading toward a breakdown because of what I experienced in my college years. This was the beginning of an emotional breakdown. The last sign of the emotional landslide was my total frustration with God. How could the Divine Healer allow His daughter have a breakdown? During my first breakdown in college I received my salvation, but what good can come out of a breakdown this time? I was so mad. This was the spiritual part of the breakdown.

I started getting counseling from a friend who was a highly respected Christian counselor. After several sessions he pointed me to a female counselor who was a Christian. When I met her the first time I was a mess. She told me that I was having a physical, emotional, and spiritual breakdown. She told me that I was like an old worn out tapestry with a frayed and faded picture of Jesus woven in it. She could tell I was a Christian. She was so good that I continued to go to her for many years.

Hitting Bottom

My emotional health was heading to the rock bottom. My doctor told my husband to have me admitted in the psychiatric hospital. My first experience in the psych hospital was positive because I rested. I was exhausted. I had no responsibilities so I zoned out by putting together lots of jigsaw puzzles-four to be exact. I attended group therapy sessions and took my new psychiatric medications. After being released from the hospital, I stayed as an outpatient for three weeks. There I had group therapy from nine o'clock in the morning to three o'clock in the afternoon Monday through Friday.

Upon arriving home, I began to find out how sick I really was. I couldn't function as a wife or mother. I couldn't fix dinner or clean my house. I couldn't even focus enough to communicate with my children. All I could do was sit around, stare at the wall, and cry. My counselor told me that I was as sick as a person who was in a full body cast. Hey God, where are You?

One day I received a letter from the Christian School where I had worked. They did not want me to show my presence there until I was well. I was devastated. I didn't feel close to my new church yet, so I had leaned on the school as my support. I was so upset that I didn't want to live. A parent from the school saw my reaction to the letter and called my husband. He came home from work and took me back to the psychiatric hospital. The social worker admitted me again, but this time I was in terrible shape.

The psychiatrist changed all my medication and I had withdrawals from the old meds. I couldn't think. I barely knew my name and address. I tried reading my Bible, but I couldn't concentrate what-so-ever so I curled up in my bed with my Bible and Smoky Mountain blanket. This blanket brought memories of camping in the Smoky Mountains and the hike on the Appalachian Trail. *God's living room* was residing in my heart. Thank You, Jesus. My hands shook uncontrollably. I couldn't eat in the cafeteria so a nurse brought food for me to eat in the community area. I was a mess.

The night I left the psychiatric hospital I had a grandmal seizure. Two days later I found myself at the community hospital under the care of a neurologist. After much testing, he thought the abrupt change in psychiatric medicine had triggered the seizure. Now I had another problem, by law I was not allowed to drive for six months. How were the kids getting to school? What about groceries? Not only could I not function socially but now I couldn't even get around.

God's Provision

In the midst of the breakdown, God miraculously met our needs. God gave me one of the best psychiatrists in our community. My loving neighbor contacted him, even though he wasn't taking any new patients. After her loving persuasion he decided to take me on as his patient. I had a wonderful counselor. My new pastor had suffered from a breakdown several years earlier so he was able to sympathize with our situation which was a tremendous help to my husband.

A neighbor from up the street arranged meals four times a week for three months. The meals came from my own church, my neighbor's church, the neighbors, many home school families, and the swim team at the High School where two of my daughters attended. She proved to be such good support and helped me greatly.

I was not able to care for my girls before or after school. Another friend of mine came by the house every morning to get my children ready for school and drove the younger ones to school. Many friends picked up my children after school and helped them with their homework. God had put together a team of Christians from different walks of life to help our family.

The holidays soon approached and God was still in the business of providing for our family. A woman, who didn't even know our family, gave us a full Thanksgiving dinner! Not only that, she gave us a $100 dollars. Christmas was equally a blessing. My children decorated the house. Some people from our church and the girl's high school gave us gifts. We were so blessed that God had not only taken care of our needs but our wants too!

Family Devastation

It took over two years of recovering before I realized the devastation that the breakdown had on my family. Roger was such a trooper. He missed so much work while I was sick. He had to be Mr. Mom, and he operated as Mr. Mom in a business manner rather than my style as a mom of mercy and compassion. The children were afraid when he directed them to keep the house clean to help me get well. He kept the girls from coming in my bedroom where I was cuddling with my Smoky

Mountain blanket. I was so sick that I could hardly communicate with my family without crying.

The children were afraid to talk to me because they were so hurt when I couldn't focus on their conversations. They thought I was rejecting them when I walked off in the middle of talking to them. I don't remember doing that. I thought I had been a good mother before the breakdown, and now I believed all the good had been undone. My teenage daughters felt alienated by me. This breakdown definitely affects more than the person who is sick, but it affects their family and friends as well.

Family Healing

After realizing that there was a chasm between my girls and me, I set out to bridge the gap. Was it too late? I reached out to the teenagers by hugging them as often as I could and I cuddled with my younger girls. I apologized to them for not listening to them when they shared their deep feelings with me. I knew I couldn't help it at the time, but my children needed to hear the apology.

Later, I talked to all the care givers of my girls during the time I was so depressed. I wanted to know their perspective of how my girls handled the situation. I then called our pastor to talk about Roger. All this information inspired me to have a round table discussion so everyone could share their feelings during the time of the breakdown. The teenagers giggled when they shared and the two little ones didn't have a clue what we were talking about. Roger shared when the sharing time was more serious. Finally, I implemented my plan I hoped could help bring restoration in our relationship. I washed each family member's feet and apologized for anything I may have done that hurt them. It was an intimate time. Everyone hugged each other tightly. Healing was taking place.

It has been several years since the breakdown and the healing is still not complete for me and the family. I still reach out to the girls and give them hugs. I encourage the girls to share from their lives. I realize it is hard for teens to share their feelings, but I know that each time they share a layer of bitterness peels off. Love can bring healing in all our lives.

Life Returns to Normal

It has been five years since the breakdown, and I am back to teaching full time with a part-time job working as a cashier. I am no longer performing for acceptance and I know how to rest. However, I am still on psychiatric medication, and may have to stay on it for the rest of my life. Life sure has its ups and downs! The ups last for a season and the downs last for a season. When life is down, it is time to really draw near to God. Just His Presence alone can bring healing.

"There is a time for everything, and a season for every activity under heaven: a time to weep and a time to laugh, a time to mourn and a time to dance..."
Ecclesiastes 3:1, 4

Chapter 6

Entering a Season of Rest

A Lifetime of Stress to Learning to Rest

*G*d loves me so much! He speaks His heart message to guide me in the direction he's taking me. This time God spoke to me while I was camping in His Living Room in the Smoky Mountain National Park. I have always been an early riser, and I love finding a place of solitude beside the Oconaluftee River. This has always proved to be a wonderful time of silence to contemplate and hear from the Lord. After arising from the night I made a pot of coffee, grabbed my camp chair, my Bible, my journal, my coffee mug, and a walkie talkie so my family could contact me when they got up. I hiked to a solitary place about a half mile up the trail. I carefully went down the bank to hide behind the trees and bushes. I set up my chair on the riverbed rocks and sand surrounded by larger moss covered rocks. I sat and looked with wonderment at the beauty that surrounded me. The sun's rays glimmer through the canopy of trees and danced on the water. The Mountain Laurel and Rhododendron covered the bank with white blooms on the other side of the river. The clear rushing water of the Oconaluftee River provided the sound and back drop for God's peace to settle me so I can hear His still quiet voice. The air smelled so fresh. This place was like a dream.

One such time I spent in solitude with the Lord, I heard His voice as clear as can be. I was watching some leaves flutter down to the center of the river and ride the rushing swirling water around and over large boulders. I envisioned myself in the middle of the stream riding the fast current of life. I could feel the tension and pressure everything that was happening in my life. The Lord told me that this was how my life was now and had been all my life thus far. I sat there quietly and contemplated these words as my eyes drifted to the small eddy along the side of the bank right in front of me. As I watched the water slowly swirl into this small pool, I felt my spirit begin to settle again. A dozen tiny minnows swam in the shallow water, while water skippers danced on the surface. It was simple yet so calm and peaceful. The Lord spoke to me again. He told me that this pool was what my life was going to become like. Peace filled my heart as I contemplated His words. Little did I know that this vision would change my life forever.

After I had the physical, emotional, and spiritual breakdown, my life came to a complete halt. I couldn't do anything except to sit and *REST*. This was such a sharp contrast to the fast pace I had led all previous forty-five years of my life. I could not teach any children, not even my own. I couldn't perform in any kind of music. I couldn't write. My mind had shut down and I couldn't think. I even had a hard time taking care of my own children with the basics like meals. I was in a season of total *REST*. I thought about the eddy on the side of the Oconaluftee River. God had brought me to a calm and peaceful time in my life. I just had to let go of my anger and embrace His peace. What was happening to me was God's doing.

Now after having the breakdown and losing the ability to perform, I discovered that this was not any easy change for me to accept. I had a really bad attitude so God had to remind me of what He shared with me while sitting alongside the Oconaluftee River. This time of *REST* was His doing. He reminded me many times of the eddy on the Oconaluftee River, but I needed Him to speak this message in my heart over and over again. Once again, I needed to let go of the frustration and embrace God's peace. This time of *REST* was a gift from God!

A wonderful new musician friend of mine sent me a card in the mail. God was once again so good to me. He used the theme of music to speak about *REST* in my heart this time. I love music and I was so open to hearing this message because of the music theme. Here is a work from John Ruskin.

"There is no music in a "rest," but there is the making of music in it. In our whole life-melody, the music is broken off here and there by "rests," and we foolishly think we have come to the end of time. God sends a time of forced leisure – sickness, disappointed plans, frustrated efforts – and makes us a sudden pause in the choral hymn of our lives and we lament that our voices must be silent, and our part missing in the music which ever goes up to the ear of the Creator. How does the musician read the "rest?" See him beat time with unvarying count and catch up the next note true and steady, as if no breaking place had come between. Not without design does God write the music of our lives. But be it ours to learn the time and not be dismayed at the "rests." They are not to be slurred over, nor to be omitted, not to destroy the melody, not to change the keynote. If we look up, God Himself will beat time for us. With the eye on Him we shall strike the next note full and clear." (Ruskin, 1925).

God's message was clear. I was experiencing a time of *REST*. Now, I had a choice whether to accept this time of *REST* from the Lord or have a bad attitude. I was slowly learning to embrace this time of *REST*. God has plans for my life even through the depression. My life is hard but I'm in His hand.

God continued to minister to me through the scripture from the 23rd Psalm. This is a passage of scripture that my Grandmother had me memorize as a child. Little did I know that God would use this verse to speak such an important message in my heart.

"The LORD is my shepherd; I shall not be in want. He makes
me lie down in green pastures, he leads me beside
quiet waters, he restores my soul."
Psalm 23:1-3

I thought about God leading me beside quiet waters to restore my soul. This was exactly what He was doing in my life. God continually reminded me of the small pool in the Oconaluftee River representing a peaceful time in my life. The rests in music play such an important part in making music so beautiful. There was no question about it, God had brought me into this season of *REST* and it was my choice whether to have a bad attitude and suffer, or accept this time of *REST* as from God and enjoy His Presence. I believe that learning to *REST* is vital in my healing from depression and is foundational to experiencing joy again.

Chapter 7

Deliverance—What Is God Doing?

Miraculous Healing God's Way

i nally, the depression will be gone once and for all! Jesus is going to heal me just like he healed in the Bible! I had a chance to travel to a three day deliverance conference with a good friend of mine. I want to bathe in God's Presence and healing power for the whole time! Halleluiah!

Before I went, I wanted to make sure that what I was going to was Biblical I looked up a few verses in the Bible. I knew Jesus healed people. He had love and compassion for His people. I found many examples of Jesus healing all kinds of diseases.

> *"Jesus went throughout Galilee, teaching in their synagogues,*
> *preaching the good news of the kingdom, and healing every*
> *disease and sickness among the people. News about him spread*
> *all over Syria, and people brought to him all who were ill with*
> *various diseases, those suffering severe pain,*
> *the demon-possessed, those having seizures,*
> *and the paralyzed, and he healed them."*
> Matthew 4:23-25

Can people besides Jesus possess the gift of healing? According to the Apostle Paul people in the church can have the gift of healing.

> *"And in the church God has appointed first of all apostles, second*
> *prophets, third teachers, then workers of miracles, also those*
> *having gifts of healing..."*
> 1 Corinthians 12:28

"Now to each one the manifestation of the Spirit is given for the common good. To one there is given through the Spirit the message of wisdom, to another the message of knowledge by means of the same Spirit, to another faith by the same Spirit, to another gifts of healing by that one Spirit..."
1 Corinthians 12:7-9

"When the apostles returned, they reported to Jesus what they had done. Then he took them with him and they withdrew by themselves to a town called Bethsaida, but the crowds learned about it and followed him. He welcomed them and spoke to them about the kingdom of God, and healed those who needed healing..."
Luke 9:10-11

I know that some Christians believe that healing was for Jesus and the early church but I believe it is also for today. I know many people who have been healed! This is what I deeply want. I heard a song found in Isaiah 61:1-3 that ministered to me greatly.

"The Spirit of the Sovereign LORD is on me,
because the LORD has anointed me
to preach good news to the poor.
He has sent me to bind up the brokenhearted,
to proclaim freedom for the captives
and release from darkness for the prisoners,
to proclaim the year of the LORD's favor
and the day of vengeance of our God,
to comfort all who mourn,
and provide for those who grieve in Zion —
to bestow on them a crown of beauty
instead of ashes,
the oil of gladness
instead of mourning,
and a garment of praise
instead of a spirit of despair.
They will be called oaks of righteousness,
a planting of the LORD
for the display of his splendor."

I was dealing with suicidal depression so I wrote this down on the intake form. After all, I wanted to be transparent before God and those with the gift of healing. I wrote down stuff about my mom while wondering if I was experiencing a generational curse.

Every morning started with magnificent worship. I love to worship God and just get engulfed in God's Presence. I *let go* of my inhibitions and danced right there in front of the whole world. I wanted to express my deep love to Jesus. As far as I was concerned if we worshipped all day and did nothing else I would have been satisfied.

There were many teachings on different aspects of healing and the uncovering of the tactics practiced by demonic spirits. One of the main topics was unforgiveness. I thought I had forgiven my mother through the years but I asked God to help me forgive her again. I had a visual image that sins might be in layers like an onion. I still might have some unforgiveness deep within me that I didn't know about. I repented of all the hatred I had toward mom. I notice that several times in the flow of the conference, one of the teachers would rebuke the spirit of suicide. I wondered if that was in response to writing suicide on the intake form. One of these tactics they mentioned was the spirit of paramecia. I was on at least twelve different meds at the time! Was this part of my problem? There were many more topics taught such as the spirit of witchcraft for which I repented. My sister had been involved in satanic practices when she was in high school and my mother was into astrology. They also prayed against generational curses.

On the last day of the conference an individual prayed for me. Of course, I cried very hard when she prayed about my relationship with mom. This was very unusual because of the amount of antidepressants. I hadn't been able to cry for years. I believed as she was praying for me, God was healing me once and for all! I left the conference feeling such peace and joy like I hadn't felt in years. It was wonderful!

Spiritual Battle

Weeks later I still felt pretty good but was not convinced that I should get off the antidepressants yet. Was this unbelief or wisdom? I could feel the depression creeping back, so maybe I needed to review the material again and claim the healing scriptures for myself, so I did that. The depression still seemed to linger and I was starting to get discouraged. Maybe I wasn't healed? Was it my fault? I could hear Satan's condemning voice in my heart. "I had not pressed into the healing enough. I was not putting on my spiritual armor every day. I am weak." Satan harassed me until I couldn't stand it anymore. I was angry at Satan and at God!

I looked up deliverance on the internet and read just one comment then I had to close it down right away. It said there were many weak Christians today. I felt judged and discouragement tried to overtake me. For some reason the deliverance movement makes me feel like I have failed. I was prayed over for healing and wasn't healed. I wondered if it was my fault. I feel judged. Maybe I have not pressed into the healing enough. Maybe my lack of confession has blocked my own healing. Maybe I haven't, in my own effort, done what it takes to be healed. I know these thoughts are not true because God doesn't need my effort at all. This is a spiritual battle.

> *"For our struggle is not against flesh and blood, but against the*
> *rulers, against the authorities, against the powers of this*
> *dark world and against the spiritual forces of evil in*
> *the heavenly realms."*
> Ephesians 6:12-13

God's healing is not based on great faith, for I know if I have faith as small as a mustard seed, nothing will be impossible, including healing. I don't know how anyone can measure how much faith a person possesses.

> *"I tell you the truth, if you have faith as small as a mustard seed,*
> *you can say to this mountain, 'Move from here to there' and it*
> *will move. Nothing will be impossible for you."*
> Matthew 17:20

Experiencing God's Grace during Life's Winter Season

Life has different seasons, and some of the seasons are very difficult emotionally. I call those really hard seasons a Winter Season. This Winter Season I am in now is called depression, and since I can't seem to get healed and I am getting really mad at God. Am I going to have to live in this depression the rest of my life? I wanted to experience God's healing grace but I didn't get to. O God, I'm crying uncontrollably with tears covering my face. It seems that life is too hard right now!

I know that miraculous healing is for today just as much as the early church and I know so many people who have been miraculously healed! However, could it be that God has another Divine plan for my life, like grace to live my life with the depression? Maybe deliverance with divine healing isn't the whole picture of what Jesus' has for me. Suffering and sickness are a part of the fallen world we live in. Not everyone is healed. Without suffering there would be no need for compassion. Jesus was moved with compassion when He healed people. Could God be teaching me life lessons about mental illness and teaching me how to receive His unconditional love even though I can't perform? Could this be God's schooling to teach me how to receive and give compassion? He wants me to have a heart full of love for people who are having a very difficult emotional time.

My thoughts drifted to Joni Erickson Tada's quadriplegic condition. She has struggled with paralysis and wasn't healed from it in all her years. Through the Lord's grace, she is now strong in the Lord. She received the Lord's comfort in all her suffering, and this has made her strong. She is now able to comfort those who are suffering (Tada, 1976). I want to receive God's comfort during this depression and be able to comfort others who are having emotional difficulties. Yes, I want to be healed from depression but more than that I want to experience Jesus' love and victory in any circumstance that I am in, whether healed or not.

God's Mercy, Not My Effort

I know that the last number of years I have focused on healing as God's only answer in my life. I was limiting God from manifesting His creative grace of love in my life. Yes, it is true that God's healing power is evidence of His grace, but God has many other ways to show His love and grace. Anyway, God's mercy is an expression of His compassionate love, and it is not dependent on my desire or effort at all.

> *"Is God unjust? Not at all! For he says to Moses, 'I will have mercy on whom I have mercy, and I will have compassion on whom I have compassion.' It does not, therefore, depend on man's desire or effort, but on God's mercy."*
> Romans 9:14-17

Chapter 8

Back to Serving God's People

Supplemental Income

As I was recovering from the severe depression, I really wanted to get out of myself and help others. We were looking for an opportunity to supplement our income. God provided me a place to serve and have a slight income. A lady from our church had been struggling with cancer. She needed someone to do the wound care on her neck and to do some light housekeeping. I was back to driving and they lived just ten minutes from the house. I really enjoyed helping her. I watered her plants, cared for her birds, cleaned the kitchen, and did laundry. I fixed breakfast and enjoyed fellowshipping with her. She was an angel, but she eventually went to be with the Lord. I miss her.

My next volunteer position was to help my daughter's High School band director. Part of his responsibility was to direct the two public school elementary bands. He played trombone. Brass instruments were his specialty. My experience was with woodwinds. I went to the schools once a week to do sectionals with the woodwind players. I substituted for him when he was out. Eventually I got on the substitute list for the School System and received some light pay for helping out.

As many families know, raising a family of seven is not cheap. Roger asked me to try to get some work so I put my feelers out. I had no idea what I was capable of doing so I trusted the Lord to guide me. My neighbor received a lead for a part-time teaching position. There was a small school just starting up that had a focus to help middle school learning disability students. I applied for the position at the school as an assistant and got the job! That first year there were just five students so it was a great environment to learn how to teach these special needs students.

The next year the student population grew and we had to move to a new location in an office building. I was promoted to a full-time teacher. I was like a sponge taking every opportunity to learn new curriculum and teaching skills to reach these students. I was teaching reading, English, and science. Each subsequent year the student population grew and new teachers were added. It was fun being in on the ground floor of such a good school.

I really liked teaching at the school. The classes were small with no more than eight students per class, but many of the classes were smaller than that with just three students. Teaching there reminded me of home schooling because the students had such diverse needs. Flexibility with a willingness to learn new teaching skills was a prerequisite for this job.

As the school grew in number the school was divided into middle school and high school. Early on I was honored to have the position of Middle School Coordinator. This position was fun but had many responsibilities. It seemed that my natural abilities didn't match the position too well so I dropped back to a teaching position.

One year I volunteered to help with the students who had to stay after school to wait for their parents to pick them up. This brought a little more income to help out the family. My hours were from 8:30 to 6:00 Monday through Friday. My day was a bit long but the work wasn't difficult. A little later I picked up a part time job as a cashier at Publix. I worked a several evenings a week and weekends.

This extra income was really helping us out. Our family was in an expensive season as we tried to help finance weddings, college education, and club volleyball. Our girls were growing up and we wanted to help them out as much as possible.

Balancing all these jobs proved to be very difficult for me so I had to drop the cashiering job and the work after school. I needed to focus on just the teaching and raising my girls.

As I was teaching, we had to have some major work done on the house. The second floor toilet had over flowed causing extensive damage to the downstairs kitchen ceiling and hardwood floor in the kitchen. The only problem was that we had hardwood flooring covering the whole first level of the house. This meant we had to replace all the hardwood flooring. We had to pack up the main level of the house and have all the furniture moved out. This was an especially huge project especially since the hardwood was glued to the sub flooring. All the sub flooring had to come up as well. At any rate, we lived in a hotel for several weeks while the house was getting repaired.

This inconvenience must have affected my ability to work. I remember the owner of the school talked to me that summer after school was out about my mental health. She was concerned and let me go. I told her that I would pray for her and the school anyway. Two weeks later she hired me back. Thank you, Jesus!

I worked the next school year but was having a difficult time. One of the new students was giving me problems and some of his behavior reminded me of my own mental difficulties. Another student had been admitted in the psychiatric hospital during the school year and suffered from similar psychiatric problems that I had. I don't really know why this year was so difficult but I ended up getting admitted into the psychiatric hospital then eventually resigned from my job. I had worked at the school for five years.

Part 2

BROKENNESS
Depression Takes Over

Chapter 9

Emotional Roller Coaster

Seven Psychiatric Hospitalizations in One Year!

*D*uring spring quarter of 2010 while teaching at the School, for some unknown reason that I knew, I was suicidal again and ended up in the psychiatric hospital. This was during the school year and my job was now in jeopardy. I was on three psychiatric meds so why was I suicidal??? God, what is happening?

The hospital was new and very nice. I wasn't crazy about my psychiatrist but that was okay since this was just a temporary situation anyway. After a couple days I went home just to lose it emotionally again. Back into the hospital I went. This time I had a female doctor who changed my medication. She took me off the SSRI medication put me on an old Tricyclic medication I had taken in college. I was on other medicines to stabilize my mood. I was also on a bunch of other medication from my neurologist, meds from my Urologist, Gynecologist, Endocrinologist, and my family doctor. I was a walking pharmacy!

When I was in the hospital, three friends approached Roger individually. They shared about their positive experience with ECT, electroconvulsive therapy. Two of the friends shared about how helpful ECT was with their mothers. The other friend was a man who used to run the sound system with my husband at our old church. He is a dear friend who is now suffering from depression. ECT has just about completely eliminated his depression. He has to go back for Maintenance ECT once in a while. He said ECT is much better than antidepressants because there is less side effects.

Instead of leaving the hospital right away, I participated in the Partial Hospital Program (PHP) for 2 weeks. I attended group therapy everyday starting at 9:00 and ending at 3:00. During this time I was experiencing a number of side effects from the meds. Music kept playing over and over in my mind, much like it did during my college breakdown. My tremor was awful and I could hardly hold anything including drinks without spilling. These side effects seem to get better as time went on but never went away. The hospital where I was in the PHP was an hour away from my home, but I wasn't driving. Roger dropped me off before work and many wonderful friends from church volunteered to pick me up. The group therapy was very good for me. I was introduced to the concept of taking ownership of my emotions. You mean I didn't have to ride the ups and downs of my emotions like riding a rollercoaster?

Is This Cocktail of Drugs Right for Me?

After the PHP was over I went home satisfied. Surely this cocktail of drugs should do the trick, I hope. The tremor in my hands kept getting worse so I couldn't type on the computer. I fell several times – I fell backwards onto the kitchen floor once while looking in the refrigerator for some taco sauce. Another time I fell sideways into the bushes as I was taking the dogs outside. I was frightened. I couldn't remember anything either. What's going on? Is this the side effects of the new medication?

I met with my outpatient neurologist and he immediately double my tremor medication, and arranged for me to have physical therapy to help with my balance. I'm just glad we had insurance. The physical therapist was very good. We worked on my balance for several weeks. It seemed to get a little better.

I joined a water aerobics class. This was an interesting experience. I couldn't do many of the exercises because of my lack of balance. In fact, one time while trying to do the abdominal exercises, I just about drown! The life guard jumped in the pool and pulled me off the bottom of the pool back to the surface! Boy was I embarrassed! I decided not to do that exercise again. I participated in the water aerobics for a month then stopped. The balance problem was too great.

Electroconvulsive Therapy

While I struggled with the side effects of the meds I was on, Roger decided to tell me about Electroconvulsive Therapy (ECT). I was very closed minded at first. It brought back memories of the psychiatrist wanting to do shock therapy on me when I was in college. I had pictures go through my mind from watching "One Flew over the Cuckoo's Nest" from years ago. No way was this an option! However, my heart softened and I decided we should at least have Roger's friend and his wife come over and share their experience with ECT. After our visit, I was very impressed with his testimony. ECT was much more sophisticated than in years past. Maybe I should give it a try.

I met with my own psychiatrist and we talked about two hospitals in the Atlanta area that do ECT. I went to the one with the best reputation. My psychiatrist filled out tons of paperwork required for treatment, which I am so very grateful.

After several weeks, my husband and I met with the psychiatrist and the nurse practitioner at the ECT lab. They sure were nice! After going over the paper work, my doctor filled out and met with Roger and me. They determined that I was a good candidate for ECT. Along with the ECT, the psychiatrist wanted to take me off all my psych meds and put me on an old MAOI antidepressant. She has had very good results with this combination. There were many food restrictions that I wasn't looking forward to. Roger suggested that I be admitted in the hospital when they took me off the antidepressants since I tended to get suicidal when I had medication changes. It was arranged that I would go inpatient at the hospital psych floor. I was so grateful to get off the cocktail of drugs and get rid of the side effects.

I was admitted to the psych unit and met with three psychiatrists. None of the other psych hospitals I had been in had a team of psychiatrists working with the patients. Every once in a while the doctors, nurses, counselors, and other pertinent staff members met to discuss each patient. They worked together. The psychiatrist was not a lone island unto himself making all the decisions. The whole staff worked as a team; I was impressed!

The doctor expressed his concern about ECT because of my memory problems. He arranged for a neuropsychologist to test me. I had difficulty with the test and didn't get good results. The doctor decided that ECT was not an option since one of the side effects of ECT was short term memory loss. He took me off all the psych meds and neurology meds but left me on one SSRI medication. He suggested that I try a new type of cognitive behavior therapy called Dialectical Behavior Therapy. I was really mad. I had hoped that ECT might be a viable treatment for the depression like it was for my husband's friend.

The doctor dismissed me from the hospital after five days but I was really having a hard time at home. I had an emotional meltdown and was suicidal again. Roger took me to the emergency room and back on the psych floor I ended up. This time I stayed just a couple days. Once again the doctor and group counselor highly suggested that I have the DBT Therapy. The counselor gave me several names to contact.

I went home from the hospital so disappointed. Now what was I going to do? After several weeks the doctor from the ECT Lab called and wanted to know if I would like to meet with her again. Why? I thought that door was closed. Did I still have hope?

Roger and I met with the ECT doctor and she told us that she couldn't do ECT on me because the hospital psychiatrist believed it was not in my best interest. However, she had a different point of view. She could contact the head of the ECT department and discuss my case with him. We agreed. She immediately contacted him and off we trotted to another building to a conference room. He was doing an ECT presentation to four psychiatrists from Texas. They all were going to meet with us! We sat in the conference room with six psychiatrists and one nurse practitioner. I was pretty nervous! This doctor asked both Roger and me a ton of questions; some of them seemed to be about Bipolar Disorder. Otherwise I couldn't tell what he was thinking. We left the meeting and walked back to the ECT Lab with the nurse practitioner. No decision had been made before we went home. Several days later the nurse practitioner called to tell us that ECT was an option for me. He wanted to know if we wanted to schedule the ECT. It was scheduled for several weeks later.

Since I was more depressed because of being on so little medication, I decided to go to another psych hospital to participate in their Intensive Outpatient Program (IOP). This program was half-day group therapy from 9:00 until 12:00, seven days a week. This program was similar to the PHP that I had attended earlier in the spring. I thought that this group therapy might help me to deal with the depression. After two weeks of group, I got severely depressed again with suicide ideation and ended up inpatient at this hospital. O brother, this is so humiliating. Not another hospitalization! The psychiatrist wanted to put me on several other psychiatric drugs besides the SSRI drug I was still on. I knew I was going to have ECT and go on the MAOI drug so I refused to take the meds. In fact, I quit taking the SSRI drug. I told him about the ECT, but he seemed to not listen to me. He kept prescribing meds. The meds nurse was very mad at me for refusing to take the meds. I wondered if this might mean that I would never get out of this hospital! My social worker finally contacted the nurse practitioner at the ECT Lab and the doctor finally let me go home before the weekend.

I began the ECT treatments on a Tuesday and I scheduled to receive eight treatments in three weeks. I wasn't supposed to eat after midnight on the night before ECT. The next morning I was pretty nervous, but all of the staff was wonderful. They hooked me up to an IV, gave me some meds, and then wheeled me into the ECT treatment room. I was met with the smiling faces of the anesthesiologist and ECT psychiatrist as well as other staff. The ceiling tiles had pictures painted on them! What a nice touch to a treatment room! The anesthesiologist explained the anesthesia and muscle relaxant to me. They put a cuff around my right ankle so the muscle relaxant wouldn't go to my foot. They wanted to watch my foot move during the seizure to see how long it lasted. The next thing I remember is the oxygen mask and drifting off to sleep.

Later, I woke up in the recovery room and felt fine. I couldn't tell anything had happened except the anesthesia. The nurse gave me some juice to drink, and I eventually got out of the bed, sat in a wheel chair, and then was pushed to designated pick up spot where Roger picked me up with the car. He informed me that I had unilateral ECT and had a one minute seizure. This was really good. I was not allowed to drive while having ECT. Later I knew why. I couldn't remember where to drive on the roads. My memory was definitely affected. I didn't have the typical side effects such as a headache or nausea, just the memory issues.

After just a couple ECT treatments, my mood was greatly improved and I was feeling much better. I ended up with eight ECT treatments and started MAOI antidepressant around three weeks into the treatment. After getting off the SSRI drug, I had to let the SSRI drug completely clear my system for two weeks before starting the MAOI drug. During that two week window with no meds, I felt great! In fact, I felt better than I had for the last eight years! I was experiencing joy again! It was wonderful! I started the MAOI drug and gradually increased the dosage until it was at 40 mg.

The two weeks of joy left a positive memory. Unfortunately it didn't last long. As soon as the MAOI drug was at 30 mg, I started getting depressed again. I had problems getting to sleep, and staying asleep. My sleep disorder neurologist prescribed sleep medicine to sleep. A week later when the MAOI drug was at 40 mg, I became severely depressed. I wanted to end my life once and for all. No more hospitals this time. I just wanted to take the whole bottle of medicine and end the misery.

The next thing I knew was that my husband was taking me to the emergency room. O brother, I was so very frustrated and humiliated at the same time. I had the same psychiatrist, and he wouldn't give me my sleeping medicine. I couldn't sleep while in the hospital, and boy did that make me mad. I told the doctor I was really mad at him, and I wanted to get off the MAOI medicine because I thought that it was messing up my sleep. I wanted to go home and take my sleep medicine so I could get some sleep. After all, I had come on a voluntary basis so I should be able leave when I wanted. He thought that was a good idea. He took me off the MAOI drug cold turkey. He didn't want any psych meds in my house. He dismissed me from the hospital and I went home.

Now those ECT treatments had a pretty severe effect on my short-term memory. I couldn't remember so many things. My mind was blank. My memory started coming back slowly over several months later and life got back to normal.

I am now off all psychiatric drugs. During the weeks of being off the medication I really had mood swings! I had not felt such intense emotions in eight years. I felt happy and even ecstatic at times. I laughed uncontrollably at the dinner table, and my family stopped eating to watch me laugh. They laughed too. While at other times I was very sad. I cried and was very hard on myself because I lacked motivation to do anything. I had a very hard time being productive. I cried at church and was embarrassed. My daughters commented on my moods being like a roller coaster, up and down! All I remember was life was extremely difficult. I was very depressed and having a hard time functioning. I wanted help but drugs weren't a part of the solution.

I went two months without any psychiatric drugs, and then I asked my psychiatrist for help. We discussed Maintenance ECT and thought that might work for me. I told him that I didn't care if I forgot things, because if the ECT worked I could be happy again. So my doctor called the ECT Lab and lined up the Maintenance ECT. They started me out with two unilateral treatments a week for three weeks. The ECT then was spaced out to one treatment a week for four weeks and then one treatment every ten days for three weeks. We would end up with one ECT treatment every other week for four months. When that is over we will discuss what to do next since I'm not taking psychiatric drugs. Maybe there will be more Maintenance ECT.

Currently I am in the fifth week of Maintenance ECT and feel great! This last ECT series has not affected my memory as much at the intensive treatment at first. The beginning of this Maintenance ECT started with two treatments a week for three weeks instead of three times a week which really affected my short term memory. Now the treatments are once a week and I can tell that my memory is affected a little, but it's worth it. I have been telling everyone that I am happy because of the ECT treatments. It is quite remarkable!

Chapter 10

God's Healing Love

"You have persevered and have endured years of depression and now you have forsaken your first love. Come back to Me my weary one and bask in My Presence and feel My love for you. Learn from Me, for I am gentle and humble in heart and I will give you rest."
Word of the Lord spoken to Stacey Smith

God's is Drawing Me Back to Himself

"Lord, where are You? I can't feel Your Presence anymore. Has the depression suppressed my ability to feel You? Is faith without inspiration the only road to You now? O Lord, I am in a dry and weary place. I feel like You have forgotten me, Lord. Have I been banished from Your Presence? Am I not Your child? Do You not love me? O God, I cannot bare this depression anymore. My anger seethes against You."

"In my distress I called out to You. I went to deliverance seminars for divine healing. I tried SSRI antidepressants, Tricyclic antidepressants, and MAOI antidepressants and many different psychotic medicines. I even had ECT. Now I'm on no antidepressants. I have had eight years of Godly Christian counseling. Many Christians have prayed for my healing, but the depression keeps coming back furiously. Lord, apparently there is no way of escape. Depression consumes my life and has all but destroyed me. Only the love for my wonderful family and inpatient stays at psychiatric hospitals have saved me. The words of Jonah might as well be my words too."

*"I know that you are a gracious and compassionate God, slow
to anger and abounding in love, a God who relents from sending
calamity. Now, O LORD, take away my life, for it is better for
me to die than to live."*

Jonah 4:2-3

*h*en I was in the hospital this last time, the first day I asked the nurse if I could meet with the chaplain. He came to my room that afternoon and we talked for an hour. He perceived that I was lamenting about all the talents I had lost because of the depression. He told me that lamenting was a word in the Bible and that it would be good for me to study this topic. He also perceived that I was really angry at God. I felt exposed. I shouldn't be mad at God! He told me God already knew I was angry and that I should tell him so. Since I have a spiritual journal, he told me I should write down all my anger. He brought me several pages of printer paper from the nurse's station and told me to write about my anger against God, front and back on the pages. After he left I began writing. He came back the next day about an hour before Roger picked me up. I was so grateful to have him speak into my life. I believe that God used him to help start the healing in my heart. My spiritual life has been so empty this last year. I had been indifferent to God and now I was seething with anger toward Him. This awareness is huge!

I really have an anger issue with God... I wrote this while I was on the psych floor hospital. So here goes...

"God, I hate You. My life is ruined and I feel totally abandoned by You. You have left me in a cesspool to rot. All the gifts you gave me such as sports, music, home schooling, teaching, and writing have passed into history seemingly long forgotten. Now all I do is journal, cry, stare at my dirty house, go to my psychiatrist, counselor, psych hospitals, and go to church. Where are You, God? Not here in me. I can't feel You. You have forgotten me so I guess You don't care for me anymore. That is why I want to overdose on psych meds. Life is meaningless without You."

My God, whom I am trying desperately to deny, is knocking at the window of my heart. Not only that, He is bringing His servants to me for encouragement. The chaplain was the first divine servant from the Lord to reach into my heart. He was God's instrument to bring this anger to my attention. My own pastor at my church was God's second servant to encourage me. He compassionately told me that people who go through really hard times seem to develop a much deeper relationship with God. But I HATE Him!

"Submit to God and be at peace with him."
Job 22:21

God Speaks in My Heart

Another divine servant from God was a counselor from church. He taught a class on spiritual disciplines for four weeks at church during the month of October. The class that reached deep in my heart was on solitude.

"Settle yourself in solitude and you will come upon Him in yourself."
Teresa of Avila

We had an opportunity to practice solitude in the last 20 minutes of class. I was scared because I knew that I would just cry. Several ladies gave me tissues to wipe my tears. Our scripture for meditation was, "Be still and know that I am God." *Be still* was easy for me to embrace but *know that I am God* was a stumbling block. I was too angry to even want to experience God. I cried so much. Even in my miserable state of mind, God spoke to me! These words were the still quiet voice of God in my mind. I knew His voice because I had heard it many times before. The Lord spoke to me three times during that twenty minute period. The first thing He told me was, "Stacey, I love you." Of course I cried because I wanted to wrap up the words and throw them back into His face. The second thing He told me was that the reason I could not sleep at night was because I had so much anger towards Him. He wants me to resolve this anger so I can sleep. The third thing He told me that was not words. It was a picture of Jesus' face. I wanted to turn away from Him or push Him away, which is impossible to do when the picture is in your own mind. Of course, I cried so much more.

God wants me to embrace solitude as a tool to release all my anger toward Him. He wants to fill me with His love and help me to receive His comfort once again. When I sit in solitude, I cry. Tears fill my eyes and run down my cheeks. Lord, is this releasing my anger? This is so difficult for me. During this quiet time, God is reaching deep in my heart to settle my mind and emotions. Swirling thoughts and simmering emotions erupt and I cried. Lord, please settle me. I need Your comfort. God is beginning the inner healing process in my heart by inviting me to spend solitary time with Him.

Experiencing God's Love

One day, after studying the Bible, I was so exhausted that I lay down to take a nap. As I was laying down to rest in my bed and I said the word REST over and over again in an attempt to fall sleep. As I rested I began to hear the still quiet voice of the Lord speaking in my mind.

The words *"I love you, Stacey"* flowed through my mind over and over again.

I wept... You love me, Lord. I hear You. I love You too, Lord. I can't believe that I said that.

You love me even when I weep. *"It's okay,"* You say to me. *"Weep for this is an inner healing."* God, You actually love me when I cry. Crying is not sin is it?

God, You love me even when I am indifferent to You, just like You love sinners before they know You. You love me even when I am seething with anger towards You. Again I hear the words, *"I love you, Stacey."*

You have been close to me all these eight long years, even though You seemed so afar off.

You love me when I can't perform. I don't have to do anything??? You love me.

You didn't abandon me to the cascading feelings of depression. You were with me all the time.

I wept and wept. I hear the word *"release"* repeatedly. Tears flowed until my pillow was wet. *"It's OK, Stacey. I love you."*

You love me even when I want to commit suicide over and over again. He spoke again, "*I love you, Stacey.*" I wept for a long time. Lord, You truly love me.

The words of David came to mind:

"LORD, you have searched me and you know me... If I make my bed in the depths, you are there. How precious to me are your thoughts, O God!" Excerpts from Psalm 13

I sense that God is tenderly inspiring me to release my anger to Him and slowly opening my heart to receive His love once again. I need His acceptance and love all the time. I don't have to feel guilty for being depressed or perform for God's love. He loves me just the way I am, a broken pot with the imprint of Jesus' on all the pieces.

Chapter 11

A New Type of Therapy

❧ ❧

Help For This Mood Disorder!

*M*y psychiatrist at the hospital believes that I have Borderline Personality Disorder (BPD) as well as Major Depressive Disorder (MDD). He suggested that I get have a type of Cognitive Behavior Therapy called Dialectical Behavior Therapy (DBT) (Linehan, 1993, p. 1). This therapy focuses on changing thinking patterns that causes behavior problems. Two other psychiatrists, I highly respect, also recommended DBT. The psychiatrists were aware of the suicide ideation that landed me in the psychiatric hospital seven times this last year. They believed that DBT would help. I have had psychotherapy for nine years which has been successful up until now. Now it is time to try something new.

As I read up on DBT, I found out that it teaches skills to help me manage damaging thought life and behavior. It teaches skills that can reduce destructive thinking and behavior. This should help me to cope with challenges of erratic emotions and suicide ideation. I will learn a variety of skills to help me regulate my emotions. I need something that will help! As I look into DBT, I began to believe that it is definitely worth trying.

Following the advice of doctors, I decided to change from my Christian female counselor to a Christian male counselor who was trained in DBT. This would give me a different perspective. I needed to change my counselor to one who will objectively help me to change my behavior with DBT. He was just ten minutes away and covered by insurance. After meeting with him the first time, I believed he was the therapist I needed. He offers weekly individual counseling and phone support in between sessions. The phone support is proving to be a much needed service since

I was dealing with suicidal thoughts so much. Wow, God's provision is wonderful! He is pouring out His grace for me. Now, maybe I can learn how to deal with these intense emotions. However, God wasn't through providing support. He provided a DBT Group Therapy that is covered by insurance. It is on the north side of Atlanta and my husband is willing to take me. I hope this new direction with the Dialectical Behavior Therapy will teach me skills that will help me overcome the emotional landslide into suicidality once and for all.

Learning New Skills

One of the new skills I'm learning from Dialectical Behavior Therapy is that emotions come and go on their own. I want to have patience with myself when I'm feeling so sad. The sad emotions will go away in time. Another skill I learned is that we have an emotional part of our mind as well as a reasonable part. We are at our best when we use both of them together. When I get very depressed and suicidal, it is very hard for me to be reasonable. I really want to be balanced so I try to settle myself down and use my reasonable mind to think through the problem. It is the reasonable mind that has kept me alive! I focus on my family and realize if I were to commit suicide, the devastation to my family would be unbearable! That thinking is an example of a balanced mind and the power of love. During those dark moments of depression and suicide ideation the words from my counselor comes to mind, "Expose the darkness and bring it into the light. Tell someone." This is so hard to do when I'm in crisis. I just don't want people to know I'm in such a desperate place. Eventually, I tell my husband. Sometimes just talking to my husband helps me, but other times my husband ends up taking me to the hospital. I really need to learn to ride out the erratic emotions so I have to learn some new skills to help me.

Now I believe I should embrace and apply the Dialectical Behavior Therapy because I desperately need help. God will go to great lengths to help me get well. I am going to trust that He is providing DBT as a life preserver to save me from the tsunami wave of depression to suicide.

A Year Later: The New Therapy Changed My Life!

It has been a year since I began learning Dialectical Behavior Therapy, and I can honestly say that I am much more stable now. The skills have helped my thought life and emotional life become more stable. I believe that learning the new skill called mindfulness has stabilized my emotions and brought me closer to God than ever before. I now know deep inside that God loves me unconditionally. He even loves me when I suffer from suicidal depression and reject Him! I now know that there is nothing I can *do or think* that will separate me from God's love. His love for me is not based on what I do, but who I am. I don't have to perform for His love. Oh yes, there are things that I can say or do that brings grief to God, but He loves me so much anyway. He is going to continue to help guide me on this path of inner healing.

Applying the Therapy to My Life

One of the most important aspects I learned from all the types of therapy is that I must apply it to my life and my faith. I have learned skills that are foundational in dealing with my inner world that has been in so much turbulence. One of the skills I learned is meditation, and it seems to be pivotal to my healing. When I am meditating, I use as time to embrace intimacy with God. I try to focus on the skills that I am learning so I can internalize them and apply them to my life. The most important part of meditation is drawing close to God. I hear His voice in my spirit and He reinforces His love for me. I receive inspirational thoughts to write in my journal. I feel God's tender love while I meditate, which inspires me to keep drawing near to Him and apply what I'm learning to my life.

Digging Deeper to Help Apply the Therapy

Sometimes I study the skill I'm learning by looking up synonyms and antonyms of certain words. For example: judgmental. As I studied the word judgmental, I found out that judgment can mean condemnation. I found out that opposite to condemnation is compassionate love. I went to my Bible and studied the scriptures using these two words. Learning to stop condemning myself and replace it with compassionate love has brought me great comfort.

Saved from Condemnation

> *"For he stands at the right hand of the needy one,*
> *to save his life from those who condemn him."*
> Psalm 109:31

"Jesus straightened up and asked her (a harlot), 'Woman,
where are they (those who wanted to stone her to death)?
Has no one condemned you?'
'No one, sir,' she said.
'Then neither do I condemn you,' Jesus declared.
'Go now and leave your life of sin.'"
John 8:10-11

The Healing Power of Compassionate Love

"Jesus replied: 'Love the Lord your God with all your heart
and with all your soul and with all your mind.'
This is the first and greatest commandment.
And the second is like it: 'Love your neighbor as yourself.'"
Matthew 22:37-39

"Turn, O LORD, and deliver me;
save me because of your unfailing love."
Psalm 6:4

"I will be glad and rejoice in your love,
for you saw my affliction
and knew the anguish of my soul."
Psalm 31:7

"May your unfailing love be my comfort,
according to your promise to your servant.
Let your compassion come to me that I may live,
for your law is my delight."
Psalm 119:76-77

"The LORD is gracious and compassionate,
slow to anger and rich in love.
The LORD is good to all;
he has compassion on all he has made."
Psalm 145:8-9

The whole study helped bring enlightenment to what I was learning. It was easier to apply to my life because I could see that God really does care, even when I was overcome with depression. I was learning to not judge or condemn myself or others but have compassionate love instead. One application of compassionate love is to quit judging myself when my mind is bombarded by negative thoughts and emotions. I get so mad at myself for not feeling well. This doesn't help me get better. I need to accept and love myself when depression or racing thoughts descend upon me. God accepts it all. I desperately need God to heal my inner life and my relationships. I am way too emotional. Learning to love myself unconditionally is such a great a tool that bring healing.

Learning and Applying Therapy Brings Inner Healing

Learning different forms of therapy from various therapists can be helpful, but faithfulness to a single therapist is very important. The real secret to overcoming emotional problems is to apply the concepts and skills that the therapist teaches. Being accountable to a therapist is a healthy a way to overcome emotional issues. Now for me, I knew I needed help so I worked hard to learn what my therapist told me. I worked hard to apply the skills I was learning. I would pray and seek God for His grace to change the way I think and act. My work with the new therapists has been a time of soul searching with deep intention to get well. I needed to learn to love myself unconditionally; loving myself through all the painful emotions. The pain signaled me that inner healing was still needed. Overcoming negative emotions with my therapists has caused me to embark on the trail of inner healing. It is the hardest thing I have ever done in my life, but it's worth it!

Chapter 12

Root Issues

My Close Companions—Rejection and Abandonment

*h*ere are two destructive issues from my childhood that drive the downward spiral of depression in my life—rejection and abandonment. I seem to be very sensitive when Roger has to work late, especially if it is a busy season at his job. I fall into the negative feelings of *abandonment*. I know this is a feeling from my childhood because of my workaholic dad and alcoholic mother. I was neglected as a child, but my husband is not neglecting or abandoning me. We talk on the phone off and on during the busy times. We stay in touch. Yet, a feeling of sadness over takes me that I can't seem to shake. This feeling of abandonment descends on me when Roger is involved in coaching volleyball, especially on the weekend tournaments. Sigh, he needs to play once in a while. This abandonment feeling descends on me when my friends are busy and have little time to get together. I feel sad and have a hard time giving them space to deal with life's demands. The issue of abandonment contributes to the depression that I feel.

The other really destructive issue is rejection. O boy, this is a huge! I have come to realize that I can spiral into deep depression whether I am rejected or perceive that I am being rejected. Let me expound on what I mean when I use the perceive word. The rejection probably isn't rejection at all! Here is an example: When I was at the drug store selecting some body lotion, I picked out a store brand lotion that was comparable to a major brand. I was quite satisfied that this lotion would do the trick. My wonderful husband was with me and asked me if I picked out the best lotion! Here were my inner thoughts. "He doesn't trust my judgment! Am I not capable of selecting what I want?" At any rate, I spiraled right down into deep depression right in the middle of that store isle! Now I had to engage my reasonable mind to this emotional situation. I told myself first that Roger loves me. Second, that he meant nothing about his comment, he was just being his cerebral self with a man comment. As I focused on these truths about my loving husband's comments, my emotions started to become more stable.

Here is another example of perceived rejection. I called an ECT nurse practitioner about some emotional fatigue I had been facing. I wanted to know if the emotional fatigue was due to the anesthesia from ECT or something else. He commented that the fatigue was not caused by the ECT but probably due to lack of stamina or possibly depression. I found his comment very insightful. I asked some questions about Maintenance ECT. However, after our brief conversation I perceived that he was giving me the cold shoulder because I wasn't his patient anymore. I forgot to ask an important question about driving and Maintenance ECT so I called him right back. He didn't return my call. Of course my emotional mind told me that since he didn't call back that he really was rejecting me. O brother! For some reason my reasonable mind would not engage. Now to top it off, I called Roger at work and asked him to call the ECT nurse. He commented that he was very busy at work and didn't believe he would have time to call. Oh no, more perceived rejection! I called my Physician's Assistant at my psychiatrist office to talk about Maintenance ECT and she told me to talk to my counselor about it at my next appointment. She said she would talk to me about it in two weeks. Oh brother, more perceived rejection. I spiraled into deep depression with out-of-control crying. This lasted for hours. I did do something constructive while uncontrollably crying. I hung up my clean clothes and cleaned the shower, even with my wet face and snotty nose. That night I had DBT Group Therapy which I couldn't miss. I was an emotional wreck so I took one my emergency medications with the hope it would help me to pull my emotions together. It helped; I was just weepy. Roger drove me through downtown Atlanta during rush hour to DBT Group Therapy.

Now just to tell the ending of the story: Roger did call the ECT nurse practitioner and left a message. He didn't reject me at all. The ECT nurse called Roger back and answered the question about driving during Maintenance ECT. Based on what he said, I believe that Maintenance ECT was probably a viable option. To top it off, the nurse apologized for not calling back right away. He had been very busy. See, he wasn't rejecting me at all! The next day I called my Physician's Assistant at my psychiatrist office to tell her to schedule Maintenance ECT in a week and a half, right after Thanksgiving. She agreed to call. See, there was no rejection! This perceived rejection is a real problem for me. My emotional mind way over reacts to the feeling of rejection, whether real or perceived. Once my emotional mind takes over dealing with the pain I'm feeling, my mind can't balance out my emotions with reasonable thinking. This is a dangerous time when I can't think with a balanced mind.

Grasping Coping Skills to Deal with Suicidality

I have tried to understand why I have these emotional landslides with the hopes that this understanding would help me to stop having them. I know that the root problem is probably neglect and rejection from childhood.

> "I can understand why you'd want to understand why rejection is such a hot button feeling for you. I think it'd be helpful on some level, too. But I don't think it's as much of a priority as being able to change the connection between rejection and suicidality" (B. Boden LCSW, personal communication, October 3, 2010).

I have been so focused on finding the root of the depression, and this isn't bad, but I never thought that the priority should be focusing on breaking the emotional landslide from depression towards suicide ideation. Suicidality is a more serious issue right now. This is why I have been in the hospital seven times in the last nine months. I need to learn to manage my emotions. This should be my focus.

The next day I called my DBT Group leader to discuss how to implement mindfulness during the times when my emotions are so out-of-control. She was very supportive and acknowledged that learning this skill is very difficult. A good friend of mind gave me the money to order this book, *The Mindful Way through Depression* (Williams, 2007). In the meantime, I said a prayer concerning getting in God's Presence during my morning devotion.

> *"O Lord, I hear your call to engage in solitude. I need you to help me get out of my emotional state and enter Your Presence. Yes, I lose sight of You, Lord, as I engage in the battle of irrational thoughts and emotions. I get caught up with ruminating on vain thoughts. The mental tapes play repeatedly. Lord, calm my spirit once again, and help me to put my trust in You. Help me to be mindful during my most desperate times. I need to*

live in the present moment let all other thoughts drift away. This is impossible for me without Your help, Lord. Let Your peace that passes all understanding descend upon me and help me learn how to nurture and affirm myself during this depression."

I have meditated on the concepts *rejection* and *abandonment*. They have such a destructive role in my life right now, but with God's grace one day their presence may have far less power over me. This is my hope. I believe that as I accept God's acceptance of me no matter what mood I find myself in that I will learn to accept His unconditional love in my life. God's love is not based on my mental health. He loves me even with the feelings of *rejection* or *abandonment*. He loves me greatly and is always ready to give me the grace to combat these negative thoughts.

Chapter 13

Take Every Thought Captive

"For though we live in the world, we do not wage war as the world does. The weapons we fight with are not the weapons of the world. On the contrary, they are divine power to demolish strongholds. We demolish arguments and every pretension that sets itself up against the knowledge of God, and we take captive every thought to make it obedient to Christ."
2 Corinthians 10:3-5

Depression Leads to Stinkin' Thinkin'

The basic problem I struggle with when I feel depressed is stinkin' thinkin'. I will cut to the chase, I ruminate on negative thinking. The thoughts may be true or may not even be true at all, such as a wrong perception. It doesn't seem to matter. I just feel so bad that I let myself sink to the point of despair. However, I am beginning to learn that I can release these negative thoughts to God through mindfulness. When I am caught up in this stinkin' thinkin', releasing these thoughts seems impossible. I need God to intervene and He usually does. I imagine sitting next to God and hearing His words of love. He Helps me to focus on His grace, and release the negative thinking.

"Come to me, all you who are weary and burdened, and I will give you rest. Take my yoke upon you and learn from me, for I am gentle and humble in heart, and you will find rest for your souls."
Matthew 11:28-29

I get so weary from focusing on the negative things in my life from growing up and the last several years, especially the feelings of failure with my family. Every once in a while I see and hear words of encourage-ment that God's grace has covered my family while I have been sick, then those negative thoughts try to consume me once again. Discouragement frequently knocks at the door of my heart. Isn't this thinking vain imagi-nations? I know so. Even though there have been negative consequences because of not being able to train my children, and a shortfall of funds due to my inability to work, I need to look for the good. For some reason, the depression clouds my ability to see the evidence of God's grace in my life and in my family member's lives. Focusing on the negative feelings and events in my life makes my life miserable.

Worrying about the present is vain. I remember these words my father used to say, "Worrying is like a rocking chair. It goes back and forth but goes nowhere." Isn't that true! During this season of depression, wor-rying about the future seems to come natural. I used to be optimistic about the future but now I am very pessimistic. I feel like I won't have the grace to handle what life may throw at me, and that the depression will never end. I tend to believe I will feel miserable the rest of my life. Depression lends itself to worry which feeds the depression and makes the burden unbearable. Sigh...

> *"Therefore I tell you, do not worry about your life, what you will eat or drink; or about your body, what you will wear. Is not life more important than food, and the body more important than clothes? Look at the birds of the air; they do not sow or reap or store away in barns, and yet your heavenly Father feeds them. Are you not much more valuable than they? Who of you by wor-rying can add a single hour to his life? Therefore do not worry about tomorrow, for tomorrow will worry about itself. Each day has enough trouble of its own."*
> Matthew 6:25-27, 34

It would be easy for me to focus on misery, weariness, and bur-densome. That's the life I now feel because of depression. God on the other hand does not want to leave me in this cascading emotional time of depression. He has infinite grace to help me fight the good fight. He has given me weapons and power to demolish strong holds, vain imagi-nations, and arguments that are contrary to the knowledge of God. I'm going to take captive every thought to make it obedient to Christ.

Fighting the Good Fight with Love

Now I want to point out that my energy level is perilously low, so drumming up the fortitude to fight the good fight has to come from God. After all, I am His child and He doesn't want me to live a miserable life.

One of the first lessons God is teaching me in this fight is that He loves me no matter what, even in the midst of depression. He loves me when I can't perform for my family or anyone else. He loves me when I am sitting in a heap crying. He loves me when I withdraw to my bedroom or when I am in a psychiatric hospital. "I can do nothing to separate myself from the love of God." (Romans 8:39, personalized) This is a foundational truth to hang on to and never forget!

The second lesson God is teaching me in this fight is to fully trust in His love. I know He loves me and will never forsake me, even when I turn my back on Him with tremendous anger and when I'm so hurt and frustrated; He still loves me. His love is so unconditional, that no matter what state of mind I find myself in He still loves me. I am going to trust in His unfailing love. You are my God and this time of depression is in Your hands.

> *"May the God of hope fill you with all joy and peace as you trust in him, so that you may overflow with hope by the power of the Holy Spirit."*
> Romans 15:13

The third lesson God is teaching me in this fight is to get quiet before God. The verse from Isaiah helps me, "In quietness and trust is my strength." Isaiah 30:15 (Personalized). This verse is a foundation in my moment by moment walk with Jesus. When I feel the depression or anxiety start to surge up, I try to quiet my mind and trust God to take care whatever the thought is stirring up. John says, "Do not let your hearts be troubled, trust in God; trust also in me (Jesus)." John 14:1. During the moment of negative thinking I have to quiet my mind and trust in God. Usually this is a process because negative thinking wants to come back over and over. I have to practice releasing this negative thinking and quiet my mind. It is very difficult for me.

The fourth lesson God is teaching me in this fight is how to deal with my intense emotional moments. When my emotional mind takes over then I anticipate that peace will come in time. My thoughts betray me, condemn me, are not based in reality, and have some self-destructive moments mixed in. I suppose this might be my most insane time in my depression. *"Jesus, help me! Only You can bring me inner peace once again."*

I am learning several new skills to help me when I have an emotional meltdown.

1. DO NOT ISOLATE!
2. Expose these thoughts to the light of Jesus by either telling someone or getting together with someone.
3. Practice mindfulness meditation by bringing the thoughts to the present moment. Sit in a chair, focus on the breath, and release the many tears of sorrow without judging myself. Remember, Jesus loves me right now, even in this moment. Draw near to Him and absorb His love. Trust Him to help.
4) Anticipate the depression lifting and peace returning. Remember that depression is like a wave in that it flows in and out. The feelings of despair will go in time. Be patient.

"My Lord, I call out to You for help! When I collapse into deep depression, I need You to help me rise above my circumstances. Sometimes deep depression sits on the throne of my mind, so it is hard to live in the present moment. I just seem to think about what I have done in the past, or the what I can't do now or won't be able to do in the future. O Lord, I need You to reach down from heaven and envelop me with Your love. This love needs to be so powerful that it overcomes my negative feelings. Thank You, Lord, for Your intimate love for me. I am truly blessed."

I am eagerly waiting for the Lord to teach me many more skills to help me deal with the multi-facets of depression. I am willing to learn all God wants to teach me, with a flame of hope that I could experience joy again. I want God to help me express meaningful love to my husband and children once again. It is just very hard to dig out of the pit of depression and walk in love towards myself, my family, and my friends.

Chapter 14

Depression, a "Thorn in the Flesh"

*"There was given me a thorn in my flesh, a messenger of Satan,
to torment me. Three times I pleaded with the Lord to take it
away from me. But he said to me, "My grace is sufficient for you,
for my power is made perfect in weakness." That is why,
for Christ's sake, I delight in weaknesses, in insults,
in hardships, in persecutions, in difficulties. For when
I am weak, then I am strong."*
2 Corinthians 12:7-10

Depression Is an Avenue to Receive God's Grace

*Th*e apostle Paul was given a *thorn in the flesh* to torment him and he pleaded three times with the Lord to take it away. It is interesting to note that Paul asked the Lord just three times to take the *thorn in the flesh* away. That's it, only three times. There is no more mention of the *thorn in his flesh* in the scripture after that. From this absence of words, I suspect that Paul received God's grace and walked on in God's strength.

Could this major depression be a *thorn in the flesh*? Maybe God doesn't want to heal me from depression yet. Maybe His grace is sufficient for me like it was for Paul. God just might want me to learn to walk in His grace through the depression.

I have asked God for eight years to take this depression away. I don't think that I have received God's grace yet. I think that my discontentment and anger have blocked me from receiving God's grace. Paul gladly boasted about his weaknesses. I know I haven't boasted about this depression. Paul delighted in his weaknesses. I haven't delighted in the depression. Paul realized that when he is weak, then he is strong. I need to realize that when I am weak because of the depression, then I am in a position to receive God's grace and become strong!

Experiencing God's Grace

What is grace and how can it manifest in my life? Grace is kindness from God we don't deserve. There is nothing we can do to earn this favor. It is a free gift from God.

> *For it is by grace you have been saved, through faith—and*
> *this not from yourselves, it is the gift of God—not by works,*
> *so that no one can boast.*
> Ephesians 2:8-9

Grace is associated with mercy, love, compassion, and patience. God loves me in this way all the time. He doesn't get mad at me, but He is patient and kind. I have experienced God lots of time in my past such as when I accepted Jesus in my heart and became a Christian. My problem now is that I am experiencing depression with its dark cloud encompassing my life. It has become very difficult to think positively about my life. I usually beat myself up for feeling so depressed. I think that people don't love me. My worse thoughts are ones that lead to rejecting Jesus and overcome with suicidal thinking.

"O God! How can you love me in that point of despair?"

I need to remember that God loves me even with my negative thoughts and suicide thoughts. He extends His grace out to me during those difficult times. He loves me in my worst times just like He loved me in my dark time before becoming a Christian.

Now the real challenge is to have grace with myself even though I'm depressed. God loves me, so I really do want to love myself just the way He does. One act of showing myself grace is to forgive myself when I have really negative thoughts. It is hard to forgive myself after plummeting into a deep dark pit with suicidal thoughts. I don't want to fall into the pit of being judgmental with myself, because Jesus loves me with the depression. My moods don't dictate when God shows me mercy and grace. As I experience times of victory over the depression, I want to express my gratitude to God.

"My Lord, I want Your grace so bad. I don't want to succumb to depression and let it destroy my life. Please move on my heart so Your love can manifest itself in my life even in the midst of the depression. Lord, as I meditate on Your love, I realize that You have manifested Your love directly to me during the last eight years. You spoke very comforting and intimate words in my journals, and Your people have shown me love in so many diverse ways. But Lord, I need You to help me to be grateful for what You are doing in my inner life now. I can say in all honesty, I have not been gracious with love towards myself with the depression. Change me, O Lord."

Meditating seems to be one of God's best tools to help me receive His grace. During this time with the Lord, I don't want to focus on my miserable emotional state. I want to settle my mind and allow God's transforming Presence to descend upon me. I can relate to Ruth Haley Barton's words, "I am a word person. My life as a writer and speaker revolves around being able to make sense out of things by putting them into words... I couldn't imagine letting go of my own efforts to fix and solve and make progress in my spiritual life. After all, I am an achiever" (Barton, 2004, p. 29). I want to yield my body, soul, and spirit to God's Presence and *let go* of my desire to *fix myself*. I want to receive God's grace, even when it is beyond my understanding. I just want to bask in God's Presence because I love Him deeply.

Experiencing God's Peace

One beautiful fall day, while meditating and practicing sitting in solitude, I focused on the word *peace*. My mind drifted to the verse that says "And the peace of God, which transcends all understanding, will guard your hearts and your minds in Christ Jesus" Philippians 4:7. I have a deep desire to experience this kind of peace even in the midst of major depression. I continued settling my mind, while focusing on my breath and the concept of *peace*. As I settled my mind, I could feel God's Presence surround me. It was amazing! I didn't want it to end, so I basked in God's Presence for a half an hour. God's Presence is so peaceful, and even in my emotional state I could feel God's peace.

Experiencing Acceptance with Love

A little later while I was sitting in solitude before God and practicing my new DBT skill of meditation, another word entered my mind, *acceptance*. As I meditated on *acceptance*, I realized that for the last 8 years I have not accepted myself with the depression. I have fought the depression with great fervor. My spirit became agitated and I tried to redirect my thoughts to *peace* but to no avail. God was doing a big work so it was time to write what He is impressing on my heart.

In DBT I am learning to accept and not judge my present experience. So often my present experience comes in some form of depression or anxiety. Sometimes the cascading emotions cause me to lose hope and want to quit. This depression, anxiety, and unstable emotions are a part of who I am now. Is this okay, Stacey? Can I accept the depression without judging myself? I will meditate on acceptance in the weeks to come. I want to sit in solitude with God and practice meditation while focusing on God's mercy. His mercy is full of acceptance. He is so merciful with me even with the depression. God wants me to be merciful and walk in acceptance with who I am now even with the depression. This will be a huge change for me! Is this the beginning of contentment? Could I delight in the opportunity to grow in grace through depression? Is this the path to receive God's grace and become strong?

Receiving God's Multi-Faceted Grace

Several months have passed since I wrote this chapter, and I have been reading it every day for weeks. I can say in all honesty that God's grace is finally manifesting itself in my life. I am grateful for all that God has brought me through with this depression this last eight years. This is amazing! I am accepting myself with the depression in my life. I am no longer mad at God because of it. I am learning how to deal with the depression and am hoping that one day I will be able to help others that deal with depression.

One important lesson God has taught me is that His grace can manifest itself in many different ways. In the area of depression, God's grace could manifest itself through divine healing. I pursued divine healing by going to deliverance seminars, but I wasn't healed at the time. Unfortunately that made me mad at God which didn't help me get better. What I learned this last year was that God's grace can manifest itself in more ways than just healing. I need to be open-minded to anyway that God's grace could manifest Himself in my life. His grace could be a medical treatment that relieves the depression. Antidepressants and ECT are ways that can help to relieve depression. Currently I am experiencing ECT and it's helping me to be stable. I know that another manifestation of His grace is to bring someone to my side to teach me how to think differently through counseling. God has brought several friends to me that are full of tenderness and wisdom.

"O Lord, thank You."

There are many different approaches in counseling that are effective in helping those who are depressed. I have experienced several techniques in counseling that have been very helpful. This last approach in therapy that I am experiencing has been very helpful I have an individual therapist and a group therapist. These wonderful people are helping me to accept myself even with the depression which is a manifestation of God's grace. God has brought supporting friends into my life that love me even in the midst of the depression. That's a manifestation of His grace too. I am seeing God's grace manifested in so many ways that my heart is filled with thanksgiving!

God is teaching me to be kind to myself, even when I am depressed, feel anxious, or have an cascading emotions that causes me to lose hope and want to quit. I am learning to embrace acceptance for my *thorn in the flesh*—depression.

> *"God will show the incomparable riches of his grace,*
> *expressed in his kindness to me in Christ Jesus."*
> Ephesians 2:7-8, personalized

Mercy through Love

God shows me mercy through His Divine love. May I imitate God Almighty by being merciful and show myself love as well? Nurturing myself is still so difficult for me.

> *"Therefore, Stacey, as God's chosen daughter, holy and dearly*
> *loved, clothe yourself with compassion, kindness, humility,*
> *gentleness and patience toward the depression. Bear with*
> *yourself and forgive whatever grievances you may have against*

the depression. Forgive as the Lord forgave you.
And over all these virtues put on love..."
Colossians 3:12-16, personalized

Here are some definitions to go along with Colossians 3:12-16 to help deepen the meaning of how God loves me even when depressed. He wants me to have these qualities, and treat myself with His love. Can I love myself this way?

- compassion (sympathy and concern)
- kindness (the tendency to be sympathetic and compassionate)
- humility (modest, meek – submitting to God's will, and respectful)
- gentleness (kind, mild, gracious, soothe myself, and be tender)
- show patience (endure waiting without becoming annoyed or upset, persevere calmly)

God wants me to bear with myself (endure the depression without great distress or annoyance) and forgive myself (stop being angry with myself) for the depression. Remember, the Lord has forgiven me and loves ALL of me including the depression. I will meditate on all these concepts as I practice mindfulness in the weeks to come. This is huge! This could be a giant step toward my inner healing!

One of the great manifestations of God's grace is that He is teaching me to love myself through His Spirit. I know that He loves me, even with the depression. He wants me to love myself as well. All my life I have learned to be critical of myself. I had the false belief that in order to be of any worth in society I had to perform to the utmost. This belief system has just about destroyed me. If I can't perform, then somehow I believed that I was worthless. I have not been able to perform at anything this last year because of the depression so I was thinking about suicide, but I'm still here... God intervened and showed me that He loves me even with the depression and inability to perform. He showed me that He loves me even if I have negative thinking and just sit in a chair for hours and ruminate. I can't perform at anything right now and that is okay. The amazing thing that is going on in my mind is that God is teaching me to love myself just like He loves me!

Now it is not easy to teach this old dog new tricks. God is using my *thorn in the flesh* called depression to teach me how to love myself. Wow! Can good come out of suffering from depression? Can I learn to love myself with mercy as Jesus does? This is a new skill to embrace. I practice loving myself several times a day when I practice meditation with my mind focused God. I think the following thoughts often:

- God wants me to have compassion by showing sympathy and concern for myself.
- God wants me to have patience for myself.
- I need to endure and persevere calmly when I am feeling bad.
- God wants me to forgive myself when I get depressed.
- God wants me to love myself just like I love my children.

"Remember, Stacey, God loves you with a divine tenderness. He wants you to show compassion to yourself. Love yourself the same way as God loves you." This is my nurturing parent inside of me speaking!

Chapter 15

Am I Really Okay?

"When I said, 'My foot is slipping, your love; O LORD, supported me.'"
Psalm 94:18

Grasping for God's Grace in the Midst of Depression

*h*e last two days I have suffered from depression, because we have had a snow week. Basically the city is shut down due to snow. This includes all my emotional support system. The ECT lab has been closed all week so I missed my ECT treatment. The DBT Group Therapy was cancelled and so was my counseling session. That's not all. Everything was cancelled including the girl's school and Roger's work. Roger worked from home and was pretty focused on that. I have had no one to lean on so I had to put into practice the things the Lord has taught me. This is really not a bad situation; I crawled right into my Creator's lap while meditating on His love. I wanted to receive His comfort and guidance. God is pouring out his grace on me, and contentment filled my mind. However, at the end of the week the depression set in big time. I suppose it is because I didn't have ECT and the DBT support. I began slipping into my old habits of rejecting myself.

It was now time to practice the skills God taught me the last two months. I need God's grace big time. Everything seems so much harder to implement when I'm really depressed. When I meditate, I just sit in my chair and ruminate on how bad I feel. O brother... I have to focus on my breath like I learned in mindfulness. I just want to settle my mind. When I do that, I cry. I am learning to accept myself no matter what mood I'm in. This is unconditional love. I go to the DBT Self Help website and watch the *Radical Acceptance* video (Dietz, 2003, http://www.dbtselfhelp.com/html/radical acceptance_part_1.html).

It is really hard to accept myself right now when I feel so bad. I feel like a wet washrag thrown in a heap in the corner of the bathroom floor? I am just a mess right now. Acceptance is very hard.

One of my problems is that I am a social person at the core of my being and I have cabin fever big time. I sent out at least ten emails hoping of getting some kind of response. I really want to connect with someone. One person called me and told me that what I had to say was very encouraging. That was great! I honestly tried to not have any expectations about others but I did have a desire to hear back from more than one person. I didn't hear from anyone else and it left a hole in my heart—rumination material.

I tried calling many people to make a connection with someone. Now I don't want to just talk about the negative, because I did connect with a couple of people midweek: a friend, my counselor, and another counselor from my insurance company. I connected with a friend at the end of the week and she encouraged me to take my p.r.n. medicine. At the time I talked to her I was in trouble, having some thoughts of wanting to hurt myself. I had called several support people and left messages but no one else called. I called Roger at work and he came home as fast as he could on the ice covered roads. After a couple hours he got home and was a tremendous support.

These thoughts have flooded my mind the last couple days. I'm lonely for friends. No one calls me these days, even if I request a call. No one visits me either. In fact, as I think about it, I don't think anyone has visited me in months. No one emails me either, even if I email them. I used to meet with some good friends for tea once a week but that has stopped. Does anyone love me—again, more rumination material?

My wonderful husband and I discussed my problem of not being able to connect with people. This could continue to be a challenge since I am not allowed to drive because of ECT. We discussed another tool that might help me to connect with people and that is Facebook. I feel a bit intimidated with Facebook because I really don't want to advertise my depression all over the internet. He said that he would teach me skills that would help me to keep my messages private. I am going to pursue this when I'm feeling better.

The cause of the depression appears to be missing ECT treatment on Monday, missing DBT therapy, and a shortage of friends. I can't do anything about any of those reasons, so here I sit with tears in my eyes, my (rescue) medicine, and God. I am in God's hands now so I have to totally rely on His Presence and His Word to help me. I have to trust in His loving grace!

The last couple days my *thorn in the flesh* depression has been staring me in the face big time. I thought about how Paul dealt with his *thorn in the flesh*. God's grace was sufficient. I desperately need to experience God's sufficient grace. God's power is made perfect in my weakness of depression. How does that happen?

"O my God, I need you, Lord! You said that your grace is sufficient for me so I call out to you for more grace right now. I need You for there is nowhere else to turn!"

"Turn, O LORD, and deliver me;
save me because of your unfailing love...
I am worn out from groaning;
all night long I flood my bed with weeping
and drench my couch with tears...
The LORD has heard my weeping.
The LORD has heard my cry for mercy;
the LORD accepts my prayer."
Psalm 6:4-9, personalized

Practicing Mindfulness and Acceptance

I believe at this time that the two most helpful skills the Lord has taught me to help deal with depression are mindfulness and acceptance. I will start with mindfulness. I have been *waiting on God* several times every day all week. It truly has been a life line to me. God has given me great insight and even ability to write. However, now that I am at the end of the week, depression has set in big time and *waiting on God* has become very difficult. My mind seems to only ruminate about how bad I feel. This morning as I focused on solitude as I sat with the Lord, I pictured myself in *God's living room* on top of Balsam Mountain in The Great Smoky Mountain National Park. I love Balsam Mountain and the colorful wildflowers and refreshing smell of the spruce/fir forest. I imagined it in my mind and pictured Jesus walking with me on the trail. After a while my heart got very heavy and I cried because I felt so awful with depression. I began focusing on my breath. This is a technique I learned from studying mindfulness. I just needed to stabilize my mind and not give in to the rumination.

As I sat and focused on my breath, I started to calm down and enter Jesus' Presence. Jesus, the God of all comfort was still with me; He was comforting me as I suffered from depression. Peace began to enter my mind. The God of all comfort was with me. Thank You!!!

I thought about accepting myself. I just felt awful with depression and didn't want to accept myself in that state of mind. All I could think about was how I must not be a very friendly person any more since I had so few friends. I heard so many other negative thoughts in my mind. I don't want to write these thoughts down because they aren't even true. Depression is ruling and rumination has taken over. Accepting myself is too hard right now so I will focus on how much God loves me.

God's Mercy and Unfailing Love!

> *"Remember me... O my God, and show mercy*
> *to me according to your great love."*
> *Nehemiah 13:22*

> *"Do not withhold your mercy from me, O LORD;*
> *may your love and your truth always protect me."*
> *Psalm 40:11*

> *"I trust in God's unfailing love for ever and ever."*
> *Psalm 52:8*

These verses from the Bible talk about God's mercy and unfailing love. I spent a half-an-hour reading about how much God loves me. I know He loves me, even when I feel awful with depression. God's love is unfailing. Yes, I feel like a wet washrag thrown in a heap in the corner of the bathroom floor right now, but God still loves me! This is amazing! I spent some time meditating on God's unconditional love that He has for me. As I meditated, I began to feel God's love and the depression seemed to lift a bit. Then another thought entered my mind, "Stacey, do you love yourself?"

"O God, I don't love myself like this!"

Everything came to a halt! I don't like myself depressed so therefore I can't accept myself in this depression. Acceptance is impossible right now! Wow, it is time to read my DBT Group notes again and focus on God's love. If God loves me, how could I not love myself? I need God's merciful grace to love myself in this depression. He loves me and forgives me. My emotional mind is ruling my life and I need to engage my reasonable mind to help me love myself right now.

Struggling with Self-Acceptance

DBT teaches that I need to "decide to tolerate the moment I am in." This is called ACCEPTANCE (Linahan, 1993, p. 176). I need to tolerate the depression right now. This doesn't mean that it is good. It just is. Even as I write this I realize that accepting the depression right now doesn't mean I judge it as good or bad. It is just depression and that is where I am living right now.

Now as far as loving myself goes, I am not sinning just because I'm sad. It is not sin to have a chemical imbalance such as depression that ECT can fix. So should I dislike myself because I am emotionally sick? Sigh... Where is my sympathy, and concern? How can I be kind to myself? Can I be gracious with myself and soothe myself with tenderness? Can I bear with myself without being annoyed? Can I stop being angry at all the pain the depression has caused? "Stacey, focus on loving myself and accept myself even when I'm depressed!" (This is my newly formed nurturing part of me speaking.)

"God, I will meditate on your unfailing love."
Psalm 48:9, personalized)

Enduring Depression with Mercy

It is now time to sit quietly before God. I started this morning imagining that I was on Balsam Mountain up in the top of the Smoky Mountains. It is time to meditate on mercy and forgive the depression. I need to encourage my mind to be filled with love towards myself. I will embrace concepts like compassion and mercy for myself. God has shown me compassion and has been so merciful, so I want to soothe myself with mercy and tenderness too. I know that God loves me in these ways, so I want God to pour out His grace to help me love myself in these ways too.

It is later and I am sitting in solitude with God for a while. He is helping me to accept the depression. It helps for me to remember that I am sick with a chemical imbalance in my brain which causes the depression. This idea helps me to have compassion for myself. I am now being gracious and tender with myself now and guess what? The rumination has stopped. I feel so much better, but I'm still depressed. I want to stay in this loving state so I will sit in God's Presence with the intent to embrace God's merciful love. I know He loves me. Applying mercy to my real life is difficult, but vitally important. We needed to go grocery shopping. I was still struggling with depression as I was shopping but I was gracious with myself. God helped me to be kind to myself. These are such good skills to learn. They help me to embrace emotional healing with a merciful attitude.

"Give thanks to the LORD Almighty, for the LORD is good;
his love endures forever."
Jeremiah 33:11

"O Lord, I am okay. You poured your grace on me and I'm learning to love myself even when depression overcomes me. This is huge! Your loving mercy is encompassing my life even while depressed. This is amazing! Thank You, Jesus."

Chapter 16

Control vs. Trust

"When I am afraid, I will trust in you.
In God, whose word I praise, in God I trust; I will not be afraid."
Psalm 56:3-4

In Quietness and Trust Is Your Strength

a t again! I woke up in a really lousy mood! Did I get up on the wrong side of the bed? No one has done anything to deserve the wrath I feel inside. This is a day to zip my lips so I don't spread my wrath and depression all over the people love. I have had ECT. I have had counseling. I have had DBT Group. So why do I feel so bad??? Once again, I seem to not be in control of my mood.

The good news is that I am not ruminating, just sad and aggravated with myself. I quieted myself by meditating for an hour, but why can't I be happy again? I took the dogs on a walk, but that didn't help my mood either. Eventually, I took a nap with the hope it would get rid of the bad mood.

An hour later I woke up from the nap and yuck! The mood is no better. In fact, I am super depressed and don't know what to do. My husband is leaving to coach volleyball in Alabama. Is this why I'm depressed? I called the emergency lines for the psychiatrist at the ECT Lab, my own psychiatrist's office, and my counselor, and they all told me to not go in the hospital but apply my DBT skills. Sigh, I can't go in the hospital. I'm not on meds right now and am having ECT once a week. None of the hospitals can accommodate me with the treatment I need. What DBT skill??? Which one can help me in this depressed mess? *"Jesus, help me!!!"*

One of the problems with the depression I experience is that I can't control my mood. Now that I think about it, I have trouble controlling most of things in my life. I used to be an immaculate housekeeper, but not anymore. I used to teach Bible, but not now. I used to raise five daughters and home school, but now I can barely connect with the two daughters that are still at home. I don't have the ability to control anything except maybe the kitchen where I cook. I think my *used to control list* is pretty long but I seem to not have the strength to do those things right now.

I used to be a control freak! It's hard to emotionally *let go* of controlling. I get the false sense that I am a weak person now because I can't control things like I used to. However, now I sit here and realize that maybe I'm in a better place. I have to relinquish all the control to Jesus. He is in control of all of my life now. Of course, He always has been in control but I didn't always acknowledge it. I have had so many talents, and just plowed right on through life with all of them.

The LORD Cares for Those Who Trust in Him

Since I am currently living in my emotional state, I have to lean on Jesus. I can't control my mood most of the time and can't seem to manage my home and family. Since I have no control, I have to trust Jesus in every area of my life, even with my emotions and my family. The first act of trust is for me to quiet my spirit by sitting at Jesus' feet and entering into a quiet time. I don't know where to begin when lifting my needs to Jesus, so I just take everything and pile them in His lap. I surrender everything to Jesus, and sit in my recliner while trying to quiet my thoughts and emotions. Sometimes when I'm really depressed I practice meditation and focus on my breath, in and out, over and over. I have to *let go* of my negative feelings, and give them to Jesus. Now when I give everything to Jesus, I have no expectations of what happens next. I just focus on Jesus' unconditional love, even when I am super depressed and have a raunchy attitude. Once again, I *let go* of the yucky mood and focus on Jesus' love for me. Allowing God to be in control of the depression is surrendering it all to Him: giving Him the sadness, the apathy, and the right to think I have to be happy.

> *I will say of the LORD, "He is my refuge and my fortress,*
> *my God, in whom I trust."*
> Psalm 91:2

*Trust in the LORD with all your heart and lean not
on your own understanding;
in all your ways acknowledge him, and he will
make your paths straight.*
Proverbs 3:5-6

Trusting in God while depressed encompasses the concepts of acceptance along with the surrender. So much of what I experience in life doesn't make sense, I have to accept and surrender the situation to God. However, I have to trust that God loves me where I am at, and will give me the grace to deal with it even if I don't understand. Understanding is not a prerequisite for God's love and grace, but total acceptance is a prerequisite for happiness. Challenges and difficulties in life give me an opportunity to really exercise my faith and trust that Jesus is really in control.

Trusting Jesus??? Is He sovereign in every aspect of my life? I can say in all honesty that believing He is sovereign over the depression is a really tough one for me. I have thoughts like, "Why me?" all the time. I have pity parties, and I regret the way things are in my life. I am a perfectionist and depression doesn't fit in the formula. I know I'm not trusting Jesus in this area of my life, and this lack of faith is making my life absolutely miserable. I have been applying mindfulness when I practice meditation, but right now I think my problem lies in the fact that I don't trust Jesus is taking care of me while I feel this emotional pain. I don't accept that God can do great things through the depression in my life. This thinking needs to change for me to get better.

"Jesus, You want me to accept things exactly as they are in this present moment. You want me to search for Your way in the midst of the depression."

Unconditional Love

Unconditional love helps me give all the depression and the problems it causes completely and totally over to Jesus and putting Him in charge. Jesus loves me no matter what mood I find myself. I have to trust Jesus. Accepting myself with love when I am depressed is really hard. I learned some steps to help learn help me to apply what DBT calls is *Radical Acceptance*. (Dietz, 2003, Radical Acceptance, http://www.dbtselfhelp. com/html/radical acceptance_part_1.html.)

1. Accepting that reality is what it is.
   I do accept the reality that I am depressed. I'm not in denial of that fact.
2. Accepting that the event or situation causing you pain has a cause.
   It is not too hard for me to accept that the depression is caused by a chemical imbalance. ECT stops the depression. I'm trying to take care of myself by going to a natural pathologist who is hopefully correcting all the hormones, minerals, and vitamin levels in my body. Maybe this will help me get rid of the depression.
   Could there be a Divine cause for this depression? Is there a purpose for all the suffering I'm going through? I know that God can make me strong through the depression. Do I have to suffer to become strong? I know that I have a tremendous amount of mercy and compassion for those who suffer from a physical or mental illness. Could that be one of God's purposes?
3. Accepting that life can be worth living even with painful emotions.
   Accepting that life is worth living with the feeling of depression is *really* hard for me. Is life worth living when I am overcome with depression? I need help!!! Sometimes I just want to quit trying. Could God be making me strong in the midst of this trial?

When I feel depressed, I have a pity-party or pout because I can't live up to my expectation, this leads to more depression big time. I'm a perfectionist with no room for depression. These thoughts show that I'm not totally accepting the depression. Lord, please HELP me!

Blessings in the Depression?

It has been several weeks since I have been working on loving myself unconditionally. Instead of just focusing on the negative aspect of depression which seems to come naturally, I am learning to look for the good. The good is not inside me since I feel so bad. The good is the expression of some act of compassion and love by someone toward me. I need to focus on manifestations of God's love and grace in the midst of the depression. People show me acts of love all the time! It is this love and grace that makes the depression easier to bare! I am also learning to love myself, and am learning to receive love from the Lord. God will never fail me.

"Jesus, you want me to be eager to gain all the blessings you have hidden in the depression!" I like to play a game with myself to look for any and all manifestations of God's love and grace with the depression. I

am now a *grace detector*. God's grace is the blessings that He hides in the depression! His grace is manifested through the continuous loving support of my husband and children. It is manifested through my many doctors and nurses who I see every week because of the ECT, and now with balancing out my body systems. I see God's grace manifested through my various counselors. They guide me with skills to help cope with the depression, and guide me in how to get additional help when needed. There are so many friends who drive me places, since I am not supposed to drive because of the ECT. So often they share words of encouragement when they are with me. One friend told me that she could see God's love shine right through me. Ah! What a blessing! God speaks to me through books such as the devotion *Jesus Calling* (Young, 2004). God speaks to me in my heart when I write in my journal. He helps me multiple times each day, so I continue to look for ways He is helping me, and I want tell everyone around me how good God is! God truly blesses me through the depression! I just have to ride out my depressive feeling and focus on God's love.

One thing I have figured out is when I'm depressed, I feel like I have no control over my life. It is an awful feeling for me since I love being in control. I need to *let go* of the activities and the *shoulds* in my life. This is the season for me to rest and give the control over to Jesus. Trust takes faith. I do believe in God and am working on believing that He is in charge of my life, even with depression.

Chapter 17

Martha and Mary

"As Jesus and his disciples were on their way, he came to a village where a woman named Martha opened her home to him. She had a sister called Mary, who sat at the Lord's feet listening to what he said. But Martha was distracted by all the preparations that had to be made. She came to him and asked, "Lord, don't you care that my sister has left me to do the work by myself? Tell her to help me!"
"Martha, Martha," the Lord answered, "you are worried and upset about many things, but only one thing is needed. Mary has chosen what is better and it will not be taken away from her."
Luke 10:38-42

Multitasking Expert or Sitting at Jesus' Feet

*C*rist and his disciples came to the village of Bethany to Martha's house. She welcomed them in her home, for she was the housekeeper. She was a specialist in domestic affairs but was distracted with all the preparations. She was providing for the entertainment of Jesus and his disciples. I can just imagine the hustle and bustle that went on in her home for this honored entertainment. Martha loved Jesus and wanted to give Him her best in His honor.

Now I have entertained guests in my home as well. I have hustled and bustled in my effort to serve and bless my guests, especially at Christmas time. It is truly an exhilarating experience but very tiring. I can relate to Martha.

I have raised five daughters. After many years of mothering I believe that I became an expert at hustling and bustling. I learned to serve them unselfishly and sacrificially. As I remember those parenting years, I believe that multitasking is the only way that I could get anything done. I suppose that home birth and home schooling just gave me the opportunity to polish those multitasking skills so now I am a specialist in domestic affairs just like Martha!

I have served in the church unselfishly and sacrificially. Early on during the first few years of my marriage I served in the sound ministry with Roger. I served in the nursery to help the tired mothers out so they could listen to the message from the pulpit, and not worry about their children for a time. I served in the Christian School as a teacher. I realized early on that teaching was a sacrificial job. I definitely put in more hours then I got paid for, but it was all right since teaching is really a ministry. I was serving God's children. It was an honor. I served by overseeing the home school program as a support group leader. I taught parenting classes and served in the children's ministry. Serving in the children's ministry proved to be very self-sacrificing. Hustling and bustling and multitasking skills were mandatory skills for this job! I was proud of my Martha ministry.

One thing I notice all those years of serving was I earned great respect from my children and my peers. The nice thing was that they showed me honor with compliments, certificates, and opportunities to teach the mothers. I liked being respected by my peers. Not only was I like Martha in all my serving for those thirty years, but that busy role became my identity.

I was distracted by all the serving I was doing, but even in my distraction I would spend time learning about Jesus. I went to Bible College, attended the church services, and went to women's studies. Again, I was respected by my peers because of all that I was learning about Jesus and living as a Christian. Feeling respected really feels good! During this season of my life I was focused on *doing* the expected Christian activities by serving and learning. I really believe that up for over twenty five years I was in a Martha season of my life. I am a master at living a life of *doing*.

Now Mary loved Jesus but she expressed her love to Jesus in a different way. She sat at Jesus' feet and listened to His teaching. Jesus commended Mary for doing the better thing. Now obviously we can't sit at Jesus' feet because he's not with us in body. So in my thirty-five years of serving Jesus I have learned that it is spiritual to sit and listen to someone teach from the Bible, like maybe during a church service or Bible study. It is also spiritual to read the Bible during a quiet time. But honestly, growing spiritually is a little more abstract than I care to admit.

Waiting on God

As I grew in maturity as a Christian I learned that it is spiritual to have a quiet time and *wait on God*. I knew that a quiet time encompassed reading my Bible and praying but *waiting on God*? This is definitely an abstract concept. No one seemed to be able to tell me what *waiting on God* was. I am creative so I just came up with an activity that I thought might be an expression of *waiting on God*. I selected worship music and sat in a chair listening to it for maybe a half-hour to an hour. At first my quiet time consisted of reading my Bible for part of the time and prayed for part of the time. However, for the majority of the time I tried to *wait on God*. I tried to quiet my mind and not *think* so much. My goal was to focus on feeling God's Presence. I wanted to sense His Divine Presence if that could happen. I had an intense desire to *hear* God's still quiet voice in my heart. I would *wait on God* most every day. I usually didn't hear anything while I was *waiting on God* but later during the day it seemed like I was more aware of God's Spirit. I could see how God was answering my prayers too. It just seemed like God wasn't so far off and was actually moving in my life.

I did notice some changes in my life as I *waited on God*. I realized deep in my spirit that Jesus was more than just an abstract God; He was a person! Not only was He a person but He loved me! I became more aware of the idea that Jesus was my *friend*. He was someone to get to know personally, not just learn about and serve. My teaching changed because I had a desire to introduce the kids to the person of Jesus who loves us. I started to write some of the impressions God was putting on my heart so I wrote my first book, *Children of Faith*. This became the curriculum used in the girl's program at church and shortly after implementing the program there was a revival in my class! Something really cool was taking place! Kids were getting to know a real God who cares about them personally!

Another thing I noticed is that no one knew about me *waiting on God*. If they did, they didn't say anything. I didn't talk to anyone about *waiting on God* because the whole experience is so abstract it may come across as boring. *Waiting on God* is not an activity you do to gain respect from your peers. It is an activity like Mary did as she sat at Jesus' feet and was commended by Jesus. *Waiting on God* is an activity to help experience God's Presence.

Hearing God's Still Small Voice

It has been many years since I began *waiting on God* and many things in my life have changed. The major event of change was the physical, emotional, and spiritual breakdown in 2002, nine years ago. *Waiting on God* has been a life line to God that I believe has not only kept me from committing suicide, but it is the only way I know to receive grace for inner healing from depression.

It was while *waiting on God* by the Oconaluftee River in the Great Smoky Mountains that I heard God's still quiet voice. My life has been like the rapids in the center of the river when I did many things. My life was going to change to become like the quiet eddy filled with tiny minnows and water skippers dancing on top. I have remembered this picture since the breakdown nine years ago and now I believe that my life might be like that quiet eddy now. This quiet eddy was not a time to *do* many things, such as in the Martha season of my life. This eddy represented a time to *rest* as in the Mary season of my life. This is a season to *be* by spending time with Jesus like Mary did.

For the first five years after the breakdown the act of *waiting on God* was manifested through spiritual writing. My journals contained thousands of conversations with God. God told me over and over how much He loved me. I ate it up. He offered guidance through the journaling that helped me become mentally healthier. God was not only my friend, but He was my counselor.

Distracted by Many Things

However, since I still seem to be just human, I stopped waiting on God. I had started working and got distracted teaching and running a household. My spiritual life became mundane because I was busy teaching learning disabled children and caring for my family. This all lead up to another breakdown months ago. That is when the emotional roller coaster time of my life took place and I went in and out of psychiatric hospitals many times that year. Little did I know that God wanted me to *rest* again. Once again I could not *do* things such as work, teach, or run a house with my younger two kids still at home. Since I couldn't *do* things my self-esteem plummeted and I wanted to commit suicide off and on all year.

Back to Sitting at Jesus' Feet

It took an army to get me to sit at Jesus feet. Of course, I can't do that literally but I can *wait on God* again. It started with an unsaved psychiatrist at the last hospital where I was admitted. He told me that I needed DBT so I started seeing a DBT counselor and attending DBT Group Therapy. One of the first concepts I learned was mindfulness. One of the skills with mindfulness is meditation. Meditation is like *waiting on God*. Now during that same time I attended a class at my church on Spiritual Disciplines where the counselor taught on Solitude. Solitude is *waiting on God*. I started practicing solitude and mindfulness meditation several times a day. My pastor was reading a book on solitude and wrote a blog entry about his experience practicing solitude. I ate up his words and put the concepts into practice. I started learning how to *wait on God* much like Mary did and how I did years ago.

To start with I sit in my recliner in my living room, with no music on. At first, I talk to God through prayer and I read scripture and my DBT notes during my morning devotions. Then I sit in silence and focus on my breathing and embrace the concept of accepting myself even with depression. I think about how much God loves me and focus on loving myself with the depression and inability to perform. I *wait on God* between a half-hour to an hour several times a day. The wonderful thing that's taking place is that this is not a spiritual discipline for me now; it has become a delight. I love *waiting on God*!

I know why *waiting on God* is a delight for me. God speaks to me with His still small voice. Most everything in this book is what God has spoken to me. For example, I learned the concept *acceptance* in DBT. I learned how my emotional distress was rooted in my lack of acceptance. I was really rejecting myself because of the severe depression. As I learned about accepting myself even with the depression, it felt good. God reaffirms to me that He loves me unconditionally for who I am, depression and all. He wants me to love myself unconditionally as well, depression and all. As I meditate on these concepts, I feel good. I have warm fuzzies in my heart and all thoughts of suicide flee! I feel happy and even joyful at times!

When I *wait on God*, sometimes God speaks directly in my mind with words or pictures. He usually speaks to me through people such as my pastors, doctors, counselors, family members, church friends, and neighbor friends. So often the message from these people is seed thoughts that God wants to speak to me. He seems to be looking for any messenger that will speak His words to me that will help me in my walk with the depression. My spirit is always open to God's still small voice because with His voice comes the grace that helps me in my walk. *Waiting on God* and hearing His words off and on all day have become a life line of grace. This grace has reconnected me to God and I can now feel His love for me once again. He is showing me why I have been suicidal and teaching me His whole gospel so I am beginning to understand His grace even while mentally ill.

Living Out the Mary Season of My Life

It has been two months since I started *waiting on God* by practicing meditation and focus on Jesus' loving arms wrapped around me. This is the same time that I have had Maintenance ECT, and am off all psychiatric drugs. One of the drawbacks of ECT is that I am not supposed to drive. However, this has set the stage for me to *wait on God* more. I'm also not working so I have lots of time to *wait on God* and think and write about my experience that He is teaching me. Instead of the Martha part of me getting all frustrated, the Mary part of me is excited! I am finally learning to delight in this time of am not *doing* many things. I am *resting* now, and I am living out the Mary season of my life by sitting at Jesus' feet as I *wait on God* and it is exciting! I am learning to just *be*.

Chapter 18

Waiting on God for Grace

$\maltese$ $\maltese$

*"Be at rest once more, O my soul, for the LORD
has been good to you."*
Psalm 116:7

*"Come with me by yourselves to a quiet place
and get some rest."*
Mark 6:31

The Gift of Meditation to Rest in God's Presence

e st has been a major theme in my life for the last nine years. The last couple months God is once again calling me to rest through meditation. There are other words for meditation such as *waiting on God* and *solitude and silence*. However, I have been challenged to call it meditation. The author Ruth Haley Barton challenges us to let go of our Western Ways and enter into a time of rest. "The practices of solitude are radical because they challenge us on every level of our existence. They challenge us on the level of Western culture that supports us in beyond entering into what feels like unproductive time for being (beyond human effort) and listening (beyond human thought)" (Barton, 2004, p. 31). God is really challenging me to settle my mind through the teaching of mindfulness. This is a part of ancient Christian cultures as well. Mindfulness includes the concept similar to meditation or spending solitude time with Jesus. Both concepts teach a settling of the mind to enter a state of peace and rest. Settling of the mind is difficult for me since I am a *doer* type person. It is hard to understand mindfulness, and even harder to embrace. Not only do I think I should be physically active (which I really haven't been since being depressed) but my mind is still always filled with words and pictures. It never seems to stop! I believe that the Lord wants my mind to settle and not think so much. I believe embracing the skill of meditation is a very important step toward my inner healing.

The main reason I am drawn to meditate is that I really need an intimate relationship with God. It is only by His Divine influence that I can even deal with this depression. However, I know that Jesus reached out to me first with the concept of meditation after I got out of the hospital. The first class I attended at church was on solitude. During the last twenty minutes of class we practiced solitude. This is when God opened my extremely discouraged mind to embrace His Presence. During that time I hated God for all the painful depression I had gone through, but He reached out to my hardened heart and spoke to me anyway, "I love you, Stacey." It was hard for me to receive His love at that time, but God loved me anyway. I really believe that meditation is one of the most important steps towards my inner healing.

God reached out to me first, even when my heart was so hardened and full of anger. He loved me and still loves me so much that He wants to spend intimate time with me. He wants me in His Presence to embrace His unconditional love, especially when I am depressed and emotional!

I love the Bible, so in my quest to learn about meditation I turned to the scripture to see what God has to say. This study is helping me to understand and embrace the concept of entering a deep resting period with God.

"Be still before the LORD and wait patiently for him;"
Psalm 37:7

Be still means to cease all activities and not work or play. It means to actually rest. I need to take time away from all the busy work of motherhood, homemaking, and writing. I need to take some time away from playing as well. That means the computer games, watching TV, and family games are not *be still* activities. I need to totally rest my mind.

"In repentance and rest is your salvation, in quietness
and trust is your strength..."
Isaiah 30:15

Quietness means to relax and take it easy. It means to rest, settle, and be still. It means a state of relaxation, restfulness, tranquility, calm, and peacefulness. I need to relax and take it easy from all the things I do. I need to rest, settle, and still my busy mind. This is an active process as I learn to release my many thoughts so I can enter a state of total relaxation. I want to feel so calm that I feel God's tranquility and abundant peace anywhere I am, just like I felt His peace in *God's living room* in nature.

Passion and Creativity

> *"A heart at peace gives life to the body."*
> Proverbs 14:30

The heart represents the feelings, the will, and even the intellect. I need to control my passions and protect the emotional condition of my mind. I am very creative and passionate. Roger can vouch for this! Very often my creativeness and passion take over my life. I have always thought this was good since I have become a good musician, teacher, and writer. As I sit here and contemplate the creative and passionate part of me, I realize that these qualities have been a way of escape from the emotional pain of rejection and abandonment while growing up. I poured myself into music as an escape from the pain of family life. Now, as an adult, I still pour myself into a creative outlet such as teaching and writing. The intensity in my life with the creativity makes an atmosphere of tension surround me. I have been greatly rewarded for my creativity in music and teaching and highly respected for my passionate love for the Lord and ability to express my heart through writing. However, my creative and passionate heart is not at peace. It is driven.

The things that I view as my greatest strengths, creativity and passion, might be the reasons that I have a problem with depression. I had learned to strive and achieve personal goals because of my intense desire to earn my parent's love. I am an overachiever. When I am creative, I am very ambitious, determined, motivated, and even to the point of being obsessed with dreams I want to fulfill. How do I guide my driven heart to reach a point of inner peace? How do I guide myself to only express creativity birthed from God's heart? You know, not just a good idea, but a God idea! How do I learn to control my passions? How can I protect the emotional condition of my mind? I believe as I actively practice solitude with Jesus through meditating, sitting in God's Presence, and living in the moment through Mindfulness that God will reveal His deep love for me and His empowering grace to guide me in God's Presence, even with severe depression.

I have a habit of possessing an over active mind. When I am happy, I plan things to do. When I am sad, I ruminate on past failures (or perceived failures) and future limitations (or perceived limitations.) I want to experience Jesus in the present moment more than ever. This is going to take intentional practice. I believe as I meditate several times a day that this will help me focus on the Lord. I need to be very patient with myself. I only have most of my life with a habitual over active mind to bring to rest so I can enjoy God's Presence now.

Peaceful Submission through Meekness

"The meek shall delight themselves in the abundance of peace."
Psalm 37:11 KJV

A healing spirit is made up of love and meekness with a hearty, friendly, cheerful disposition. Meekness means gentle. It means humble, not proud. The meek are happy and peaceful because they quietly submit to God's will. I want to submit to God's will and bear the depression without anger and frustration. I need to talk to my loving God about it. When I am meek, I can share my frustrations without getting mad at God because I trust that He loves me and has my best interest and my family's best interest in mind. Submitting to God's will is no easy task when feeling miserable from depression. I still want to kick and scream. This is why meekness is so important. It is the road toward true happiness and inner peace.

Humility, Letting Go of the Misery

God wants me to be humble by emptying myself in order to be filled with Jesus Christ. I am God's child and need to crawl right into His lap when I feel so miserable. God wants me to acknowledge that He is great and holy and that I need Him. Humility requires me to *let go* of the miserable pain of depression, even for several moments at a time at first, to worship God and focus on His great love and holiness. God wants me to be broken and contrite, always in want of His grace, always willing to crawl in His lap to receive His nonjudgmental love, and His unending acceptance no matter what state of mind I find myself in.

I am reminded of the last time I went to church. I felt like a sponge soaking up the worship music and message. It was as if I felt God's non-judgmental and unconditional love reached deep in my soul. I wanted to receive everything God had for me. We celebrated communion during the service. As the bread was passed to me, all I could do was stare the emblems. The words "the broken body of Jesus is given for you" flowed through my mind and I wept from the depth of my heart. Jesus could relate to the brokenness that I feel all the time now, His broken body and my broken mind. I felt very close to Him in that moment.

Chapter 19

God's Comfort

*"Praise be to the God and Father of our Lord Jesus Christ, the
Father of compassion and the God of all comfort, who comforts
us in all our troubles, so that we can comfort those in any
trouble with the comfort we ourselves have received from God."*
2 Corinthians 1:3-4

Comfort through His People

*h*ave suffered from depression for nine years, yet God has met me
with compassion and comfort every step of the way. At first it was my
neighbor, and many church members who showed me so much compassion by supplying meals for over three months! Many people showered
us with gifts during Thanksgiving and Christmas. Many people expressed
their love in so many ways through service, money, and affection. Now
I want to mention that many professional people showed their love as
well. My psychiatrist bent over backwards to accept me in his practice
and my counselor showered me with love and acceptance repeatedly
during my appointments.

It is now nine years later and many people are still showing me their
compassion and comfort. I have had many compassionate doctors in the
many hospitals where I have been inpatient and in the hospital where I
have the ECT treatments. The staff members have been awesome! I have
compassionate doctors who are helping me to get healthy so I hopefully
won't have depression anymore. I have had many different counselors
who compassionately want to help me to not be depressed. Some of
them don't even mind it when I call them between sessions. My husband
and children have been awesome showering their love on me. Their hugs
and encouragement help me to keep focused. I want to mention my many

church friends who have driven me places since I can't drive. They visited me and befriended me. I have a pastoral staff that has loved on me too! There are many people who are cheering me on in my endeavor to get better. Thank You, Jesus!

Jesus' Intimate Comfort

The greatest comfort of all is when Jesus comforts directly in my heart. This happens as I sit and focus my mind on Him when I am meditating. Often when I feel depressed, my mind is focused on Jesus holding my hands and telling me He loves me. Jesus tells me He loves me many times and guess what? I need to hear these words often. The beauty of knowing Jesus intimately is that He is always available for me to be in His Presence. This is wonderful for the times that my need for support is erratic. I don't have to make an appointment to be with the Lord. I just need to quiet myself and focus on Him. He in return affirms His love for me. This is wonderful!

God comforts me through His people but the greatest comfort of all is when God comforts me directly in my spirit. Yet because depression is what it is, I condemn myself. I don't know why I am so hard on myself. It is sin, I know. I have to stop. Now I spend hours every day focusing on Jesus' love for me and focusing on having loving thoughts towards myself. When I give God a chance to love on me, my heart gets filled with His warmth. I feel like a sponge soaking up His amazing yet intimate love.

Comforting Others

As God comforts me in this depression, I have a burning desire to bring His comfort to others who are hurting. I know first-hand that when you are depressed it is hard to receive comfort so I want to help my depressed friends learn how to receive both the comfort from people and the comfort directly from Jesus. I am hoping that since I have walked the Depression Trail, it will empower me to walk the alongside others walking their own Depression Trail. I know that when dealing with depression it is hard to receive comfort, but hopefully I can come along side God's people and because of my experience I can provide intimate comfort. My greatest desire is to help people embrace God's loving comfort.

"O Lord, I come before you while suffering from depression and ask for grace to continue dealing with it. I know that You are with Your people

who are contrite and lowly in spirit. I am contrite and lowly and need You greatly. I know that there are many people out there who need a touch of Your Spirit. Let me be Your vessel who spreads Your love to the multitudes who are contrite and lowly in spirit. May I share the comfort You have given me with others who need You so desperately."

> "I live in a high and holy place, but also with him who is contrite
> and lowly in spirit, to revive the spirit of the lowly and to
> revive the heart of the contrite."
> Isaiah 57:15

Chapter 20

Perseverance, Character, and Hope

❧❧

*"We also rejoice in our sufferings, because we know that
suffering produces perseverance; perseverance, character; and
character, hope. And hope does not disappoint us, because God
has poured out his love into our hearts by the Holy Spirit,
whom he has given us."*
Romans 5:3-5

Courage to Undergo the Medical Treatments

t has been nine years since I first suffered from depression and eleven months ago since I started the revolving door with the psychiatric hospitals. I am currently in the process of having the second round of Electroconvulsive Therapy called Maintenance ECT. I had eight ECT treatments four months ago and started a MAOI antidepressant. The ECT was a success but the antidepressant was a disaster because I experienced a near suicide attempt at hurting myself, and now I am off all psychiatric drugs. This time I will have Maintenance ECT which could be thirty or more treatments over a six month period. We are going to use ECT as a maintenance treatment without psychiatric drugs and see how that works.

I am having individual counseling sessions once a week as well as group therapy once a week. I practice mindfulness meditation at least twice a day and am learning to accept myself all day long. One thing I have learned through the last nine years is that I can't lose heart and quit treatment. My husband and all five of my girls need me to keep trying. I have a wonderful loving family. I need to persevere for them. I love them! I have to persevere through the different forms of therapy and treatment until I find the right combination that works for me.

Now I want to be real. I have been very discouraged because of the depression, especially during this last year. I have been in more hospitals, seen more psychiatrists and tried SSRI antidepressants, tricyclic antidepressants, and MAOI antidepressants, had ECT, and was guided by more counselors and social workers this last year than in all the years I have dealt with depression. Negative thinking seems to rule the throne of my mind and this continual depression is leading to discouragement. It takes great courage to undergo the various treatments. I have to persevere for my family. I love them so much!

> *"Be strong and courageous. Do not be terrified; do not be*
> *discouraged, for the LORD your God will be with*
> *you wherever you go."*
> Joshua 1:7

This is a great Bible verse because it says to be strong and courageous. I can't give in to the depression or fear of the different kinds of treatment. It takes God's strength to overcome the depression. It takes an infusion of God's courage to try new forms of treatment. My struggle with treatment is that the doctors are messing with my mind by using psychotropic drugs and ECT. I have to change the way I think and not give into discouragement even at my age. I guess this old dog is going to have to learn new tricks!

Transformed by the Renewing of Your Mind

> *"Therefore, I urge you, brothers, in view of God's mercy, to offer*
> *your bodies as living sacrifices, holy and pleasing to God — this*
> *is your spiritual act of worship. Do not conform any longer to*
> *the pattern of this world, but be transformed by the renewing of*
> *your mind. Then you will be able to test and approve what God's*
> *will is — his good, pleasing and perfect will."*
> Romans 12:1-2

The Lord wants my mind transformed by renewing it. Now I am learning to be merciful with myself even though I suffer from depression. This kind of thinking takes practice because it doesn't come naturally to me. A critical spirit tries to take over and condemn me for being depressed. This is not God's will so I have to stop judging myself. I have to accept and love myself even when I feel depressed. The way I practice accepting and loving myself is to practice meditation with the Lord. I sit in a chair and think about accepting and loving myself in all the various moods that I find myself in with the depression. Jesus accepts and loves me.

Philippians 4:8-9 teaches me what I should be thinking about. This is such a contrast to the negative thoughts and rumination that I usually think. It takes effort to focus on what God wants me to think about. It is worthwhile to think God's way. I have been coming back to this verse several times in an attempt to become healthy. I need to think these things:

Finally, brothers, whatever is true (real or correct) I need to be real with myself and accept myself the way I am. This is reality.

whatever is noble (having excellent moral character) I have been pursuing excellent character for years.

whatever is right (correct) Jesus is helping me to think correctly, that is look at myself in the same light as He looks at me, with tremendous love!

whatever is pure (not mixed with any other substance). Jesus washed away all my sin so now I am pure before Him.

whatever is lovely (beautiful and pleasing, especially in a harmonious way) I am beautiful because of Jesus, I please Jesus and I am in harmony with Jesus. I love Him very much!

whatever is admirable (deserving to be admired) What do I do that is admirable? Now that I am over hating God because of the depression, I now love Jesus despite the depression. My perseverance is admirable.

if anything is excellent (outstanding, exceptional, tremendous) Do I do anything outstanding? Oops! Not DO! but BE! I am outstanding, exceptional, and tremendous. Jesus made me excellently.

praiseworthy (admirable, deserving praise) I am praiseworthy because of what Christ has done for me. He has made me admirable!

— *think about such things. Whatever you have learned or received or heard from me, or seen in me — put it into practice. And the God of peace will be with you.*

Persevere to set mind on these things...

Romans 5:3 says, *"We also rejoice in our sufferings, because we know that suffering produces perseverance."* Lord, rejoice??? I have been meditating on this concept for days, Rejoice in the depression??? That seems impossible for me. How can I rejoice when I feel so sad?

A New Day and Rejoicing

The depression is gone for now because of the ECT and practicing the DBT skills mindfulness and acceptance! I can look back and see that the suffering does produce perseverance. I have read these definitions of perseverance, character, and hope over and over again. I am still reading them.

Perseverance (cheerful endurance, patience) My counselor said that I show perseverance because I'm not giving up. I am trying different forms of therapy such as ECT and DBT. Both require great perseverance—ECT because it takes more than one treatment, in fact, dozens. DBT requires application all day long every day. I focus on accepting myself even with all my moods. I haven't quit! I am persevering!

Character (trust worthiness) I am honest and transparent.

Hope (to anticipate with pleasure) I am hoping for healing from the depression. I hope there will be a time when I am happy again.

None of these words have a negative overtone to them. They are all positive. There are words like cheerful, hopeful, and to anticipate with pleasure. I can say in all honesty that in my experience with depression that I have not felt these positive feelings. That might be the problem. I have been very negative about the depression. When I feel depressed, it feels like I will always be depressed. This is not true. Depression comes and goes like waves. So I can endure the depression in anticipation of happiness returning at some time. I can trust the Lord to help me get happy again. I have been doing ECT and this has helped me with the depression and erratic emotions. Practicing the DBT skills of mindfulness and acceptance have been a great help with the depression. There, I do have hope. I can anticipate the time when I will be filled with pleasure.

> *"Brothers, as an example of patience in the face of suffering, take the prophets who spoke in the name of the Lord. As you know, we consider blessed those who have persevered. You have heard of Job's perseverance and have seen what the Lord finally brought about. The Lord is full of compassion and mercy."*
> James 5:10-11

Receiving God's Strength as I Meditate

Stacey, for everything that was written in the past was written to teach you, so that through endurance and the encouragement of the Scriptures you might have hope. I will give you endurance and encouragement so that with your heart and mouth you may glorify the Me. (Romans 15:4-6, personalized)

Stacey, I commend you in every way: in your great endurance; in your troubles, hardships and distresses; in My Holy Spirit and in My sincere love; sorrowful, yet always rejoicing. (2 Corinthians 6:4-10, personalized)

Stacey, I have not stopped praying for you because I want to fill you with My knowledge of My will through all spiritual wisdom and understanding. I want you to live a life worthy of Me, and please me in every way, bearing fruit in every good work, growing in My knowledge, being strengthened with all power according to My might so that you may have great endurance and patience, and joyfully give Me thanks. Stacey, I have rescued you from the dominion of darkness manifested by depression, and brought you into the kingdom of My Son, Jesus, whom you have redemption and the forgiveness of sins. (Colossians 1:9-14, personalized)

Stacey, may I direct your heart into My love and Christ's perseverance. (2 Thessalonians 3:5, personalized)

Consider it pure joy, Stacey, when you face negative emotions, depressive thoughts, and can't feel My Presence, because the testing of your faith develops perseverance. Perseverance must finish its work so that you may be mature and complete, not lacking anything. (James 1:2-4, personalized)

Stacey, depression calls for patient endurance on your part. Obey My commandments and remain faithful to My Son, Jesus. (Revelations 14:12, personalized)

Suffering from depression has produced perseverance in my life. I know Jesus loves me and is pouring out His grace in my life. He doesn't want me to lack in anything. This perseverance will yield a harvest of righteousness, peace, holiness, and maturity. Jesus is full of compassion and mercy. Hang in there, Stacey, and don't give up! God is doing a deep work in your life for your good. He loves you very much!

Chapter 21

God Sees Me as Strong???

Stacey, Stacey, Satan has asked to sift you as wheat. But I have prayed for you, Stacey that your faith may not fail. And when you have turned back, strengthen others who deal with depression.
Luke 22:31-32, personalized

The Spiritual Side of Recovery

*O*ne day I had a visit with my pastor. He was so compassionate when he told me that people who go through really hard times seem to develop a much deeper relationship with God. He said that he thought God saw me as strong to allow me to go through these troubles. Wow... I certainly don't *feel* strong! I thought of Job.

> *"Then the LORD said to Satan, "Have you considered my servant Job? There is no one on earth like him; he is blameless and upright, a man who fears God and shuns evil." "Does Job fear God for nothing?" Satan replied. "Have you not put a hedge around him and his household and everything he has? You have blessed the work of his hands, so that his flocks and herds are spread throughout the land. But stretch out your hand and strike everything he has, and he will surely curse you to your face."*
> Job 1:8-11

Here I am, after nine years, still suffering from major depression. I have learned many things during these past years and the first thing is to stand up for myself! Be my own advocate about getting help. I need God to guide me to the help I need. There are many people who want to help and actually can help! My first advocate nine years ago was my neighbor. She helped me get a psychiatrist who wasn't even taking new patients! I have had friends help line me up with really good counselors. I have made many calls enquiring for help and watched God provide help through friends, professional staff, and the professionals themselves.

Another lesson I learned is since I am made of body, soul, and spirit; treating one part of the body isn't going to heal depression. Depression affects all three parts so just treating the body alone with psychotropic drugs isn't going to do the job. Talk therapy is very important. There are many techniques that therapists use so be wise in choosing the right therapist. Now this last part the medical professions seem to ignore and that is the spiritual being. As I look back, I realize that the psychotropic drugs seemed to numb me from being able to sense God's Presence. It *felt* like God wasn't my personal God anymore so I neglected my spiritual life. Eventually I began to hate God for even allowing me to suffer with depression so long. I really believe now with all my heart that it was the neglect of my spiritual life that paved the road to my deep desire to commit suicide.

The Road to Receiving God's Comfort and Grace

"Even though I walk through the valley of the shadow of death,
I will fear no evil, for you are with me; your rod and your
staff, they comfort me."
Psalm 23:4

Maybe God ordained it that I walk in the valley of the shadow of death. I know that since I have been so close to suicidal death all year, it has given me great motivation to seek God for His comfort! I love my family deeply and know that my absence would be very hard on them. I desperately need God to help me overcome the suicidal depression since it appears that the medical community doesn't have all the answers. I am motivated to sit in God's Presence with the hope that somehow in God's mysterious ways He will guide me in the steps towards inner healing. As I continue walking the depression trail towards healing, I can look back and tell that God is guiding me! Sometimes I hear His still quiet voice in my heart but most of the time he guides me through people, and not necessarily just Christians either.

Disaster—Worship!

Job was a good man that experienced multiple disasters. The Sabeans took his herds and killed his servants. A crack of lightning struck his sheep and shepherds. The Chaldeans raided his camels and killed those servants. A cyclone struck the house and killed all Job's children. As if that was not enough, sickness was added. From the soles of his feet to the top of his head he was inflicted with sores, a sort of leprosy or elephantiasis.

These kinds of disasters, I'm afraid, would have done me in—not Job. He took it all as from the hand of God. He didn't blame anyone. He tore his robe and shaved his head then fell to the ground in worship. His first instinct was to worship God. My reaction to depression was *not* worshipping God. I wanted to commit suicide.

"Oh my God, save me from myself! Help me to not give into discouragement. Help me to worship You with the depth of my heart."

For the first eight and one half years of depression of the depression I drew close to God by having conversations with Him in my journal. I wrote down my prayers, then when I discerned that God answered I wrote it down. In other words, I was having a back and forth conversation with God in my journal! I read devotional books that inspired me to draw near to God. I worship God out of desperation. I need God to either heal me divinely or guide me to the right professionals who can. I have hope that God wants me to be a blessing to others, so I hope He will help me. I know that all the depression I have experienced has a blessing wrapped around it. My heart is so compassionate towards people. My love is deeper. God has allowed the depression to connect my heart to Him in a more intimate way.

Part 3

Treating the Whole Body

Chapter 22

Nutritional Disaster!

"Worship the LORD your God, and his blessing will be on your food and water. I will take away sickness from among you..."
Exodus 23:25-26

We Are What We Eat

i nally, it's time to work on something other than my thought life and spiritual life. My physical body needs some serious help! For nine years I have had the depression treated by drugs, talk therapy, and lately electroconvulsive therapy (ECT). No one directed me to have my body checked out until just recently. It makes sense that if I don't take care of my body then disaster could happen to my emotional life. In my case, my body is in such bad shape that depression would be the natural result!

I went to a new internal medicine doctor who is a natural pathologist. She was highly recommended to me by my DBT counselor. This doctor took one look at me and told me that I was very deficient in magnesium and progesterone. She was suspicious that I had a systemic yeast problem and a digestive system that wasn't able to absorb all the nutrition I needed. Even though I was taking a B complex supplement, she said my body was not able to absorb them. She explained to me that my nerves were so depleted nutritionally that the sheaths on the outside of the cells were damaged and could not possibly communicate correctly. She had many vials of blood drawn for testing! That first visit ended with an IV of an anti-yeast medication, and magnesium. I had two injections, one B complex/amino acids and the second was progesterone. She gave me a prescription to get rid of the yeast. She encouraged me to go on a healthy diet, and since I am my blood type is O Positive I should not have dairy, wheat, or pork. I was also instructed to cut out all artificial sweeteners. I need to focus on the natural food that I can eat!

During the following week the lab work confirmed her diagnosis. I was very low in magnesium and had no progesterone. Many other lab results were off too. As I listened to her explain how my body was deficient in essential nutrients, I decided to take the diet seriously. Now this is no easy feat! Once again I had to change, not just my thought life through DBT, but now change everything I eat. Remember, I was still having ECT and DBT Group Therapy once a week so my life was getting complicated, much like a three-ring circus! Those aren't the only things I do. I have church and a ladies Bible study meeting each week. I think this would be a challenge to most people, but I was suffering from depression which makes it way harder to stick to a healthy life style.

Now back to my new counselor. She recommended a book to order on helping to cure myself from depression with healthy dietary changes. This book confirmed that what my doctor was prescribing to help me physically was necessary for me to get better from depression. How come I didn't know about this information nine years ago?

The first week and a half on the new diet and medication has affected me greatly. Now it is probably hard to say conclusively that it was these changes that caused my discomfort, but nothing else was changed. The first thing that happened was I got a chest cold and low grade fever for a few days. I lost five pounds. I have a headache. Emotionally, I'm super irritable and depressed. My friends have told me that I am probably going through detoxification.

Life is really hard for me right now. I have been faithfully sticking to my diet. I haven't had any dairy for a week. Now I didn't have much before except the half-and-half in my coffee. It took me a couple days to give up the coffee and half-and-half. I'm drinking green tea with Stevia instead. It's a good substitute. I haven't had any bread either. I am allowed to eat sprouted bread. It is pretty good toasted with butter and organic jam on it. I cut out the eggs in the morning and have been eating sprouted bread with goat cheese. That cheese is legal. I have been eating steak or fish and a small sweet potato for lunch along with some veggies.

Living Life Moment by Moment

I have made significant changes in my diet, but I have had to fight my bad attitude: The *why me*? I struggle with a pity party that wants to take over. I need to *let go* of the frustration and accept the circumstances I'm in this present moment. I need to get a better attitude.

This new life style change has made me cling tightly to Jesus' hand. I have been so irritable and depressed that I can't even plan my day or do much at all without barking at my family BIG TIME! This has been a moment by moment walk for me. I sit in Jesus' Presence in the morning and try to clear my mind, sometimes practicing meditation by focusing on my breath. I refuse to think about the *To Do List*. It overwhelms me right now so I focus only what I am to do right now in the moment. The DBT skill of mindfulness is my lifeline to make it through each day.

"Jesus, I need to cling to your hand and have you lead me through the day one step at a time. I need you to show me what you want me to do on a moment by moment basis. For some reason, changing my diet has made me so overwhelmed that I am desperate for You, Jesus."

Grace to Follow the New Diet

Since I am a *grace detector* now, I must tell about God's grace in this nutritional enlightenment phase I'm going through. First of all, I am still not allowed to drive because of ECT. God has provided a Christian from church to provide transportation to the new medical doctor/natural pathologist who put me on this diet. This is huge since this doctor is an hour south of my house and the appointments last at least three hours. This is at least a five hour commitment for my friend. Plus, I need to add; she encourages me greatly for she has struggled with depression in the past and has seen me struggle with depression for the last nine years. She is very interested in what the doctor is saying that might help me! She is one of God's angels!

Another angelic friend is my daughter's husband's mother. She has been in the family now for ten months, since that's when our kids got married. At any rate, she is a Christian and has been on this special diet for years. She offered to have a cooking party! She filled me in on a secret like Almond Milk is a great substitute for regular milk. She has filled me in on the detoxification symptoms and has encouraged me to hang in there. It will take a while for my body to heal itself. See, God wants to bless me, even if it's hard! God pours out his grace on His children!

As one day turns to another, I have to cling onto Jesus' hand. The last two days I have had time in public, at church and at the hospital for ECT treatment. Both places I cried and cried. My friends at church brought me so much comfort. While I was at the hospital I pictured Jesus holding my hands and telling me that He loved me even though I felt severely depressed. This brought me great comfort. While at the hospital, the psychiatrist saw that I was having a very hard time so he wanted me to come back for my next ECT treatment in three days. The ECT staff was being very supportive and encouraging. God is so good to me! Hopefully this nutritional change will bring healing to my body and mind!

On Down the Road

It has been seven months since I started going to the medical doctor/ natural pathologist. I really believe she is a God send. I have had lots of connections with medical people but no one until now treats depression with a cleansing diet and supplements to make me physically healthy. One of her treatments is for magnesium deficiency is an IV during the appointment and a magnesium powder to mix with my water at home. It seems to help me. I am also taking other supplements and now I am happy! After adjusting the dose a few times my mood has become the best it has been in a couple years thanks to my doctor!

Chapter 23

Healthy Changes
Can Help Heal Emotions

"You have made known to me the path of life;
you will fill me with joy in your presence,
with eternal pleasures at your right hand."
Psalm 16:11

Depression Is Not Only a Mental Problem, but it is Physical

*h*ave had to give each moment of every day to Jesus to stay in His grace and overcome depression. Jesus has directed me on several paths towards healing: psychiatric help, counseling, and spending time with Jesus. The new path I am walking on to help recover from depression is the alternative mental health way to regain my health. I am on bio identical hormones (estrogen and progesterone), supplements with an IV of magnesium and a weekly injection of B Complex and Amino Acids. I am taking other supplements and am eating an anti-inflammatory diet. The second path for my major depression treatment is Maintenance ECT once a week and that will be stretching out to every ten days and then up to two weeks apart next. The third path I am still on is individual counseling to help correct my depressive thinking habits. I have individual therapy and group therapy every week. The good news is that at this point in my life all my hard work has finally paid off. I am happy! It has been about a year that I have suffered from suicidal depression but the last two weeks I have been happy!

This walk to regain my happiness has been a close walk with Jesus. I spend lots of solitude time with Him. I need Jesus to guide me to the right people, people, books, and internet sites for direction. I need God's wisdom all the time, so in my walk towards healing I can do my part to help bring healing. This is hard since the depression makes me want me to withdraw and go to bed. I need God's grace to implement all the changes in my life mentally and physically. I need to bask in Jesus' Presence so He can transform me from the inside—out. I want to be filled with the ability to apply what I'm learning. I know that for me to continue to get healthier I need to do research and ask lots of questions, but I need Jesus to guide me to the legitimate sources. I need Him to help my mind reason accurately so I can make sense out of everything I am learning.

Physical Changes to Help Heal Emotions

New Natural Pathologist

The first thing I want to comment about is that the Lord graciously directed me to a new Internal Medicine Doctor/Natural Pathologist. She is very knowledgeable about how to make my body healthy again. I am doing everything she is telling me to do. I am reading books about natural ways to recover from depression.

Toxicity

I have a yeast problem—Candida. I was given an IV of yeast medicine at three of my doctor's appointments and I took a prescription twice a day. However, at my last appointment she made the comment that it appears that the yeast seems to not want to leave my body. I want to continue fighting the yeast.

Toxins May Lead to Depression: I have been taking a 20 minute Epsom Salt bath three days a week. This helps get rid of some toxins in my body. I am going to talk to my doctor to find out if there is anything else I can do. I have been taking psychotropic drugs for nine years so I can just imagine the buildup of toxins!

Diet and Supplements

I am gleaning some information about supplements that will help me with the depression. I pray for God's grace to help me have energy to deal with the disciplines that are necessary to overcome depression. Walking is one discipline that helps immensely, but so will taking my supplements. They are beneficial to help my depression. My doctor has me taking an injection of B-complex and amino acids once a week. My doctor found that I have a hormone imbalance so my doctor has suggested that I take bio-identical hormones. My other hormone that is really deficient is T3. This is a part my thyroid hormone panel. I am now taking a different thyroid medication. Sigh, I have digestive woes and have to go on the Anti-Inflammatory Diet. Three sources so far have said to stop consuming all dairy products, all wheat products, and artificial sugar. Changing my diet so that my digestive system can heal and absorb the nutrients my body and brain needs is a challenge. I am taking a probiotic. I am taking vitamins and minerals that are helpful for depression.

New Chiropractor

I went to a new chiropractor that my new Internal Medicine/Natural Pathologist doctor referred me to. Of course my neck was very crooked. The atlas was rotated which can affect emotions. I have a reverse curve in my neck. The rest of my back needed work. I have gone to my new chiropractor a couple times and my neck is holding! Yea! The rest of my back needs a little tweaking but it's not too bad.

Water

I bought a new water filter and am going to focus on drinking eight glasses of water a day.

The Ongoing Journey

I started on this holistic path in my journey toward inner healing about ten months ago when I first visited my medical doctor/natural pathologist. It was a hard transition at first because I was sick from possible detoxification. I rebelled because I really didn't want to change my diet either—like most people, I like sweets (Girl Scout cookies ☹, dairy (ice cream) , and wheat (chocolate cake) . The good news is that because of the ECT treatments and DBT skills I have the ability to make the changes in my diet. Since I stuck to the changes for ten months, I am now not depressed and have been feeling happy!

I have to give credit to whom credit is due though. I have spent time in Jesus' Presence hoping that He would give me the grace to make the changes. I believe that Jesus guided me to people for medical support and showed me which books to read for a reference. This has been a faith walk. I have prayed to Jesus, listened for His answers, and acted on His direction. Jesus is guiding me and filling me with His unending grace. He has put many people in my path that have shown me love. I love Jesus and I know He loves me a lot! Thank you Jesus!!!

I really want to give credit to the medical community too. I don't believe I would have had the inner strength to live a disciplined life and take care of myself. Depression is debilitating, energy is low, and motivation is just about nonexistent. I really believe that the time I was off antidepressants and having electroconvulsive therapy (ECT) it gave me the strength to stick to the discipline to make changes. ECT ended and now I am on antipsychotic drugs which are stabilizing me so I can continue the disciplines to stick to my diet and take supplements. I just know that the answer to the Major Depressive Disorder was both help from the medical community and help from my natural pathologist who is guiding me. God has miraculously guided me through all the confusion and lead me to His healing. God is pouring out His grace to bring healing.

Chapter 24

The Natural Antidepressants

"For in him we live and move and have our being."
Acts 17:28

Exercise

t is time to take overcoming depression seriously. Since antidepressant medication is not part of the solution for me at this time, than I need to take advantage of every natural and alternative help seriously. There is no time to be slothful if I really want to get well. I need to start getting regular exercise. I need to start walking again, and go to water aerobics. One of my problems is that I have very little energy to do much of anything. It is very hard for me to exercise because I just want to sit around and go to bed. Now I want to give a little background. I have been a pretty good athlete earlier in my life. However, when I got depressed my jogging stopped. Every once in a blue moon I walk. This last year I have done very little exercise and this is the year that I needed it the most. I did start water aerobics last summer and that was a tremendous success but I had to quit in the winter because the chlorine gave me asthma. Maybe I can start the water aerobics again in the spring. My chiropractor, my primary care doctor, and my counselor want me to walk. In the mean time I am going to start walking again. I have to push myself because like I said, "I have very little energy to get out and walk." I need to make myself walk anyway. I have learned that regular aerobic exercise is as effective as an antidepressant.

Just about six months have passed and I haven't walked, not even once. Again, even though I know I need to walk, I can't make myself. Sigh... It's like shooting myself in the foot! I have had two psych hospital in-patient visits this month and it is spring time. What excuse do I have to not walk now? I don't have one. In fact, I'm trying to exercise regularly now. Yea!

1. Water aerobics three days of the week.
2. I want to walk the two dogs outdoors every morning for thirty minutes. This is doctor's orders, even though I am doing water aerobics.

Five months have gone by. I started walking regularly for a while but a change in my routine has caused me to stop walking again. School started up for my girls and daylight saving time has completely interrupted my morning exercise routine. I used to exercise at 6:30 before my family arose from their sleep, but now it is way too dark and cold. It is winter, not summer. For some reason I can't discipline myself walk at all. All my doctors and my counselor are cheering me on. I must walk again. I guess this loss of desire to walk is the depression speaking loud and clear. Next week is a new week and I will try to start walking again.

Another six months has gone by and finally I am walking. My counselor really encourages me to walk every day. I'm doing it! I now have a calendar that I schedule the walking in. A reminder pops ups to remind myself to walk.

Sleep

Getting eight hours of sleep at night is a great way to start making positive changes in my life. I have been very fortunate; so far in that I usually get between eight to nine hours of sleep a night. However, since I was in the hospital two weeks ago, I'm having a very difficult time sleeping. I wake up between 1:00 A.M. through 4:00 A.M. and can't get back to sleep. Just last night I woke up at 3:30 A.M. and couldn't get back to sleep. I took a sleeping aid for a week that helped me, but since the side effects of this drug could be depression I decided to stop taking it. Now I'm having problems sleeping again.

After many hospitalizations and months later I am still struggling with my sleep so I am taking another sleep medication prescribed by my doctor at the hospital. It has helped and isn't addicting either. However, I have wanted to sleep up to five hours during the day and well as eight hours at night. My psychiatrist told me to take one of my antidepressants at night rather than the morning. I am doing much better now.

Several months have passed. The good news is that I'm off all sleeping medication. I'm still sleeping seven to eight hours a night. However, I take a nap for an hour or two several days a week. I am just excited to be able sleep without sleeping medication! It is so refreshing to get a good night sleep. I noticed that my mood is more stable when getting good sleep.

There are a some sleep disciplines which help tremendously. Implementing these disciplines helps develop healthy sleep patterns.

1. Maintain regular bed time each night.
2. Don't expose yourself to bright light in the evening. Turn off all the lights including the TV.
3. Don't watch TV before going to bed. It's too stimulating.
4. Turn off all music and sleep in a quiet room.
5. Don't nap to close to bed time.
6. No exercising or eating 2 hours before bedtime.

Developing good sleep habits helps to cope with a mood disorder. It is foundational to a healthy life style.

I have had so many problems taking psychotropic drugs. They make me worse and want to commit suicide. It is now time to apply the natural antidepressants seriously. Exercising and developing good sleep habits should help the depression. I want to get well so much.

Chapter 25

The Multi-Faceted Treatment Plan

❧❧❧

Attacking Mental Illness from Many Angles

*T*eating mental illness isn't easy. It could be caused by physical, emotional, or spiritual problems. Someone who is emotionally ill may want to attack it on many fronts to get well. This is a challenge since it is during a time when they are paralyzed with the illness. One of the fronts to take on first is to see a psychiatrist to get medication to help with the symptoms. It is wise to address the physical issues so the body can heal itself by eating healthy and exercising, but until the overwhelming emotions is treated with medication it is impossible to implement healthy disciplines. Emotional issues are best addressed with a psychiatrist and counseling with a therapist. The most important thing to address is the spiritual aspect by spending time with the Lord. A good treatment plan includes addressing the physical, emotional, and spiritual parts of a person.

PHYSICAL

Work with the Psychiatrist

The first vital step for me was to get the correct diagnosis. This gives the psychiatrist a starting place to prescribe psychiatric medication. The only drawback is that everyone's body is different so sometimes finding the right medication is trial and error. I tried to not get mad at the psychiatrist if the medication didn't work. I know it takes a while for the medication to fully be effective. If the medication is not working, I had to be open to trying other medications and other medical treatments. I had to work with my doctors. I had to believe that they really did care and wanted to help me.

Work with the Medical Doctor

I know I have physical problems that could be contributing to the depression. My thyroid level is low, and for some reason my cholesterol is high. There are other issues that need medical attention so I need to stay connected with my doctors and take my medicine and do what they tell me to do, even when I don't feel like it.

Work with my Natural Pathologist

I now have a Medical Doctor who practices medicine like a Natural Pathologist. She looks at the depression as possibly caused by my body not functioning properly. I have digestive problems so the nutrients are not getting absorbed properly. The deficiency could be contributing to the depression. I am making huge changes in my diet to help my body heal up and work better. I am taking supplements that are helping my body heal. It's a year later and I have not been sick at all, not even a cold! The depression is gone. Doing what my natural pathologist has told me to do has been an important step in my recovery.

Take Medication and Supplements Regularly

Treating depression includes taking medication and supplements. I have a medication holder that I bought at the drug store and I fill it up once a week. This simplifies managing the medication and supplements.

Eating a Healthy Diet

No junk food! Ouch, that's so hard! I want to eat candy and drink soda. No more... In fact, my doctor is having me make lots of changes to my diet. I am off dairy, wheat, pork, and artificial sugar. There have been other foods that are restricted. Sigh, I want to recover from the depression, so I am going to do what my doctor tells me to.

Chiropractor

Going to the chiropractor can really help with moodiness. A misalignment of the top vertebra in the neck called the atlas can definitely affect the mood so keeping it adjusted helps me feel so much better.

Sleep

My body needs eight hours of sleep a night to best deal with the depression. I go to bed and arise at the same time. Since I have sleep apnea, I need to use my CPAP machine every night. I have to take sleep medicine every night. As I get better hopefully I won't have to take sleep medication.

Exercise

Exercise is a very important step in my recovery. I walk for thirty minutes every day. I love looking at the nature around me. It draws me close to God. My two dogs love going with me. I'm not sure if I like them coming along. I do water aerobics three times a week out in the sun. Hopefully these activities will help me feel better.

EMOTIONAL

Support from My Family

My family is very supportive. My depression has been so difficult for them, but they still love me very much. I do my best to show them that I love them. I am blessed that I have such a loving family.

Talk Therapy – Applying the Skills

Talk therapy is very important to help with emotional pain. Learning the skills to deal with emotional issues, negative habits, and undesirable behavior is so beneficial. It is very important to apply the skills the therapist teaches about. This is the door to inner healing and can help with emotional growth.

Writing in a Journal – An Avenue to Help Apply New Skills

Writing in a journal is a creative expression that helps to internalize the new skills from therapy. This is an important tool to help apply the skills taught by the therapist. Remember, counseling without application is a waste of time. Keeping a journal helps to internalize all that God wants applied to my life. Writing is also an expressive tool to connect with God during a time of an emotional upheaval.

Choose Positive Friendships

Positive friendships help me to feel loved. I am selective with whom I hang out since I need people to encourage me at this point in my life. Discouraging people may cause a setback in my walk toward emotional healing. People that love me with encouraging words help me to love myself as well.

SPIRITUAL

Having Faith That the Lord Loves Me, Even When Depressed

My faith in Jesus is the foundation of my recovery. Learning to spend time with the Lord is such a healthy habit to put into practice. As I spend time with the Lord I can feel His unconditional love encompass me even when I'm depressed. I try to meditate several times a day while I imagine Jesus tenderly holding me. I need to feel God's love so I can have hope in my desperate place. As I spend time with the Lord, it changes me from the inside—out. The foundation of my faith begins with the fact that the Lord loves me greatly, even when I'm super depressed.

Reading My Devotion Every Day to Draw Near to the Lord

It is so important for me to get out of myself and focus on the Lord. The tool I use is reading my Bible and reading out of my devotion book. This helps me to get my mind focused on the Lord rather than on myself. Every day I need to get out of my self-focused time by have a devotion time with the Lord.

Meditation to Draw near an Intimate God

Meditation is such a good practice to apply when facing negative feelings. It really helps me to get out of myself and focus on God. Meditation helps me emotionally and physically by resting in God's arms. Most of my meditation time is focused on God's unconditional love which neutralizes my negative feelings.

Hanging out with Supporting Friends Who Have Faith

Good friends are vital to my progress. They can see the Lord's healing work in my life. One of my good friends had a vision that I will be helping others who are brokenhearted with the lessons I am learning now. This gives me hope that I will get well one day. Good friends are such an important step in recovery.

Going to Church to Have an Avenue for Worship

It is important to go to church regularly to get outside myself. I love worshipping God during the worship service. It draws my spirit up toward God and I feel so much closer to Him. Fellowshipping with the people uplifts my spirit. They shower their love on me, even if I'm in a dark depressing time. Church is a great time to focus on something outside myself and encourage other people. There are so many benefits to attending church so I need to encourage myself to go every Sunday morning, even when I want to withdraw inwardly. Most of the time I attend church, I do feel better after going.

Listening to Bible Teachings Helps to Be Grounded in the Faith

I like listening to the sermons. Once again, it brings me outside of myself so I could embrace truth and apply it to my life. I really do want to grow spiritually by listening and embracing the message.

PUTTING IT ALL TOGETHER

Receiving God's Grace to Take Care of Myself

God's gift of healing doesn't always come instantaneous. Sometimes God heals over a period of time. He has lessons for us to learn such as

His unconditional love. God wants us to accept the path towards inner healing that He has for us. This opens a door to receiving God amazing love deep in our lives. Opening our lives for healing can be a hard journey, but one that has multiple benefits for our life as well as others we come in contact with.

One thing that helps me to recover from depression is that I'm not working. I was blessed to qualify for disability so this helps our financial situation. Now I can focus on taking care of myself. I have had so much difficulty dealing with the depression with all the hospitalizations and many doctors' appointments. Since I spend most of my time at home, I am able to work on the things my doctors and counselors tell me do. I make time to journal which helps me process all the changes I am making in my life. Staying at home has given me the time and grace to work on everything that God has directed me to implement for my healing. He has given me grace to make the changes, and this is significant because depression tends to shut me down.

One of my strengths is organization. I am so motivated to get well that I spend time organizing and planning the steps I need to take to get better. I made a chart of all my medications on the computer. I have a calendar program to help organize my time. I write in my journal to help process all the counseling I receive. All of these are very hard to implement when depressed. I just had to realize that if I didn't apply what the people that God put in my life taught me, then I might not get well. I really want to get well so this desire drove me to embrace what the doctors were doing to help me and my counselors who guided me in my inner life by doing what they told me to do. I need God to gift me with time and grace to apply the lessons He was telling me through His servants that He puts in my life.

The most important time I have is with Jesus. The time with Jesus looks like this: meditating, reading my Bible and devotions, and sit while quieting my mind to embrace God's love He has for me. Quieting myself with meditation is the hardest thing I do but it is the most meaningful. When I quiet my mind, I don't feel so stressful. It helps heal my emotions. This is a time when I can renew my mind through God's Spirit so I receive His love and grace in my life to take care of myself.

Part 4

Combating Severe Depression

Chapter 26

The Depression Trail

"Your word is a lamp to my feet and a light for my path."
Psalm 119:105

A Vision for This Season of Life

*E*eryone goes through many seasons during their lifetime. Each season is like a journey that the Lord lovingly directs us on. Most of my journeys in the natural have been on hiking trails in what my father called *God's*

living room. I grew up camping and hiking in the states of Montana, Idaho, and Washington. All my life I have visited and hiked in many breath-taking scenic National Parks: Glacier National Park, Yellowstone National Park, Bryce Canyon National Park, Zion National Park, Rocky Mountain National Park, the Grand Canyon National Park, Mammoth Cave National Park, and The Smoky Mountain National Park. I love nature and feel very close to God when I am hiking and camping in nature.

God speaks in my heart through nature. As I meditate on what God's doing in my life, I realized that I have been on journeys during the different seasons of my life. These journeys are like hiking trails. Some trails are short and some are long. Some are beautiful, some are hard, and some are tragic. A job, sickness, a hobby or a ministry can be trails. The sky is the limit as far as the different kinds of trails there are. Now God is up in heaven lovingly directing everyone's life by guiding them onto a trail and giving them grace for the different challenges on each trail.

As I thought about my life, I thought of four trails in my life where I got my identity: music, parenting, teaching, and depression. I walked the Music Trail for thirteen years. I started band in 5th grade and played clarinet. I switched to oboe in 6th grade and played oboe through elementary school, high school, college, the United States Army Band, and the church orchestra. During those years my identity was wrapped up in music. I have walked the Parenting Trail for 25 years and am still walking it. I have been mothering the miraculous gift of my five lovely daughters and they are growing up now! They are all beautiful and successful. Another long trail I walked on was the Teaching Trail. For over twenty years I taught children. I taught in Christian schools, home schooled my girls, and taught in a private school for learning disabled children. I was the home school coordinator of a large home school support group. I taught in the churches mid service children's program for many years. During those years my identity was wrapped up in teaching.

Now I'm on a different kind of trail called the Depression Trail. At first I walked a short Depression Trail for two years when I was in college and now I am walking on a longer Depression Trail lasting at least ten years. I am still on this trail. Much to my dismay, my identity seems to be wrapped up in the depression.

Now as I think about the depression being a trail in my life, I realize that God had directed me onto this trail. When I was *waiting on God* next to the Oconaluftee River in The Smoky Mountain National Park, He told me that my life would slow way down like the eddy on the side of the river. This was my God lovingly letting me know that I was going to enter a season of REST. I just didn't know what that season would look like. It turned out to be the depression.

Resisting God's Inner Work

I had a huge problem; I didn't want to go on the Depression Trail, so I sat at the trailhead for years. I didn't think that my loving God would guide me onto a trail where there was emotional pain. That's not God! God only lets good things happen in my life. Anything bad is from Satan. Depression is from Satan. That's what I thought. I was mad. This depression was not supposed to happen so I totally rejected it. I had put God's grace in a box. I believed that the only grace that existed in this situation was Divine healing. Everything else was from Satan. As time progressed and I wasn't healed, I thought the only way out was to commit suicide.

Now I had another problem. I wanted off the Depression Trail so the only way I knew to get off this trail was to commit suicide. But I had a loving family. I love my husband and my five wonderful daughters, and didn't want to ruin their lives. Suicide and love don't mix. This suicide/love inner conflict has gone on for years but it intensified the last several months and I was admitted into three different psychiatric hospitals several times each, had many ECT treatments, and went to three different group therapies in the course of a year. I was still having individual counseling but things weren't getting any better. Eventually the suicide/love internal conflict became so intense that I hated myself and began to hate God. I was in denial about this hatred and didn't know until the Chaplain on the psych floor at the hospital compassionately confronted me. After spending an hour with him, my heart was softened and I listened to him tell me about this anger, then realized that God still loved me! This was huge! I was in such a mess at that time so God used an unsaved psychiatrist to guide me on a path of inner healing. It turned out that the Chaplain and psychiatrist had pointed me on the trail where God's grace would manifest in my life—that is DBT.

God Brings Inspiration from His People

God doesn't lead us on a trail that His grace isn't available. I wanted healing from depression so bad that I was blinded to all manifestations of God's grace for this journey. This made me so miserable that I wanted to die. I really don't know why, after eight years of feeling miserable and during a time when I was so deeply depressed and suicidal, how did I actually listen to the chaplain and the psychiatrist at hospital? Right after getting out of the hospital, I attended a class on solitude at church. I even listened to this Christian counselor and started practicing solitude as I quieted my mind as waited on God. During one of the solitude times God reminded me of Joni Eareckson Tada. She had to travel the Quadriplegic Trail and was in such deep despair at first that she wanted to commit suicide. Jesus saved her from herself. The amazing thing is that even though she was never healed she received God's grace in such a big way that she is now able to minister to millions of people (Tada). I thought about the grace in her life even though she is still paralyzed. Could what I'm going through end up as a big display of God's grace too?

As I sat at the trailhead of depression where I had been for the last eight years and somehow started embracing the truth that God still loves me even though I was so depressed and hated Him. I realized that God loved Joni and poured out His grace on her even though she wasn't healed. This gave me much to think about. Going to DBT counseling and learning to meditate with mindfulness was so helpful. I would sit before God in solitude and feel God's love pouring out on me. All I did was quiet my mind and I could hear God's words, "I love you, Stacey." God wanted to pour out His love on me. I realized that I needed His transforming Presence to help me embrace His love, and receive His mysterious grace even in the midst of depression.

One of the things I finally realized is that I can't put my trust in man to be able to help me because they don't know what is needed to help me. The psychiatrists have given me so many different antidepressants and add-on meds that haven't worked. They don't know what I need and are making educated guesses. Counselors don't really know what I need either, but they did show me much care and concern. They offered good advice and pointed me to Jesus. My spiritual leaders showed me compassion and concern and pointed me to Jesus. But no one could reach way down in my heart and spirit to heal me. Only God can do that, and the only way I knew that God could heal me was to sit in His Presence.

Teach me your way, O LORD;
lead me in a straight path because of my oppressors (depression).
Psalm 27:11, personalized

God's Direction on the Depression Trail

I have sat at the trailhead of depression for eight years, most of the time in misery. It was time to head up the trail but I didn't know where to go. Sitting quietly while in solitude with Jesus and practicing mindfulness meditation is the best way for me to find out what the trail markers say. The first trail marker said to embrace DBT counseling. The depression was making my mood so erratic and DBT taught me that emotions are like waves that come in and go out. DBT taught me that I have an emotional mind but I also have a reasonable mind too. My emotional mind was ruling the throne of my mind, so now I needed God to help me use my rational mind to balance it out with my emotions. The second trail marker said to embrace mindfulness and unconditional love. These skills gave me the foundation to have a loving relationship with my God even though I still suffer from depression. The skills mindfulness and unconditional love gave me the grace to love myself even with the depression. The third trail marker said to get Maintenance ECT. ECT helps me to not feel depressed so now I have the grace to apply the DBT skills. ECT gives me grace to show my love to each of my family members. ECT gives me the ability to sense God's Presence, since I'm not so consumed with the feelings of depression. Quietly sitting before the Lord and practice meditation has become my life line. I am experiencing God's transforming Presence and am experiencing inner healing. There are times when I am genuinely happy again. But I need lots more healing and direction on this trail. I don't have the mental ability to walk this trail alone, but with God's Presence we can walk it together. I have to totally trust Him.

> *You have made known to me the path of life;*
> *you will fill me with joy in your presence,*
> *with eternal pleasures at your right hand.*
> Psalms 16:11

Intimate Time with God

One morning while sitting on the Depression Trail, I decided to just embrace the beauty that surrounded me. I wanted to practice mindfulness meditation with total intent to focus on God. I meditated on the verse, "Be still, and know that I am God." I settled my mind and pictured myself on a trail in The Great Rocky Mountain National Park admiring the mountains. I have a deep love for the mountains that began when I was a young child in Montana. I have a deep love for God and thought about how wonderful He is as I pictured the mountains in my mind. This stretch of time was so peaceful that I could have sat there for hours.

Near the end of this delightfully peaceful time, God told me two words: control and trust. I thought about the four major trails that I have been on in my life: music, parenting, teaching, and now depression. They are so different from each other. I realized that music, parenting, and teaching involved connecting with people and fulfilling the roll of controlling. I had many peers in music and when I taught and was parenting I was in control of people. Now I have a peers that are close friends on the Depression Trail. Most people seem uneasy about the depression and stay away to watch from the side lines. I'm not in control anymore. The depression has made it mentally impossible for me to be in control. The problem is I realize that I have been a control freak all my life, so not having the ability to be in control has shaken me in the core of my being. I have leaned on the guidance of so many different people (my husband, psychiatrists, counselors, pastors, and friends) this last ten years but deep down I haven't really wanted to *let go* of the control. Maybe that is why this trail is so hard for me. I'm a people person who likes to be in control. Now I am learning to rely on God to be my friend. I have to totally trust Him to guide me and relinquish all control over to Him.

Trusting God to Help Me Release Control

As I sat on the Depression Trail gazing at the majestic mountains and thinking about God, I realized that nobody can help me get better because they don't know how to. Psychiatrists have had a difficult time trying to help me with the depression and have given me various medications. ECT helped for a while. Counselors and Pastors try to give me advice to help me with the depression and yes, some of the advice helps. However, I'm still depressed. I still desperately need help in the secret areas in my life that only God knows about. One time He revealed that one secret issue that I have is that I am a control freak. Now I need God to reach deep within my being and help me to *let go* of all my desire to control. I just have to trust Him to take away that desire to control. There's that word trust again. I am going to put my trust in God by sitting in His Presence during my Meditation time.

> *Whom did the LORD consult to enlighten him, and who taught him the right way? Who was it that taught him knowledge or showed him the path of understanding?*
> Isaiah 40:14

Walking the Depression Trail

I believe God allowed me to experience the breakdown to take me on this Depression Trail for my good. He wants me to slow down so he can teach me Divine truth. He wants me to experience His amazing unconditional love and learn to love myself unconditionally too. God wants me to learn to rely on His loving grace no matter what my mood may be. He wants me to realize that His grace can manifest in ways that I never could imagine. These are two deep revelations that I didn't learn on the other trails. I know there are many more lessons.

Instead of sitting at the trailhead any more, I will walk the Depression Trail every day now. I have finally accepted that God put me on this trail and it is not a *bad* trail. He doesn't have bad trails, just some very difficult ones. The most difficult trails I have hiked in the natural have been in the top of the Rocky Mountains, but they are the most beautiful. I picture this Depression Trail to be like one of those difficult Rocky Mountain trails. Every step that I take on this trail takes a measure of grace because it is rocky and steep, and I had no idea what lay around each bend. So often the scenery is so beautiful that I stop hiking and stare at what God had made: the mountains, streams, waterfalls, lakes, moose, mountain goats, or sheep, bears, and the many trees, flowers, and grasses. As I experience walking the Depression Trail, I have no idea what will be next in my life. Sometimes I don't even know what is happening in the present moment. I just have to trust God. There are beautiful times on this trail when God brings wonderful people in my life, but the best times I have are when I sit in meditation with God. God's Presence is beautiful and His love brings me so much comfort. God's Presence is my anchor for emotional stability. His Presence is my guide. I am going to trust God for His grace for every step on this Depression Trail.

"I AM LEADING YOU ALONG THE HIGH ROAD, but there are descents as well as ascents. In the distance you see snow-covered peaks glistening in brilliant sunlight. Your longing to reach those peaks is good, but you must not take shortcuts. Your assignment is to follow Me, allowing Me to direct your path. Let the heights beckon you onward, but stay close to Me" (Young, 2004, p. 19).

Chapter 27

The Tsunami Wave of Emotions

"Let the morning bring me word of your unfailing love,
for I have put my trust in you.
Show me the way I should go, for to you I lift up my soul.
Teach me to do your will, for you are my God."
Psalm 143:8, 10

God, It Doesn't Feel Like You Are in Charge

*h*is time my wave of emotion has lasted six days. It's not over though. I still get very easily upset at next to nothing today, but at least I don't want to kill myself. Oops, I shouldn't say that! I should keep it a secret that I have plummeted to that depth. Sigh… Yes, it was a 911 day yesterday and that is what this chapter is about. The good news is that I rode it out (with help) and I am still at home.

Let me give you some back ground. I used to not be this emotional. Not at all! I lived a normal life, but I had this breakdown nine years ago. I was on antidepressants for eight years. At the end I was on three drugs, an antidepressant and two mood stabilizers. I was on other meds for other health problems like cholesterol, reflux, and other things. A year ago I started getting suicidal and visited many psychiatric hospitals. Eight months ago my husband, my doctors, and I figured that maybe the anti-depressants that were supposed to be helping me were making me sui-cidal so I came off all psychiatric drugs and started having ECT to control the depression. That was a smart move except I didn't anticipate having such a hard time experiencing my emotions again. I lost my ability to handle emotions plus I was experiencing depression again. A smart move was eight months ago when the psychiatrist from the psych floor at the hospital guided me to DBT. I guess I was really the smart one and listened to him. I am now involved in group therapy and individual therapy. I'm learning skills to help handle these intense emotions.

Things have been clicking right along. I am in month six of DBT and in three and a half months of a six month treatment of Maintenance ECT. Both of these have been very helpful. I am going to an alternative doctor and have made huge changes in my diet and supplements. My hormones have been adjusted and I'm getting rid of a yeast infection. These changes have helped feel much more stable. I have experienced three weeks of happiness for the first time in a year! Of course I'm not experiencing that happiness right now and I'm really frustrated about it!

Just a little more background: I am at home every day since I had to resign from my teaching job a year ago. I go to church every Sunday and attend a woman's Bible study on Tuesdays. We are learning ideas that reinforce what I am learning at DBT Group Therapy. Sometimes I can share things from the DBT group with these ladies such as learning to *live in the moment*. My wonderful husband has a great job of over thirty years and he's flexible to take me to ECT once a week in the Atlanta downtown area for ECT treatments. I still have two of my five daughters living at home. One is sixteen and the other is twelve. My other three daughters are either happily married or about to get married. One has a great job at a pregnancy center and the other two are in college. One will be graduating from nursing school at ABAC in a couple months and the other applied for nursing school at Georgia State University and just got accepted. Other than my emotional health not being so good, the rest of my life is great! The amazing thing is that none of my daughters struggle with depression at all. I have a good life except these crazy emotions!

Getting back to a Sound Mind

Now back to the topic of this chapter—emotions. I don't know why my Emotional Mind is sitting on the throne of my life this week but it is. I have been practicing the mindfulness skills with the hope that my Rational Mind could engage and I could use my sound mind. I think that my sound mind is engaged today so I want to write down how I got from emotional suicide thoughts of yesterday back to my sound mind of today. I really get very emotional if anything goes wrong still, but at least right now I'm not suicidal any more.

One of the basic skills I have been putting into practice is meditation from mindfulness in DBT, which I call sitting in solitude with God. My God, somehow I have to get a grip on my emotions! But I really need to get myself in a position where Jesus' love can perform surgery on my emotions. I need an emotional miracle! I usually sit in my recliner in the living room, close my eyes, lay my hands in my lap, and focus on my breath and my mind on being still. The words *"Be still and know that I am Lord"* flow across my mind. I then pictured Jesus holding my hands and telling me that He loves me, even when I am emotional. It's okay. I sit there anywhere from 20 minutes to an hour. I have to remind myself that Jesus is in charge of my life, even though at times I don't *feel it*. I can see evidence of it during the day. His love and grace manifest often in my life often. Remember, I am now a *grace detector*! I do see His loving grace in my life! O my God, even though all I want to do is collapse in a heap and cry, Jesus you are still real and love me!

This morning, while I was at the chiropractor's office laying on the roller bed I decided to meditate. I didn't meditate for long before the Presence of God filled my being, and I pictured myself curled up in Jesus' lap. I was crying. He had His arms wrapped around me and was silent. There were no words exchanged between us, just loving tender affection. My thoughts drifted to all the different times when His grace was manifested in my life in the last five days. I felt His amazing love for me and was so thankful! I was still crying. I am still very emotional. But it's okay. Jesus still loves me and reassured me that He is still in control even though it doesn't *feel* like it. My emotions are *temporarily broken*—I am emotionally sick; it's not sin.

Here is the order of events from this last week. First of all, I had an appointment with my regular psychiatrist of nine years last Thursday, five days ago. Since I'm not on meds, I don't see him as often so I filled him in on the details of the ECT and my medical doctor/natural pathologist who is trying to heal my body so that the depression might go away. All the info got transferred and then my psychiatrist informed me that he didn't need to see me again since I'm not on meds. He put my care under my counselor's care. We departed with an affectionate hug and I went on my way. The only problem is that my emotional mind started taking over. Even though I really don't need to see him anymore, I felt like he dropped me. I just stewed about what had happened and seemed to get more emotional as time went on.

Friday was ECT day. The treatment went as planned with no real event. Later that day I prepared to go to a church woman's retreat at Callaway Gardens, and then rode with a friend for the hour drive to the gardens. We set up in the cabin and attended the first hour meeting. The message was great! We ate at one of the cabins, and then attended another meeting. That second meeting really ministered to me so I talked to the speaker afterwards. She gave me a paper full of scriptural prayers and then prayed for me. I was blessed. My encounter with her was an expression of God's grace in my life. Her love for Jesus and her prayer life really ministered to me. The rest of the retreat was great and I really enjoyed being with the ladies. I'm usually at home alone so the socialization was a gift from God. I went out to lunch and came home Saturday afternoon.

Sunday I attended church, and my husband was away coaching volleyball. I was feeling pretty lonely and just sat alone. I was very aware of the fact that I needed more close friends, not just people who say hello to me. Several ladies greeted me with a big hug but I needed more. I was lonely. I needed someone to talk to beside doctors and therapists. I thought about all the time I spent during the week at home that I didn't even have friends to call or go out to lunch with. There needed to be a change in my life. I had the seed thought that maybe I needed to change churches – just a thought.

A Cascade of Emotions

Later Sunday I received a call from the office where my alternative doctor worked. I had an appointment with this doctor the next day, but she had left the practice. They welcomed me to see the nurse practitioner in her place. I made the appointment with the nurse practitioner and arranged for my ride to take me there. After the business was taken care of I started to get very emotional. I lost two doctors in one week. My psychiatrist dropped me and my alternative doctor abandoned me. This was not good.

I knew I needed to trust that Jesus was in charge, and that He would work everything out. But I was scared. For some reason I felt shaken to the core of my being. Why? Jesus was my source of stability, not the doctors. Yet, I was so frightened. The more I thought about my doctors the more scared I became. Fear was beginning to rule in my heart. I started to cry. My husband tried to talk some sense in me but I was too emotional. I thought I was still using my sound mind about the situation with the doctors. I was making plans to call doctors on Monday, but my husband wanted me to wait and email my alternative doctor. He felt pretty confident that my psychiatrist was still available for me if I really needed him. I felt those doctors were history and I needed to find new doctors. I felt like my husband was rejecting my ideas. He wasn't but that's what it felt like. At any rate, my husband and I had a major conflict. Even though I thought I was using my sound mind, hindsight reveals to me that it was my emotional mind ruling! I was not rational at all!

Monday, my husband went to work and I made many phone calls and sent many emails. I got several rejections from psychiatrists who couldn't help me out because I was not on meds. This really upset me. I feel sicker then I have ever been, yet these doctors won't help me. I couldn't get in touch with alternative doctors. I sent an email to my DBT group leaders to fill them in on the emotional pain that I was feeling because of losing my doctors. I emailed the nurse practitioner at the ECT Lab to fill him in on what was going on with my doctors. Since he was in charge of my ETC, I thought he would want to know and inform my doctor there.

A little later my friend arrived to take me to my appointment with the alternative nurse practitioner. That appointment was a very good visit. The nurse practitioner gave me my doctor's email address and comforted me in my pain of losing my doctor. She ended my visit with a big hug! My friend who transported me was great! She loves Jesus and greatly comforted me in my pain.

Later that Monday my husband arrived home from work then drove me through downtown Atlanta to my DBT Group Therapy in Buckhead. After dropping me off he went to visit our middle daughter and her husband who are going to school in downtown Atlanta. They regularly get together for pizza on Monday evenings during my group. (I'm jealous.) I attended group and it went very well. We were learning about how to deal with distress. Hmm, I was in distress so I needed this group.

My husband picked me up afterwards and we headed back home through town. About half way home I received a phone call from my pastor's wife about the Tuesday night woman's meeting. She wanted to encourage me to not share so much so other people would have more time to share. I heard her loving heart and knew that she just wanted to give some of these folks more time to process the material and share. But I started to cry. For some reason I felt like I was being kicked while I was down. I listened to her kind gentle words and believed that what she said was right. I just couldn't handle it emotionally though. I wanted to be strong but there was no grace left in me. All I could do was cry. My husband tried talking to me but I didn't answer. I cried the rest of the way home, then walked into the house and headed straight up to bed. I didn't even greet my daughters. I changed and climbed into bed and cried some more.

God Manifesting His Grace

My husband called the associate pastor and invited him and his wife over that night to help me. I changed back into my clothes and went down stairs to sit in the recliner. I really love this couple. They had ministered to my husband and me many times before. He had experienced a breakdown years ago so he could relate to the pain I was experiencing. As I waited for them I sat and cried and cried until they showed up at the house.

Their presence was a manifestation of God's love and grace once again. This pastor was scheduled to teach that night but none of the twelve people that were signed up to attend his class showed up! I guess he was supposed to visit me! He told me that it was so evident that I was embracing Jesus' love in my life. He thought it was amazing that I accepted the depression and accepted Jesus' grace to deal with it. He continued to encourage me for two hours. Jesus loved me deeply through this couple. God's amazing grace was manifested. He showered His love on me through these wonderful people!

Riding an Emotional Rollercoaster

The next morning I woke on the wrong side of the bed! I felt awful! I knew I was in trouble. I wanted to quit. I had no more grace to deal with life. I thought about suicide. I thought about going back to the psych floor in the hospital. But would that really help? What did I want? What did I need? I really wanted Jesus' love, and knew that I should trust that my Jesus was in control of my life. It didn't *feel* like it. Had He abandoned me by taking away my doctors? O brother. I didn't even need my doctors because Jesus could heal me without any doctors, but I wasn't healed. O God, my thinking was full of confusion and fear. I thought maybe that if a Christian friend could stay with me at the house all day maybe I would be all right.

A Manifestation of God's Grace and Love

I called my Christian friend and invited her over to sit with me all day. I knew she had dealt with depression before so I could be open and honest with her. I told her I was suicidal and needed someone to sit with me at the house. She gladly accepted and told me she would rearrange her day. As I waited for her to come I called 911. I wanted to know that if

I really needed help, could the ambulance take me to a specific hospital. I couldn't go to any other hospital because I was getting ECT every week. I needed to go to a specific hospital so they could arrange to take me to the hospital where I was having ECT treatment. The gal on the other end of the phone line reassured me that they could take me there. She kept asking me if I was all right. I told her yes, and that my friend was coming over.

My husband and two girls woke up and started to get ready for work and school. My husband asked me if I was going to be all right. I reassured him that I was fine since my friend was coming over. He wanted to know if he needed to stay home. I told him to go on to work. (I secretly was afraid he would lose his job if he stayed home. He already missed a lot of work transporting me every week for ECT and to the other many medical appointment around the Atlanta area.) My husband left for work and my youngest daughter got on the bus for school. My older daughter was still home when a deputy stopped by the house. He was there in response to my 911 call. He was just checking up on me. He was rather nice and we talked for several minutes. I told him that my friend would arrive soon. He encouraged me to get outside today since it was going to be such a nice day. I thanked him for coming and sent him on his way. My daughter was a little disturbed by his presence.

My friend showed up and her presence was a manifestation of God's grace and deep love. I didn't really need her to do anything specific but just be there. I basically sat in the recliner and talked with her. Her faith was such an inspiration to me. After while I decided to read several chapters out of my book about other times when God poured His grace out on me when I was having such a hard time. I was using the DBT skills. I was so amazed at the wisdom and comfort God shared with me during those stressful times. I was comforted greatly by how God loved me during all the times when I was distressed over the last several months. God really does love me.

I then talked to my friend about my loneliness. She shared with me that people at church were somewhat intimidated with the depression I was going through, and were afraid to get close to me. She told me that my depth of faith might make some people feel uncomfortable. She told me that I would face this relationship difficulty at any church. She knew everyone at our church pretty well so she helped me come up with a list of people to try to connect with that wouldn't be intimidated and might be able to help me. One of the people on this list knew about my situation this very day and was praying for me. She encouraged me to get with some of these people outside of a group setting so that we would really have a chance to connect. I was so encouraged. By the way, I called this girl later in the day and was so encouraged by her faith and humor. I might be able to befriend her, praise God!

All morning the word *trust* kept popping into my head. I had been feeling the *fear* consuming my heart. I know Jesus loves me and is taking care of me and my doctor situation. I need to trust Him. I just don't *feel* the peace that comes from trust at all. My friend told me she could tell I was trusting God but because my emotions are sick I can't experience *peace* right now. That means that I can love and trust my God in faith, but even though I don't *feel* peace doesn't mean that I do not love my God. My feelings can't manifest the fruit of my faith right now. That doesn't mean I don't have faith!

My friend and I had a healthy lunch together, and then we walked the dogs around the neighborhood. After the walk I felt much better so I sent my friend home. I knew that I was going to be all right now. I wasn't suicidal any more. At this time the nurse practitioner from the ECT Lab called me in response to my emails. He had called my psychiatrist and talked to his nurse practitioner. Just like my husband thought, my doctor had not dropped me. I had over reacted. I was humbled by his comment but I respected him and accepted what he had to say. I knew for sure at that point that I was totally emotionally minded and there was no rationality in my thinking. Sigh... This is embarrassing but now more than ever I needed Jesus. I needed to love myself unconditionally even though I was an emotional wreck.

The amazing thing that happened later that day was that I decided to go to the woman's Bible study. I felt love for the pastor's wife and had no hard feelings. I believed that I would be all right if I went to the meeting with her. I really enjoyed the meeting and everyone was inspired in my relationship with Jesus. I was transparent with the ladies and told them I was having a hard time and needed their prayers. I didn't tell them everything though. Later, I arrived home and went to bed.

I woke up Wednesday morning and felt like I was back in my sound mind once again. I wanted to write down what had happened. I called my counselor and was amazed that I could make an appointment that afternoon. God manifested His grace again. I talked to my counselor about my emotional meltdown and wondered why I even had the meltdown. He thought what might be driving this emotional meltdown was the abandonment issue I felt as a child. Wow, I thought that was behind me a long time ago! How can such a painful time I had with my mother play such havoc on my emotions forty years later? How on earth could I help that not to happen again? Wow, I still have so much to learn and overcome!

Another Manifestation of God's Grace

Wednesday night I had another Bible study to go to. My husband was coaching volleyball and my daughters were attending the youth group meeting at church. I might as well go to another Bible study! This was a small group and we were studying the book of Ruth, but we didn't tonight! We ate dinner and I shared a little about my week. We then talked about overcoming difficulties from our childhood! Everyone participated in the discussion and I learned that the man of the house, who was a pastor, had written a curriculum and drew charts in how to overcome past pain in our lives. I was amazed at what was talked about! Everything applied to my life! I shared about when I was in emotional pain that I would crawl into Jesus' lap and *feel* His love. I know He loves me just as much when I am in emotional pain as when I am happy. I don't have to settle with just head knowledge or wait until I go to heaven, but I can experience His love in my heart right now. I realized as we talked that I had already begun this journey of learning to experience God's love just a couple months ago. This was amazing and now I was seeing where God was taking me! I had only begun to experience His love and He had so much more love to share with me! This was amazing!

We talked about the reason that I was experiencing so many emotions was due to coming off antidepressants. Since I had been on antidepressants for eight years, it probably was going to take a while for me to get use to these emotions again and learn how to manage them. It might take a while for all those drugs to leave my body so I could experience normal emotions.

As I sit in Jesus' lap and experience His love, I meditate on the many facets of God's love as well. I now know that God is in the process of healing me! It's not just wishful thinking. I know that after ECT ends in a couple months that I will be so full of God's healing love that my emotions are going to get better! I can see it already! This is amazing!

The Faith Walk

Even though the medical community can't heal me and they are running out of ways to even help me, Jesus has stepped in to continue my healing process! Coming off the antidepressants was the beginning of

Jesus' miraculous power manifested in my life. All I have to do is spend lots of time with Jesus and allow His loving Presence to change me on the inside. I have to listen to Jesus' promptings and do what He tells me. Sometimes it's hard to discern what He is telling me to do but I have learned that it is better to step out in faith and do what I think He wants me to do rather than sit back and do nothing. At least when I step out in faith I have a chance of doing His will. If I miss His will, He loves me anyway and I will at least learn from my mistakes and grow in wisdom. I know that Jesus loves me more than I could ever imagine, and He is taking me on a journey to learn to experience this amazing love!

> *"But I am like an olive tree flourishing in the house of God;*
> *I trust in God's unfailing love for ever and ever.*
> *I will praise you forever for what you have done;*
> *in your name I will hope, for your name is good.*
> *I will praise you in the presence of your saints."*
> Psalm 52:8-9

Chapter 28

Mindfulness

"May the words of my mouth and the meditation of my heart
be pleasing in your sight, O LORD, my Rock and my Redeemer."
Psalm 19:14

Learning to Apply Mindfulness

*t*r ust that You, O Lord, are guiding me toward inner healing through the people that You have put in my path. You gave me the doctors in the hospitals and the outpatient doctors and staff that are guiding me toward Dialectical Behavior Therapy. You gave me the Christian counselors that are guiding me in DBT. They are helping me learn and apply mindfulness to my life. They told me that mindfulness is crucial to my recovery. You have given me Christians who love me and are guiding me in Your amazing healing love in my inner life through mindfulness. God, I am going to put my total trust and confidence that You are in charge of my emotional healing!"

Mindfulness is taught in many religions including Christianity. Becoming aware of my thoughts and emotions has been a revelation for me. There are many skills related to mindfulness such as learning to accept myself all the time and to not judge myself or others. A critical spirit doesn't help my mood. I learned to suppress my emotions all my life, and have really suffered the consequences. I am learning and applying mindfulness skills and getting to know my inner life so my emotions don't play so much havoc in my life. It is working for sure but it takes time practicing mindfulness for my emotional life to be healthy once again.

Embracing the Being Mode of Mind

Mindfulness encompasses the concepts of the *being mode of mind* which focuses on who I am and the *doing mode of mind* which focuses on what I do. The *being mode of mind* is simply exemplified by the New Testament woman named Mary who sat at Jesus feet to listen to His teachings. The *doing mode of mind* can be exemplified by Mary's sister, Martha, who was a wonderful servant of God who expressed her gift through hospitality. There was a problem in that Martha was frustrated that Mary just sat with Jesus instead of helping her. Jesus responded by saying,

> *"You are worried and upset about many things,*
> *but only one thing is needed.*
> *Mary has chosen what is better,*
> *and it will not be taken away from her."*
> Luke 10:41-11:1

It is time to not just live in the *doing mode of mind* where I excel, but to embrace living in the *being mode of mind* where I can grow in intimacy with God. Critical thinking and analyzing why I am suffering the emotional pain are expressions of the doing *mode of mind*. I excel at analyzing why I'm suffering in my attempt to help myself overcome. Once again I excel at *doing!* Not judging myself when I feel bad and accepting myself with unconditional love are two expressions of the *being* mode of mind.

Still Learning Mindfulness Six Months Later

I have had a hard time learning to receive God's love through mindfulness. Now that I think about it, my counselor has been encouraging me to embrace in the *being mode of mind* for many years. It is time to take my learning to a new level because I'm having such a hard time walking in Jesus' love and acceptance when I feel so emotional. I will read and embrace mindfulness skills to help me be nice to myself. Hopefully I will be able to embrace mindfulness more fully and live in the *being mode of mind* like Mary. I want to learn to love myself unconditionally as Jesus loves me and accepts me!

Journal Entries: Applying Mindfulness

The following paragraphs are applications of mindfulness entries from my journal. I want to apply mindfulness into my life and experience inner peace from being in God's Presence. Learning mindfulness takes time so I want to be patient with myself. Each day as I embrace mindfulness I will give my expectations to the Lord. God will bring the results in due time.

Journal Entry: Mindfulness Meditation

I met with my counselor yesterday evening and he encouraged me to use my mindfulness CD. It is a guided meditation CD. I never got around to listening to it the last three months. Since my counselor suggested I listen to the mindfulness meditation CD, I did. Here was my experience. First of all I meditated with the CD continuously while listening to the whole CD. I have no idea how long that took, maybe an hour. What I learned is to let out the *welcome mat* to the emotions that I feel. I cried a few times while meditating even though I had no particular thoughts on my mind. In other words, I thought I had no reason to cry, but I *welcomed* the tears anyway. I need to keep letting out my emotions. Meditation is bringing inner healing.

This is the season to allow myself to feel and release my emotions. In fact, the last six months is the first time in my adult life that I have allowed myself to feel so many painful emotions. I suppose that getting off antidepressants has helped make it possible for me to feel and express my emotions. The problem is that I am usually very critical of myself for having painful feelings. I am learning to let out the *welcome mat* to these emotions. Even as I sit here I want to cry. My counselor just called and I cried while talking to him. I don't have any idea why I'm crying, but it is okay to cry. I'm not a bad person because I cry.

I suspect that I have bottled up sadness that has been simmering under the surface for most of my life. I never allowed myself to experience sad emotions. In other words, I suppressed my emotions. Even most of my Christian walk I have been good at suppressing my emotions. After all I had to be emotionally well to have a sound mind and live respectfully amongst my Christian friends. Now that I think about it, it is amazing that I could suppress them so well even through five pregnancies, homebirths, raising all those babies, and home schooling. Even the hormones and stress of raising five kids and serving in the church as a teacher in many areas didn't cause me to come unglued until the breakdown ten years ago. I have always been a *doing* expert! I am now learning to *be* by allowing myself to just experience life fully in the present moment. When I am practicing meditation, I try to apply the *being mode of mind* and live in the present moment, but simmering emotions erupt. I am learning to let out the *welcome mat* to these emotions and express them freely.

Now I want to say this: when I let these emotions out, I don't sin against anyone. I don't take out any anger on anyone or bad mouth anybody. I feel love towards people and express positive words towards people. My emotions of sadness erupt as tears and the emotions of anger expressed through words of anger at something or throwing or hitting things. Sometimes I have no idea why I am feeling these emotions. Other times I feel negative emotions towards myself because of passing judgment on myself. This is a lack of love and mercy for myself. Sometimes I'm mad at God.

Mindfulness can be manifested in my life by allowing myself to experience the *being mode of mind* when I live in the present moment. I can let myself experience the emotions that surface at any moment. Letting out the *welcome mat* to emotions is allowing myself to totally be me. It is an expression of self-love. I know Jesus loves all of me, even the part of me that was emotionally hurt as a child and was never allowed to express the pain. He's telling me that expressing emotional pain is not only good but it is healthy! In other words, crying is good. When I cry Jesus is performing a miraculous inner healing. When I get mad at myself for crying, I'm not exhibiting self-love. I want to be emotionally stable with a sound mind. This is a good time to learn to show myself total love by walking in mercy and compassion with myself. When I get mad at God, I am expressing my lack of understanding that God is trying to heal me. It is time to exercise my faith and believe and trust that God really is in charge and that He loves me so much that he has made an opportunity for me to learn to love all of me.

Wow, I am becoming aware that I use my critical thinking skills to the max to try to *fix* my emotions! The result → depression → ruminating, → inpatient stays at the hospital! Using my *doing mode of mind* is not the best tool I have to help myself overcome depression. I need to use my *being mode of mind*. In other words I need to continue to learn about mindfulness and quit analyzing why I am so moody.

"Come with me by yourselves to a quiet place and get some rest."
Mark 6:31

Journal Entry: Living in the Present Moment

My mindfulness meditation experience today was very positive. I was aware of all my body sensations. I noticed that I didn't experience any emotions this time. My thoughts drifted off minimally onto the dogs in my lap and only moments of the to-do list. I was very much aware of what I was experiencing physically and the feelings of contentment and peacefulness.

The good news is that I am aware that I am getting better at applying mindfulness over the past several months. I am definitely living in the moment so much more. I like to meditate several times a day. I am living and experiencing the REST season of my life! I just still need some growth in mindfulness so I can live in the *being mode of mind* even more and not judge myself. I need to grow in love so I can learn to accept myself even while I am emotional!

I had this important thought—Jesus inhabits my presence when I live moment by moment. He's here with me now! He doesn't inhabit my past because I am really not there anymore. He doesn't inhabit my future because I am not really there yet. My past and my future only exist in the confines of my mind through my imagination. I only really exist where I am living in the present moment. This doesn't mean that I don't learn from past mistakes and successes or seek God about my plans for the future. I'm just not living in those places at this present moment. Truly God's Presence exists in this current moment so learning to live mindfully helps me to become more aware of Jesus' Presence right now as life unfolds. I enjoy what I am experiencing in life right now as I live in this moment!

Journal Entry: Applying Mindfulness to Unpleasant Emotions

My mindfulness meditation experience this morning gave me an opportunity to let out the *welcome mat* to an unpleasant emotion. One of my dogs jumped into my lap and I got mad! Boy, did I get mad! I lost all focus and the anger simmered and wanted to erupt. As I became aware of this I consciously let out the *welcome mat* to the feeling of anger. I stepped back in my mind just to experience the anger then refocused my mind onto the meditation. The anger drifted into the background of my mind. My dogs sat comfortably in my lap as I continued to meditate. The intensity of the anger lessened as the meditation time came to a close. This is a good example of emotions being like waves—in and out.

In the evening I had another opportunity to let out the *welcome mat* to a difficult emotion. Once again depression descended upon me and I don't know why. As I sat in my recliner I wanted to cry so I did. I released the emotion. I felt miserable so maybe I should just go to bed and allow myself to experience the emotional pain. I was tired anyway since I got up early this morning – 4:00 AM. I had a short nap but I was still tired tonight anyway. I told my husband that I was going to bed. He observed my tears and asked if I wanted my back scratched. I said sure!

I lay in bed and released the tears. A short time later my husband rubbed and scratched my back. At first I just cried and cried and felt awful. As my husband scratched my back my thoughts drifted to the mindfulness videos from dbtselfhelp.com that I watched earlier this afternoon. Pictures from the "Be a Tree" and "River Rock Mindfulness" meditation videos flowed through my mind (Dietz, 2003, Instant Mindfulness). I remembered the word *wise* from one of the videos and thought that maybe I was being wise by embracing this mindfulness moment. I liked to think about several camping experiences in The Great Smoky Mountains. I loved the beauty of hiking the Appalachian Trail with my daughters and the beautiful scenery of tall grass and the spruce and fir trees in the woods surrounding Clingman's Dome. As my husband continued to scratch my back and these beautiful pictures flowed through my mind and the depression slowly lifted! Peacefulness and contentment filled my mind again. Hey, I experienced victory! I didn't succumb to the *doing mode of mind* by analyzing the emotion which brings more misery, but I embraced the *being mode of mind* and loved myself with the depression. I applied the mindfulness skills I had learned and the depression lifted! Wow!

Journal Entry: Living Moment by Moment

My mindfulness meditation experience over the last several days has been awesome! It is now many months later since the other journal entries but I am still practicing mindfulness. I was in the psych hospital again a few weeks ago, and now I am motivated to do whatever I need to do to keep out of the hospital! I am thankful for the new medications that are helping with the depression. I am thankful for the mindfulness skills that God I am able to learn. Living in a moment by moment basis with depression helps me to focus on loving myself instead of giving in to anger towards myself. Mindfulness Meditation is very healing.

I am learning skills to help me REST my mind, and to distract myself from focusing on negative thoughts. I am listening to music and watching nature scenes, both things I love. I know that experiencing nature while camping both as a child and as an adult has been God's gift to me. Playing music for so many years is a gift from God that I enjoy now. I am so thankful.

The first moments of REST I embraced are watching and listening to the videos called *Radical Acceptance* and *Turning the Mind* from dbtselfhelp. com (Deitz 2003, http://www.dbtselfhelp.com/html/radical_acceptance_ part_1.html and http://www.dbtselfhelp.com/html/turning_the_mind1. html.)

These videos help me to get my mind off the painful moment I am experiencing and back to loving myself. I am embracing my favorite times when I am camping and spending precious time with God.

The next expression of mindfulness is when I listen to classical music and watch the nature scenes on You Tube. The three pieces of music I like the most are Die Maldau by Smetana, Air Suite No. 3 by Bach, and Canon in D Major by Pachelbel. When I watch and listen to these videos, the thoughts from the day drift off and I focus on the current moment I am experiencing. I am so grateful for learning how to rest my mind by I appling mindfulness. *"Thank you Jesus for giving me tools to help embrace Your love so I can enter a time of REST and inner peace."*

Learning the mindfulness skills has been an ongoing process. It has settled my mind so that many emotions from the past could finally be released. The time that I have set aside to practice meditation has become a source of major inner healing. It is a time that I can open up my mind to something other than the to-do list, home life, or the depression. It is a time that I can embrace Jesus' amazing love. Mindfulness has given me tools to embrace inner peace. Focusing on the present moment has made it possible to enjoy the fresh air, flowers, and birds on my morning walk. Learning mindfulness has encouraged me to imagine a camping trip I have been on, and place myself in the magnificent scenery in my mind again. As I imagine this camping while I meditate, I enter a state of inner peace.

Mindfulness: The Foundation for Inner Healing

It has been a year since I started practicing mindfulness and the depression is lifting. I practice mindfulness in various ways all day long every day of the week. I wait on God through meditation, and I am learning to not condemn myself but love myself unconditionally. I am learning to live in the present moment so that I won't feel overwhelmed. I want to continue experiencing God's peace. Mindfulness has become the foundation of my time spent with Jesus. This is a time for me to slow down and enjoy being in God's Presence. Mindfulness has truly been a foundation to the healing of my difficult emotions.

> *"Do not withhold your mercy from me, O LORD;*
> *may your love and your truth always protect me.*
> *For troubles (emotions) without number surround me;*
> *my sins (judgments) have overtaken me, and I cannot see.*
> *They are more than the hairs of my head,*
> *and my heart fails within me."*
> Psalm 40:11-12, personalized

Chapter 29

Self-Talk: Condemning or Loving

> *"You are a forgiving God, gracious and compassionate,*
> *slow to anger and abounding in love."*
> Nehemiah 9:17

Oh No! I Condemn Myself All the Time

i fe is so difficult right now, and now I am learning that my self-talk is very condemning. No wonder I feel so bad. If anyone heard the voices in my head, they would assume I hated myself. I condemn myself for being depressed all the time. I condemn myself for not being able to perform. I can't do anything I used to do. I feel worthless? The depression has paralyzed me so I can't do anything and don't want to. I don't even want to get around people. Tsk, tsk, tsk. Unhealthy thinking makes me even unhealthier.

Jesus Loves Me in All My Crazy Moods!

> *For great is your love toward me;*
> *you have delivered me from the depths of the grave.*
> *But you, O Lord, are a compassionate and gracious God,*
> *slow to anger, abounding in love and faithfulness.*
> *Turn to me and have mercy on me;*
> *grant your strength to your servant*
> *and save the son of your maidservant.*
> *Give me a sign of your goodness.*
> Psalm 86:13, 15-17a

"O Lord, do You love me even though I have suicidal ideations and sometimes get so mad that I reject You? How can you love me this way? You don't condemn me, Lord. Wow... This kind of love is so incomprehensible. No one loves me like that. You are full of compassion when I am hurting so bad. You care for me even when I am sinking into suicidal ideation. Sometime I just get so mad at You that I want to quit. You, O Lord, hold me close to Your heart. You love me in all my pain. This is just amazing! You have mercy on me, and are a good God. Lord, I want to experience Your grace to love myself in the same way. I need to be changed on the inside. How does this happen? I want to abound in love towards myself. I really want to experience Your compassionate love so I can love myself. Can I learn to love myself and stop condemning myself as well?"

Learning to Love Myself

My own self-talk is so negative. Do I show myself unconditional love like God does? No. Do I even love myself like God does? No. Can I show myself some grace and encouragement? I need to. I know it's so hard when I'm depressed, but that is when I need to love myself the most. I have the gift of encouragement and find it easy to encourage others. Can I love myself and encourage myself when I'm depressed? Not yet. I need to put loving myself into practice.

"O Lord, it is so hard to love and accept myself in this emotional state. Everything in me says I'm an emotional disaster! How can You even love me when I'm so depressed and possess so many negative thoughts, Jesus?"

I know that Jesus' love is unconditional, but my love for myself is full of conditions. I need to stop condemning myself.

"Lord, I need Your help so much."

I want to embrace loving myself unconditionally with compassion like Jesus does. He has so much compassion for me. My counselor told me that I need to learn to nurture myself like a mother nurtures her child. I didn't get that growing up so it is time to embrace Jesus' love as much as humanly possible and learn to love myself as well.

Learning to Love Myself without Judging

I need to learn to not judge myself as good when I'm happy and bad when I'm depressed. Judging myself when I feel bad only makes the depression worse. I need to learn to accept myself with tenderhearted love when I am depressed. Imagine being tender with myself when I'm depressed. This is so hard. When I feel depressed, it is an opportunity to nurture myself with God's unconditional love. This is so hard for me.

In real life, sometimes when I am depressed with irrational thinking it goes on for days. I feel embarrassed and judge myself. Being critical of myself makes me feel even worse. How can I not judge myself when I have made an absolute fool of myself? See the word fool. That certainly is a negative judgment. Sometimes the fruit of judging myself is suicidal thinking. It honestly *feels* like I'm not in control of my emotions! How on earth can I accept myself when I'm an emotional wreck? How can I love myself like this? Since I have been sick with depression, just about all my self-judgments have been negative. It's like digging my own emotional grave. Judging myself has become a bad habit. Something has to change!

The best skill that helps me to overcome depression is focusing on unconditional love while I meditate. I meditate every morning and ask Jesus to help me not to judge myself. One of my most meaningful secrets I have is to wrap my favorite Smoky Mountain blanket around my shoulders and pretend that Jesus is holding me. I hold the blanket tightly as I imagine Jesus holding me tightly. He's tender love is comforting me way deep down and healing me of my condemning thoughts. I desperately want to be in His Presence so that He will change me from the inside—out. As I spend time in Jesus' Presence, I sense His unconditional love for me, even when I'm an emotional wreck.

185

I can *hear* God's still small voice in my heart telling me, *"I love you just as much when you're emotional and sad as when you are happy! My love isn't based on your mood!"*

God wants me to love myself in the same way! This kind of love is unconditional and totally accepting. If Jesus loves me this way, how could I not love myself this way too? *"Jesus, help me!"*

Another way that I am learning to love myself is to apply unconditional love to my self-talk. When I judge myself, which is often, I try to reword the comments into something that is positive. I do this as often as I need so that I can break the habit of condemning myself. When learning to be nice to myself, it is very helpful to learn not to judge other people. It is a way of letting go and giving all these things to God. *Let go and let God!*

I need to focus on the fact that my emotions are not wrong. Since I am off the antidepressants, which had made me suicidal, my emotions seem to rule the throne of my life. I'm having ECT to try to stabilize me. I'm having DBT Group Therapy to learn skills to manage these emotions, and getting individual counseling to help bring inner healing to the root that is causing these emotions—rejection and abandonment issues from my childhood. I must remember that my emotions aren't wrong. Jesus loves me greatly when I'm happy as well as when I'm depressed!

Learning to Accept Myself While in a Crisis

I have many opportunities to show compassion to myself by accepting any mood I find myself experiencing. Life just isn't very easy for me right now and I need to accept where I am in my life rather than get mad. Acceptance embraces the concepts of *Love* and *Trust*. Jesus loves me in my moods and He is in control even if I don't understand what is happening. Accepting myself when I'm depressed is hard, but Jesus wants me to and He will help me.

As I sit here and reminisce about this last month, I had such difficulty with my emotions which led to suicidal thinking. Everyone I came in contact with – my husband and my daughters, the medical professionals at the psychiatrist's office, Sunday's church congregation, my group members and counselors, my friends, my counselor, and the professionals where I get ECT all showed me so much love. They all encouraged me to hang in there, and I know to focus on Jesus' amazing love. I realize that I need to have compassion and learn to love and accept myself!

It is later in the week and how come I can't seem to pull it together this time? I am still depressed and upset with myself. It has been days that I have had a *bad attitude*. I want to quit and don't want to go to church tomorrow. I am so embarrassed about my intense deep depression this whole week. Once again my emotions are so intense and I am not accepting of myself with unconditional love. Am I'm giving in to this depression? I know Jesus doesn't want me to give up. The people at church love me just the way I am with all the emotions. They accept me just the way I am. I need to hang around these people so hopefully their love can rub off onto me. Even though it feels like I can't take it anymore, I need to embrace unconditional love and accept that these emotions are not wrong, even though they are intense. I just need to give myself grace, and give myself time and space to learn to manage these emotions. Remember, Jesus loves me in the deep recesses of my heart; He wants me to love myself deeply where the depression resides. Jesus also loves me unconditionally. Can I learn to love myself unconditionally too? I want to.

I went to church but didn't want to sing or fellowship with my friends. I felt awful!!! Sigh... When is this going to end??? When I got home I called the emergency line at my psychiatrist's office and the nurse practitioner at the ECT Lab. We discussed the possibility of going in the hospital again. I'm going to try to hold out until Monday. I hope that I may start a psychotropic medication to help me get more stable. Can I love myself in my situation this time? Jesus loves me even in this mood. Can I accept and love myself? I'm not there yet...

Psychiatric Hospital Again

I ended up in the hospital and wanted to work on loving myself and my situation. It was so hard because I was so moody and embarrassed being in the psych hospital again. The good news was that I heard many encouraging comments of how good I have been doing the last six months since I hadn't been in the hospital. The psychiatrist said that she can tell that I have been working hard at DBT. Her words were very encouraging! She noticed that I am deeply spiritual! Of course, I'm working on loving myself with compassion and acceptance. I still have a ways to go.

Using the Resources Available

Just for the record, I have been watching the dbtselfhelp.com website video called *Radical Acceptance* many times over the past month (Dietz, 2003, Instant Mindfulness). It is helping me to accept myself with my crazy emotions. However, I still need to work on this skill a lot more! It is really hard to accept the crazy emotions that make me feel so distressed. I am going to keep watching this *Radical Acceptance* video and practice accepting myself with unconditional love.

Learning to love myself compassionately with acceptance is the foundation to my progress in healing. Basically I am learning to love myself unconditionally by not judging myself for being depressed. I want to love myself even when I'm moody and my thoughts plummet to suicidal thinking. Loving myself when I'm sick is helping me get better. Instead of getting mad and wanting to quit life when I'm depressed, I am now focusing on Jesus' love for me and learning to love myself. He doesn't judge me negatively but is full of compassionate love and acceptance. This is huge!!!

Chapter 30

A Serious Emotional Relapse

"TRUST ME, and don't be afraid. Many things feel out of control. Your routines are not running smoothly. You tend to feel more secure when your life is predictable. Let Me lead you to *the rock that is higher than you* and your circumstances. *Take refuge in the shelter of My wings*, where you are absolutely secure"* (Young, 2004, p. 110).

Suicide Ideation Leads to Hospitalization

*b*elieve it is time to be honest. Yes, I suffer from Major Depressive Disorder and Borderline Personality Disorder. I have shared many struggles with my emotions and shared how God's grace was manifested through doctors, ECT, DBT, my counselors, family members, my loving friends, and most importantly through the faith I have in my Lord Jesus Christ.

I have told story after story of how emotional victory was won, and now here is another difficult story. This one is really hard to write. Everything in me wants to keep my suicide ideation a secret. I certainly don't want to tell the whole world the details of falling into the depression again and ending up suicidal again. Wouldn't they judge me negatively? When anyone really wants to commit suicide they hide it from everyone. This time the only reason I am here to write this story is that I couldn't hide it from my husband. I was withdrawing and crying. He knew the telltale signs and would not leave me alone. One thing led to another, and I am now at the hospital on the psych floor again writing this story.

Why am I in the hospital anyway? The doctors won't give me medication to help with the depression? At least for now I am safe and have time to ride out this painful emotional wave. If I am going to get better, I have to use the tools that have worked for me like watching DBT videos on the DBT Self Help Website (Dietz, 2003, Instant Mindfulness). Writing has been very therapeutic and one of the best tools to help me overcome painful emotions.

First of all, I do have good emotions like happiness and joy, and I am actually glad I do! I am not hooked on depression like it is a habit, I hope. Just last week I spent three wonderful days in Nashville at my husband's family reunion. I had a very peaceful, happy time, and truly enjoyed it. I don't know why this week I'm so depressed again, but I know it is time to write to help me overcome these negative emotions. This time I am in the hospital writing yet another story. Writing has worked like a charm in the past so here I go again.

It Started with Distorted Thinking

I will start at the beginning which was yesterday at 4:00 a.m. at home. I woke up early for some unknown reason and went down to my laptop to write in my journal. Of course, I checked my email and read my devotion about trusting Jesus first. I then wrote about my DBT Group Therapy experience from the night before in my first paragraph. I wrote about the nice compliment my DBT group counselor made about me. She told me she was very impressed with the amount of work I had put into DBT. Most people don't work that hard. I then wrote down the compliment that the psychiatrist from the Hospital told me two weeks ago. She told me she was very impressed with the progress I had made in DBT. She could tell that I had worked very hard. I had not been in the hospital for six months. She did tell me that I had made the right decision to come in the hospital at that time since I was struggling with suicide again. I felt so encouraged. I then wrote the comment that the medical community that works with me is so encouraging and uplifting. I paused for a moment and soaked up the positive feelings. Tackling painful emotions with therapy is way harder than with drugs.

While I was reminiscing over the good memories a thought popped in my head. The other people in my life aren't always so encouraging. In their attempt to offer help, they sometimes say things that are damaging even though they don't know it. I wish I could just brush it off and keep on going but apparently I can't right now. Two close family members told me that I'm too self-focused. One of the members quickly commented that he just believed that I needed to take a break from working so hard and play. My pastor's wife told me to not talk about myself so much but focus on other people during the women's Bible study. As soon as I finished writing these thoughts in my journal I felt my emotional mind take over. I cried and cried. I felt like the work I was doing in DBT and writing was possibly too self-focused and wrong! O God! I began to feel awful so I decided to go back to bed. It was 5:00 a.m.

I lay in bed feeling so bad. Why did I have those thoughts? I was fine earlier. How on earth could I ever overcome my crazy emotions without being self-focused? Applying DBT skills is *really* hard! It is next to impossible to change the way this 53 year old woman thinks without writing and talking about it. O God! This is now the main tool I have to overcome depression. How can people who love me the most make such discouraging comments? Guess what? I was ruminating and it made me feel worse, much worse! I knew I was in trouble so I went back downstairs to my recliner to practice meditation. I was a pro at this because I have been practicing meditation and waiting on God while I practice solitude for the last six months. I did this for up to thirty minutes twice a day and it has truly made a positive change in my life. I am really focusing on meditation so this I thought would be my best tool to use to stop the ruminating. It didn't work. I just cried and ruminated. My emotional mind was on the throne and I was miserable. In fact, I felt so awful that I just wanted to die so I planned to slit my wrists.

As I look back on this moment I realize that I must have been in some alternate state of mind. I was all emotional and could not reason at all! The emotional pain was greater than I had ever experienced before! I remember pushing Jesus away. I didn't think about my loving husband or five wonderful daughters. I didn't think about the reality that these negative feelings would eventually go away like a wave that DBT taught. All I could think about was how awful I felt and this had to stop. The only way I knew how to end it was to kill myself. I sat in the recliner and made plans in how I was going to kill myself. I was serious this time. I wasn't scared at all. I planned to slit my wrists as soon as my two girls were off to school and my husband was off to work. That would leave me alone all day before anyone would know. I didn't think about the fact that my daughters would have been the ones that found me in the afternoon and the damage it would do to their emotional lives. No, I was in so much emotional pain that all I could think about was my pain.

I did my morning duties of making coffee for my hubby and sandwiches for my girls. Suicide plans consumed my mind but I didn't talk to anyone. I couldn't without crying. I didn't want to do DBT anymore. It's way too hard! What about Jesus? Forget it. How could He be real and let me go through this much emotional pain anyway? I knew I didn't want to go to the hospital either because they couldn't or possibly wouldn't help me. They wouldn't give me drugs to numb the pain so there was no reason to go! Death was the only thing that would take away the emotional pain. I was determined that I was going to slit my wrists this time.

I had one problem. My husband knew something was really wrong and wouldn't leave for work. What was I going to do now? He kept asking me if I was okay. I lied to him and said "yes" with tears all over my face. I wanted to die and it looked like this wasn't going to happen. Now there may be no relief for the pain! O God, what was I going to do???

I grabbed my cell phone and went upstairs to my bedroom. I called the emergency number to my counselor and left this message, "I quit. This is Stacey." I hung up and went to bed crying. Several minutes later he called back and I told him how bad I felt and told him my suicide plans. He told me to call 911. I told him I wouldn't call. He asked me if anyone was with me. I told him my husband. He wanted to talk to him so I gave my husband the phone. They talked a little then hung up. He told my husband to call the nurse practitioner at the ECT lab and that he was going to call us back as soon as he arrived at work. I just lay in the bed and cried.

Later my counselor called back and scheduled an appointment at 11:00. I agreed to see him. I then called the ECT lab and talked to the nurse practitioner. I told him about what I was feeling and my suicide plans. He told me that I needed to apply my DBT skills and that in a few hours I would be alright like the many times before. I remembered two weeks earlier when this happened and I went in the hospital just to get dismissed 24 hours later. I really do have a problem with suicide ideation and don't have the DBT skills to overcome the suicide plans yet. This time was very different. I wasn't scared and I wasn't thinking about my family. My only focus was to escape the emotional pain. The nurse practitioner did tell me to call him back in a couple hours. My husband was still with me.

I met with my counselor at 11:00 and told him what was going on. Near the end of my appointment my husband joined us. Both my counselor and my husband decided that I needed to go back in the hospital. My counselor called the nurse practitioner at the ECT lab and told him how sick I was so he made arrangements for me to be admitted into the hospital. I left the appointment pissed off! I knew those doctors wouldn't help get rid of the emotional pain! They wouldn't give me anti-depressants. I did know that I would be safe from suicide but I wanted relief from the emotional pain!

Not another Hospitalization

After getting to the hospital I met with the doctors and of course, they wouldn't give me anything to take away the pain. They talked about DBT and asked me what skill I could use to help. I have no idea. Meditation isn't working right now. I don't know what to do and I don't want to do DBT anymore! I told them my DBT group was about to end anyway. The doctors decided to contact my DBT group therapists and work on getting me into another DBT group in Atlanta somewhere. They were making arrangements to get me with another individual therapist that could teach me how to apply the DBT skills when I am suicidal. They would be available to coach me over the phone during a crisis.

I left that session with those doctors still in emotional pain. I knew they wouldn't help me with medication, and of course they didn't. I wasn't disappointed because I knew they wouldn't give me drugs, but I was still in pain. I knew that the only way I was going to get out of this suicidal time was to kill myself. At least I was safe at the moment.

An Invitation to Write

While in the hospital one of the group therapy sessions was on journaling! Isn't that amazing? Writing is one of my best tools for dealing with my crazy emotions, so I decided that writing while here in the hospital might be the best way to start helping myself get better this time. I asked the nurse at the nursing station if they could give me a pencil and some paper so I could journal. I went to the cafeteria and boy did I write! I must have had ten pages telling my story of this suicide thoughts leading to the hospitalization I was now going through.

Healing Is Happening

1) I've been in the hospital for over 24 hours and the emotional pain lifted. What a relief! Why? I think there are three reasons:

2) Emotions are like waves in that they come and go. The emotional pain subsided for now.

3) I'm not ruminating about the topic that started the whole emotional landslide in the first place. I have been distracted by just by being in the hospital.

4) I wrote this experience down on paper and for some reason that is a great therapy tool I have to help overcome the crazy emotions.

Now here's the important question – am I still suicidal? I was three hours ago, but since I wrote this experience down on paper I'm not anymore!

What is next? As I sit here, I'm in shock that this whole suicidal experience happened and I ended up in the hospital. I guess if I responded right, I would try to learn from the experience so hopefully it won't happen again. But since it possibly will happen again or more likely probably will happen, it would be wise to learn how to ride out the intense emotions skillfully at home. I need to deal with the suicidal thoughts, and try not to end up in the hospital. I don't know how to deal with that right now so I am going to have to seek out help from somewhere. I will start with my individual counselor.

Overcoming Sad Emotions While Still in the Hospital

It is now the next morning and I'm still in the hospital. I woke up at my usual time at 5:00 a.m. and practiced meditation. It was hard. I did the standing yoga then sat down and focused on my breath and Jesus' name crossed my mind a few times. I began to cry. These tears felt like healing tears this time. I told Jesus I was sorry for pushing Him aside and cried some more.

First of all, my faith is *really* important to me but when I am suicidal I reject my faith. When I quit DBT, I also quit believing in Jesus. This time I even lost the desire to fight the emotions for my family. I really did give up. For those who don't struggle with depression, think of depression like terminal cancer. Even though you can't see the cause of the emotional pain, it is as real and as painful as cancer.

I have learned from DBT that emotions aren't wrong. One of the victories I'm experiencing at the moment is that I'm not judging myself for being really depressed and in the hospital. I am letting out the *welcome mat* to the painful emotions that I am feeling right now. Somehow I think letting out these feelings through crying is a part of inner healing. I have no particular thoughts except Jesus is with me. I get the sense that He wants to love on me. I am going to settle my mind for a while through meditation and open up my spirit to Jesus amazing love. I know that He loves me just as much when I'm sad as when I'm happy. I know He still loves me when I'm suicidal and push Him away. There is nothing I can do *or think* that will separate me from His love. These are the thoughts that I am going to focus on while I meditate.

As I meditated I thought about unconditional love. I have been focusing on loving myself off and on all day long this last month and guess what? I am accepting myself for having to go to the hospital! I'm not judging myself! I love myself even though I wanted to commit suicide! Jesus loves me anyway! I'm not a bad person. I'm not foolish. I'm just human and made a mistake because I'm hurting. It's alright. I'm okay. I do have wisdom, both spiritual and emotional. Sometimes it's just not manifested. I'm still learning. This is the first time I didn't judge myself badly for being in the hospital and I'm proud of that!

Damage Control

One of the questions the doctor asked me is what DBT skill could have I used to help in this situation? I tried meditation but the emotional pain was far too great that all my mind would do is focus on ruminating. The collapse into despair happened so fast that I gave up fighting. I threw away my progress and reverted to the impulse to hurt myself. How on earth can I stop this cascading of emotions and use damage control? What damage control?

My emotions were ruling on the throne of my life, and my rational mind was on vacation. Damage control skills were non-existent at the time. Anything I use can't involve thinking, at least not at first. Maybe a bubble bath or an outdoor walk would have stopped the ruminating. Of course it was very early in the morning when this happened and everyone was sleeping and it was dark outside. Maybe I should have got my husband up and asked him to love on me by scratching my back or rubbing my feel? The only problem is that he would have wanted to know what was going on. I usually don't want to talk about my suicide thoughts, and I know from experience that a conversation between my emotional mind and his technical mind usually doesn't go well. I am going to talk to my counselor about damage control skills when I meet with him next week. I need to humble myself and seek wisdom. I need help so hopefully I can learn how to stop this emotional landslide to suicide.

It is several hours later and I have slipped into judging myself several times. I am still very emotional. I decided to read what I had written about Jesus' unconditional love, and the victories I have had in not judging myself. This helped me to feel loved. I know that I have to turn my mind from this self-judgment to acceptance with love over and over again. I learned this from DBT. I asked several staff members here in the hospital if I could brag. They said, "Yes," so I told them about my victory over judging myself about being hospitalized. Of course, they encouraged me. I bragged to several of the patients about this victory. I did this to reinforce my victory and hopefully to encourage them to have positive thoughts as well. As I hung around the other depressed patients I could see that the negative thoughts that I struggle with are definitely a symptom of depression. This is another reason not to judge myself.

Back at Home—Could There Possibly Be Additional Help?

It is the day after being in the hospital and now I am at home. What has changed is that I am having these emotional landslides into suicide two times in the last couple weeks? Could it be that since the ECT treatments have spaced out to every 10 days? It has affected me greatly. I know they were supposed to space them out weeks ago but I just wasn't stable enough yet. I have ECT on Monday and I think I will make a plea to the doctor that just possibly could they have the next couple ECT treatments closer together. I was hoping this might help keep me stable so I won't end up in the hospital again.

Around three weeks ago, I remembered that my ECT doctor had suggested possibly trying one of two medications. I listened to her because she, like the other doctors at the hospital, was adamantly against me taking medications the last five months because of the negative side effects I have experienced taking the many psychotropic drugs. I perceived that she could tell I was still having a great deal of difficulty managing my emotions and seemed to really want to help me. I was beginning to wonder if DBT alone just was not enough to help me control the emotions. I think I need some extra help.

> "Blessed is the man who perseveres under trial, because when
> he has stood the test, he will receive the crown of life that
> God has promised to those who love him."
> James 1:12

Chapter 31

A Walk Down Memory Lane

Discerning What God is Doing in My Life

e membering what God has done in my life seems to be the message the Lord is speaking in my heart this morning. It's 4:30 in the morning and I have been up since 1:00 a.m. and can't get back to sleep. I keep remembering what the doctor told me in the hospital a couple days ago. Since my memory is not the greatest right due to the depression and the ECT, I will just have to paraphrase what I remember. She said, "You have been like this all your life." I think she was referring to the suicidal depression due to Borderline Personality Disorder. I told her she was wrong and told her that she didn't know me. My past accomplishments include a thirteen year music season in my life which ended at the end of my Army tour with the Forces Command Band with orders cut to be the oboe instructor at the United States Army/Navy School of Music in Norfolk, VA. I declined the offer so I could marry my wonderful husband. We just celebrated 31 years of marriage. My teaching season of my life includes receiving a degree in Christian Education and having twenty years of teaching experience which included overseeing fifteen home school families. My mothering season of my life includes delivering all five of my daughters at home and home schooling them for 12 years. I did acknowledge that I have had some minor emotional problems all my life but not with suicidal depression until just this last year.

I briefly remember that the doctor believed that I had been dealing with suicidal depression and Borderline Personality Disorder all my life so I needed to practice DBT to overcome this pattern in my life. I knew she was wrong. I came down to the computer and decided to read this book about my own history from my childhood up to a year ago before all this crazy emotions started happening. As I read it, I was deeply moved because of the miraculous things God has done in my life! My life wasn't easy, but God met me every step of the way. I have been a sane and reasonable person with tremendous faith in God most of my adult life. Life was challenging but I was inspired to grow in my love for God during all the situations I experienced.

What is God doing in my life now anyway that I can't do music, can't teach school, can't teach the Bible to children or adults, can't clean the house, can't teach my own two children at home how to clean and cook, and can't do many other things, as well as can't control my emotions? I seem to be able to write and talk still. I seem to have the ability to learn DBT skills and the lessons that God is teaching me. I still seem to have faith in my God, even after all I've been through this last year. I still want to be close to Jesus and discern His will for my life. I really want to walk according to His plans for my life right now in this moment. I seem to have a deep desire to share what He is doing in my life with others.

As I sit here I realize that I have lots of faith in God. Through the years I have been gaining experience serving God and my faith has been growing by leaps and bounds. I was getting to know my God in a deep personal way and was experiencing His power in my life. Now I seem to be in a season when my faith is greatly challenged, but I find it is really getting deeper. Satan wants to destroy me, but Jesus is reaching deep down in my heart and spirit and ministering to me. Jesus has miraculously saved me from hurting myself so many times by the movement of His Spirit directly in my mind. My husband and friends have helped me so much.

"O Lord, could you bless them?"

I have been able to feel Jesus' healing love minister to me which lifts me out of the cascading of my emotions coming from the severe depression which leads to suicide ideation. Jesus has miraculously saved me from hurting myself so many times by moving on others who reach out to keep me safe and send me to the hospital. This act of love buys me time to get into my reasonable mind so I can embrace Jesus' love again. Now I believe Jesus wants me to learn skills that will help me not to have the emotional landslide to keep me safe from attempting suicide.

I want to ask God the question, "Why suicide?" It is interesting that I am not rubbing shoulders with believers as much as I rub shoulders with unbelievers. I have many contacts with the medical community and many people that are dealing with mental health issues. Many of these people don't know Jesus in a personal way, and many patients are so much overcome by their mental illness that if they have faith, it has been greatly challenged. I can relate to their pain and loss of faith so I can share personally about my negative experiences and share about the loving compassion that Jesus has given me while *in the trench*, especially when trapped in suicide thoughts. This love is so abstract that most people don't know anything about it. I have experienced Jesus' love and it has saved my life many times, and I want to tell about it! In fact, I can't seem to stop writing or keep my mouth shut!

Maybe this is why I am so intense and self-focused. I am in God's university gaining real life experience and skills in how to deal with mental illness from a personal point of view. God wants me to help those who have experienced mental problems and their family members. Maybe God has me in this spiritual university to prepare me to love these wonderful people that He loves.

I can say in all honesty that my life hasn't been easy, but God has really blessed me. However, this last year has been so difficult that most of the time I wonder if I can learn what Jesus wants me to learn. It is way too hard, but now I wonder if it is that way because God is really preparing me to help those who are very sick. I know that I have a huge amount of compassion and understanding of how they really feel. I have gained some knowledge through my experience with all sorts of psychotropic medication, ECT, many different techniques of individual therapy, group therapy, and spiritual experiences, and experience in how to receive God's grace and healing love.

I don't know how much longer this training is going to be, but I have to rest in the fact that Jesus will not put me through more than I can handle. I have to rely on His loving grace so I can tackle each and every moment I face victoriously. I know that I need God's tremendous grace to help me be emotionally stable during the times people communicate challenging words to me. I have to seek and rely on God's wisdom in how to communicate what He's teaching me to any person He brings across my path. I know that I need wisdom when to keep quiet. I have to trust that Jesus is absolutely in control of every aspect of my life even though often it doesn't feel like it. I need to always remember that no matter what I go through that God's love for me is way greater than I can ever imagine! This is a fact that I can rest in!

Chapter 32

Experiencing Inner Healing

*"God anointed Jesus of Nazareth with the Holy Spirit and power,
and how he went around doing good and healing all who were
under the power of the devil, because God was with him."*
Acts 10:38

Expressing Emotional Pain from a Long Time Ago

*a*m currently listening to the *Radical Acceptance* video from the DBT Self Help website again (Dietz, 2003, Instant Mindfulness). I have been watching and listening to it several times a day for over a month, but this time I'm not watching the slides but just listening to the background music. I remember the emotional pain surrounding my relationship with my mother when I was a teenager. I'm not thinking about specific memories but I am but am letting out the *welcome mat* to the emotions from long ago. I hope that my God can bring inner healing to my emotions as I sit in my recliner and cry in His Presence.

I am crying as I experience these emotions. I don't have any specific reason to cry, so why am I crying? Could this be the emotions I have suppressed all my life? Could these feelings be driving the anger that is causing me to have suicidal thoughts? The memories of mom's suicide attempts with a gun and the comment that she loved me only because she was my mother but she didn't like me are still in my memory bank, but I purposely don't focus on these painful memories. I certainly don't want to remember the emotional pain either, but maybe I should allow myself to experience the emotional pain just to release it appropriately without the suicide thoughts or an attempt to commit suicide.

I have one more memory about mom. I remember this while attending college. After recovering from a breakdown, I went to see mom in her bedroom and apologized for being such a rebellious teenager. I asked for her forgiveness. After a short time, she refused to accept my apology. I was really hurt, but right at that moment I realized how sick my mother really was. I believed that even though I was emotionally sick, she might even be more emotionally sick than me, and I need to start separating my emotional attachment from her and go on in my new adult life.

I am sitting here quietly while I continue to let out the *welcome mat* to more painful emotions. I don't have to have words or pictures in my mind, just tears. It's okay, Stacey, to feel sad. This is my newly budding parent part of me that was nonexistent six months ago. I am nurturing myself for a change! I am learning how to comfort myself. Jesus loves all of me unconditionally too, even this really hurting part of me! I don't have to bury it any more.

I'm sitting in my recliner again, no words, and no thoughts – just painful feelings with tears. I know they are healing tears for they are not as intense as emotions could be. I picture my Jesus' wrapping His arm around me tenderly comforting me as I cry. I am feeling very loved right now. Remembering, negative emotions aren't necessarily wrong. I believe that emotions might be a gift from God! I just need to release them appropriately without hurting myself. Crying is good.

I remember some specific memories of my mom's suicide attempts while I was in high school and that is that I didn't cry back then. I had to be strong to help my little sister through her pain. I didn't have any emotional response back then when the suicide attempts happened. There was intense fear, but no tears. I think the emotions were released when I was in college. I poured out my life onto music, but spring quarter I had an emotional breakdown. Could I be releasing the anger I had suppressed? It took a year to recover from the breakdown. I now wonder if that was some of my suppressed emotions being released.

It is over 34 years later, three years of service in the army band, 31 years of successful marriage and after having 5 daughters (my youngest is now 12 and oldest is 25), many negative emotions are surfacing again. They have surfaced off and on for the last year with ten psychiatric hospitalizations (twice in the last month). I have finally learned that my Lord Jesus loves me unconditionally, even with these memories and feelings of extreme sadness and tears with suicide ideation. I am learning to love myself as well, and be nonjudgmental of my past and my present. I am learning to love myself unconditionally, all of me, even the part with the painful emotions and suicide ideation.

Anger Expressed Inwardly → Depression and Suicide

Could I really have an anger problem that expresses itself by wanting to hurt myself? As I listened to my counselor today, my spirit could bear witness to what he was saying. He suggested that I might have been mad at those I loved and connected with the most. They don't understand that I really want to work hard to keep myself alive so I don't commit suicide. Writing is my rescue tool; it helps me to remember the DBT skills and work hard try to apply them. I really do want to live and not die, except when I'm in crisis. As I sat in God's Presence, I realized that I was mad at my husband. He suggested I take a break from writing so I could watch TV. (I don't like TV, except maybe nature shows, anyway.) He wants me to play games! How can I play games when I'm in a life or death state of mind? He thinks I should distract myself from the painful emotions.

Perceived Rejection → Suicide

As I sit here, I am reminded of my root issues of rejection and abandonment. My cognitive distorted beliefs about my root issues and my irrational emotional response to them are a major problem that could lead to suicide. This is a serious problem that I don't know what to do about. I know that the last two times I had suicide thoughts, they lead to two hospitalizations. These were caused by my distorted perception of rejection from those that love me the most: my husband, my daughter, my counselor, my psychiatrist, and my alternative medical doctor. I had an irrational emotional response when the rejection button was pushed. I immediately plummeted into suicide ideation and plans. Oh my God, how do I deal with the rejection button that just about destroys my life???

Suicide Ideation → Writing Helps

I'm sitting here thinking about how I can overcome the emotional cascade into suicidal ideation. I noticed that this last time the suicide thoughts couldn't be stopped with any skills I had learned. I tried hard. My husband and I walked the dogs around the neighborhood, but I was too far into my emotions, and was totally focused on plans to commit suicide for this walk to distract me. I even met with my counselor, but that didn't get me out of my suicide ideation. I ended up in the hospital. What can get me out of this emotional state??? Writing seems to be a good tool for me. It helps me to get stable so I don't focus on suicide anymore.

When I was in the hospital, the doctors really did nothing to help me get out of my emotional state. At least they accepted me on the floor of the hospital which kept me safe so I could get stable through writing. Writing really does help.

Embracing Jesus' Unconditional Love

Once again I'm sitting here quietly listening to Celtic music, but this time my mind and heart are embracing Jesus' love for me. Jesus loves *all* of me; He's holding me with His arms wrapped around my shoulders right now. There truly is nothing I can do *or think* that will separate me from His love. Even though sometimes I push Jesus away and think about committing suicide; He still really loves me deeply. This is amazing! He is still holding me tightly. He's gently holding my hands in His hands while warmly looking into my eyes. He's tenderly stroking my arms and touching my face. He wants me to receive His healing touch by receiving His tremendous love for me. Once again, my performance or lack of has nothing to do with His love for me. Jesus died for my sins, including suicide thoughts, and He wants me to *let go* of them and bask in His love through His Presence.

Until I learn the DBT skills that will help me overcome suicidal tendencies, I will continue to bask in God's Presence for His love for me is unconditional. I'm safe in His arms. I pray that Jesus will continue to help me let out the *welcome mat* to painful emotions and help me release these emotions in a healthy way. It is okay to get angry and release this anger without hurting others or myself. Often times I cry. That's okay too. I hope as I bask in Jesus' Presence that a supernatural inner healing will take place deep down in my life.

Chapter 33

Shame??? Not Again

"In you, O LORD, I have taken refuge;
let me never be put to shame."
Psalm 71:1

Forgiving Whole Heartedly to Get Past the Hurts

ometimes I think this journey on the Depression Trail is too difficult. That is how I have felt most of this week. Even with the momentous joy filled experience of watching my daughter graduate from nursing school, I have experienced intense moments of sadness and crying. I can't seem to shake the feeling that I just don't measure up. I know it's a lie from Satan, but why does my emotional mind embrace that pain? I know that Jesus loves me just the way I am and I don't have to perform for His love! He has looked in my eyes and tenderly touched my arms and face showing me His love! He has held me tightly in His arms and wrapped me in His love! He has welcomed me into His lap to curl up and cry while He hugs me and tells me over and over that He loves me! Just last night I lay in bed filled with tears and Jesus lie next to me and hugged me with squeezes and tender strokes of intimate love. I know Jesus loves me by reading about it in the Bible, but that's not all; I know Jesus loves me in my heart and spirit because I experience His love anytime I need to. I spend intimate time with Him several times every day as I practice meditation. Experiencing total unconditional love deep in my heart is not an automatic feeling. That is a feeling that I have to consciously embrace, especially during the moments when I feel like I don't measure up.

I have learned through wise counseling that when we experience emotional trauma early in our life, but don't express the emotional pain during the time of the trauma but suppress it instead, then we may experience this pain later in life. I think this is what has been happening to me this last six months. I feel emotional pain that I don't seem to have specific thoughts that triggered them. I don't know where the tears are coming from. I am learning to let out the *welcome mat* to these emotions. All my life I have earned a 100% A+ for suppressing emotions. I'm so good at suppressing negative emotions that I don't even realize that I'm doing it. Not good... Now I am letting out the *welcome mat* to these negative emotions but sometimes I don't even know what is causing them. I have been crying in my bedroom. I cried in the restaurant and in the van. I cried at the kitchen table. I cried during the whole church service. I cried in the car driving home from church. The tears have no discretion when it is appropriate to come to the surface. I need to let out the *welcome mat* and cry anyway. I believe that I am releasing pain from my teen years. Praise God, I won't be carrying this burden anymore.

God loves me so much and is definitely guiding me on this journey. I went to Emotions Anonymous on Monday and picked up a couple brochures on *Perfectionism* and *Shame*. I read the *Perfectionism* brochure and of course could relate to this difficult character defect. It fits with the other character defect of having to *perform* for love. Since I can't *perform* now and most certainly can't be *perfect* during this season of my life, I have the devastating belief that I don't measure up and most certainly am not worthy of love. I know this is a lie from Satan, but this is where my feelings are. That's not the worst though, even though that's bad enough.

Shame

The other Emotions Anonymous brochure on Shame was an eye opener! It gave a name to the emotional pain I was experiencing. Shame's root started at home, and is manifested now because I have rejected myself because of this depression I'm suffering. I read this brochure several times and let myself cry more each time. "Shame is a painful emotion which can be caused by feeling guilty. Guilt says, 'I made a mistake.' Shame says, 'I am a mistake,' (*Today*, April 1.) Shame is devastating to us as it feeds the feelings that we are worthless and inadequate." I feel the shame from my childhood, but I feel shame because my extreme emotions and depression that I have experienced this last couple years. It is hard for me to not think I'm an emotional wreck, worthless to everyone, and inadequate to do much of anything. O God, help me! "Self-talk such as this may be very deep in our subconscious, but it can be at the root of our feelings and perceptions." (Shame, Emotions Anonymous)

"Hiding shame even from ourselves will keep us from becoming healthy. We will continue to reject ourselves and others until we deal with our humanness. We must be willing to accept ourselves each day, and not be discouraged if we fall short of our ideals. We look for the positive and learn to accept that we are doing the best we can." (Shame Brochure, Emotions Anonymous)

I often feel worthless because I can't perform. That is a lie from Satan. I am now learning that my worth has nothing to do with what I do, but it is rooted in who I am. Jesus loves me just the way I am, emotions and all.

"O my God! How can I feel worthless and inadequate after all the love You have poured out on me?"

If I'm truly honest with myself, deep down inside I feel worthless with this depression. Sometimes I feel that the depression is my fault. My mind has truly become a battle ground for Satan.

Shame probably entered my life in my childhood. I remember when Mom said, "Shame on you." My mother also told me she loved me because she was my mother but she didn't like me. I remember feeling devastated! Mom didn't seem to care what I was doing. She didn't come to my music concerts and sports events. When I received awards, she never gave me praise. I remember lots of indifference on the part of my mother, and I remember the pain associated with it. I didn't let myself experience the pain, because it wouldn't do any good or change anything. The emotional pain would just ruin my life so I suppressed them. Now that I am an adult, I need to forgive my mother totally but this is hard and will take time. Hiding the shame from myself has been so damaging to my life. Deep down I have been rejecting myself. I believed I was not worthy of love.

"O God, even as I write this I want to cry. There is still pain from rejecting myself. Help me to love and accept myself just the way I am. I don't have to perform."

Flesh Pattern

As I remember the intense shame I felt as a child—I want to comment that this is the first time this pain has had a label—I realize that I had a deep desire the feel loved and respected. The best way that I could figure out to be respected was to do well in school. I was an "A/B" student. I joined the band and became an excellent musician, and was an excellent gymnast. The better I performed in school, in band, and in gymnastics, the more respected I became. The *performance* pattern in my life was forming. When I joined the Army Band, my ability to *perform* for respect was solidified especially when I was offered a teaching position at the Army/Navy School of Music as the oboe instructor. I served in the church and *performed* by serving and doing all the Christian things to *perfection*! I earned a Christian Education Degree. I taught in Christian Schools and lead the Home School Program at church for years. I taught Parenting Classes, I was the leader of the Junior Handmaiden Program at church, and wrote and published Bible curriculum. I was also a great mother after having a five of my girls at home with a midwife and home schooled for twelve years. I have done so much more. I was highly respected! This flesh patterns of *performance* and *perfection* has been an effective coping mechanism for the intense emotional shame that I really felt deep in my heart for over thirty years. Nine years ago my flesh pattern stopped working and I had a breakdown. Medication helped me deal with the emotional pain but it has been only this last six months since being off the medication that Jesus has begun really healing my heart! It is time to reprogram my mind where I can experience Jesus' love and acceptance all the time even without performing. This changes me so I can love and accept myself all the time.

I find it so interesting that it has been over forty years since I was a child and felt all this shame, but now that I am in my fifties the feelings of shame have come back with a vengeance. I have been serving Jesus for over thirty years and know well that I am precious to Him. I have nothing to be ashamed of, yet deep down I still feel shame. It is obvious to me now that knowing scriptural truth doesn't necessarily heal the pain that is in deep dark recesses of my heart alone. Knowing scripture is only the beginning. I need to apply the scripture to each and every moment of my life so it can bring inner healing. For me, it's also letting go of my failed attempts to perform for perfection as I try to overcome the shame. Jesus loves me just the way I am. I *don't* have to perform for His love. I just want Jesus to help me love myself too.

Jesus to the Rescue!

Now my Jesus is reaching way down in the deep recesses of my heart and taking me on a path towards inner healing from shame. This is such a painful journey as the emotions come to the surface and I cry. I have nothing to feel shame about any more. Jesus is healing me!

"O Lord, not only do you love me deeply, but I am valuable to You just the way I am. This is amazing! It is so amazing that You love me in the dark places. I don't have to feel shame at all, for Your love covers a multitude of sins. I am loved and accepted by You even with the feelings of shame that haunt me from my childhood. Help me to continue to release the tears from the pain of shame. I know that You love me in the midst of the shame, but You want to heal me."

Forgiveness to Heal the Shame!

> *"Then Peter came to Jesus and asked, "Lord, how many times shall I forgive my brother when he sins against me? Up to seven times?" Jesus answered, "I tell you, not seven times, but seventy-seven times.""*
> Matthew 18:21-22

Once again I have been challenged! I have forgiven my mother zillions of times and believed that I walk in forgiveness all the time, but I still have emotional pain associated with my childhood—shame. Have I forgiven each offense whole heartedly so now I genuinely want to bless her? Probably not. It has been so many years since I experienced the painful situations and comments that hurt me; I don't even know if I can remember them. I have chosen to not recall them for the last thirty years, but instead I suppressed them. I just want to go on with my adult life. However, emotional issues have come back to haunt me so it is time to deal with the source of the emotional issues by dealing with the rejection and abandonment from my childhood. It is time to revisit forgiveness for any and all offenses I have with my mother.

I am thinking about loving myself unconditionally; this is an action of mercy. I have been learning to accept myself even with the painful emotions. I am learning to forgive myself for rejecting Jesus when I'm really hurting emotionally. I am also learning to accept myself with all my crazy emotions and even with the suicidal thoughts that lead to hospitalization.

"Lord, I want to thank You for helping me to forgive my mother. She hurt me bad emotionally but I believe that she didn't know it. She was living a life with skeletons in her own closet. Drinking didn't help either. I

am so glad she took care of me growing up as a child, but my teen years were turbulent. Mother had her own problems that were affecting me greatly. God, I forgive her and lift her up to you. Work in her life so that she can embrace Your love for her. Thank You, Jesus."

I hated my mother in the past but I repented. God has forgiveness for this hatred that goes deep into my heart. There is nothing that I have done or think that the Lord doesn't forgive. This is amazing!

"Lord, help me to learn more about forgiveness and most of all help me to walk in forgiveness for my mother every day. Help me to forgive people in all areas of my life."

"Lord, I have forgiven my mother and am now working on my own feelings of shame. You are healing the shame that is way deep in my heart. I have to be patient with myself while these overwhelming tears and feelings of shame are being transformed by Your healing love. You, O Lord, made me just the way you wanted. You are helping me to walk out this healing by helping me release the healing tears of shame from my childhood. Lord, your tender touch in my life is resulting in healing from the deep pains of shame."

Chapter 34

Trust during Times of Transitions

Believing that Jesus Is Really in Control

*u*ring times of transition, it is very hard for me to trust that Jesus in control. Fear grips my heart! I have to remind myself that Jesus has been in control all my life, especially this last year while walking on the difficult Depression Trail. Jesus' provision includes amazing family support, wise medical help, wise counselors, friends, money, and the list goes on and on. It has been astounding!

Over a month ago when I thought my psychiatrist dropped me and my internal medicine doctor abandoned me, fear gripped my heart! This quickly became a transition time, but because of feelings of rejection, abandonment, and fear, I couldn't think rationally at all! People all around me tried to help me see that these doctors were still available. I didn't believe them because my emotional mind took over to the point where cognitive distortions took over. I couldn't reason. I was experiencing too much pain, so I plummeted to wanting to commit suicide. I had to go in the hospital for 24 hours. As I look back, I realize that I just didn't trust that Jesus was in control. I was too scared. Is fear the opposite of trust?

Right now I am in another time of transition. I started a new mood stabilizing medicine a week ago. This one is very different than any other drug I have been on so I'm hoping I won't have negative side effects this time. *"I have to trust You, Jesus, to take care of me."*

My DBT group ended Monday evening. I'm not comfortable without group therapy. The DBT group leaders think I need another DBT group lead by an intensively trained therapist. The psychiatrists on the floor at the hospital think I need another DBT group too. It is very hard to find a DBT group that we can afford! Most DBT therapists are not covered by our medical insurance. So what do I do? I have to trust that You are in charge of this situation, Jesus. It's hard to trust when call after call is either rejection because therapists have no openings or they're not on our insurance plan so their fee way too much for us to afford!

I am not feeling too well at the moment. This is a time of transition and gloom and doom wants to take over my emotions. My emotional mind surfaces time and time again and I want to cry. I feel scared because I don't want to suffer from suicide thoughts and end up in the hospital again.

"Jesus, You know that I'm needy; You know my trail has been difficult and draining me of strength. I need to get in Your Presence to receive Your nurturing love right now—I'm doing that now."

I sat in Jesus Presence for around 20 minutes. It was hard this time because my mind wanted to ruminate so I had to refocus my mind over and over on Jesus' love for me.

It has been several hours later and I believe that Jesus spoke in my heart! He responded to my prayers, my friend's prayers, and my intense desire to know what is going on. One of my friends called me. I told her about the DBT group ending and the difficulty trying to find another one. I then told her something very true that I didn't realize before. I commented that I learn and apply the DBT skills best when I read and watched the videos on the dbtselfhelp.com website (Dietz, 2003, Instant Mindfulness). I really learn them best on my own! Now that I have become aware of all the DBT skills from this last DBT Skills Group, maybe I don't even need another DBT group.

I do know that I need to get with people though. I am not a loner. Maybe I could attend an Emotions Anonymous group. I looked up a hospital website that offers EA groups every night of the week for free. This might be a better experience. Since EA refers to a Higher Power, then maybe I can share about how Jesus is helping me! This hospital has a crisis line. Could this be my God providing a group for me?

My friend commented at the end of our conversation that she can see me ministering to many people. There are people everywhere who deal with emotional issues and since I have received God's grace to deal with severe depression and intense emotions, I can help them. I have a gift to be able to express emotions in words. This helps people to really open up. She told me that I have such a heart for God's people. I was so encouraged! Could it be that attending Emotions Anonymous could be a better environment to learn about emotional difficulties in people's lives? I'm thinking that many people may not be able to afford DBT therapy anyway. I am reminded that what I am going through is not only for my benefit, but it is an opportunity to learn how to minister to the people God puts in my life.

I just talked to an intensively trained DBT therapist who has many years of experience. I explained my situation and she told me the research evidence shows that if you follow the protocol, DBT really helps suicidal clients stay out of the hospital. She said I would never have to go in the hospital again. But in order for this to happen I would need to do the following:

- Attend a full year of DBT group lead by an intensively trained DBT therapist
- Get an individual DBT therapist who is intensively trained in DBT
- Make sure I would have phone support in between therapy sessions

As I talked to her my heart was really drawn to her. In other words, we really hit it off! I told her I looked on the DBT Self Help website frequently. She loves that site and refers to it often! She gave me a place to look on the site that has already helped me. It provided a tool that might help me to get out of a suicide crisis. It is answering certain questions from the site in my journal. She told me that meditation was not a good tool to get out of a suicide crisis. No wonder that didn't work before. She knows so much! The only problem is that she's not taking new clients for another month and would be out of network in my insurance plan. She's an hour away, up by my husband's work, so I would have to drive through downtown Atlanta. This gives me a lot to pray about.

DBT teaches me skills to help deal with my intense mood swings and possibly help keep me out of the hospital, but would it treat the underlying issue of my mother not loving me as a child? My current Christian DBT counselor is helping me with that, and helping me to realize that I suppress many negative emotions. These negative emotions surface with great intensity at the most inconvenient times! I need to focus on affirming myself and receiving God's unconditional love. These two skills are very helpful for me.

"Jesus, even though during times of transition it is hard for me to trust You, I have to be patient with myself. I also have to pray that You will help

me to not to succumb to fear then plummet to the point where my emo-tional mind is ruling my life. When this happens, I end up wanting to quit and have to go to the hospital. That's what happened a month ago. I need to remember that You have always have provided the support I need, just not always the way I think the support should be. I can't have a precon-ceived idea of how or when You are going to provide support. I just have to keep my mind open to all the creative possibilities You support me. Jesus, I need your grace to trust that You still love me and are in control of my life during these transitional times."

Of course transition times involve trusting that Jesus is in control and helping me to make decisions. I just made a decision to enter a Partial Hospital Program (PHP). I was having a hard time and I couldn't get a hold of my psychiatrist. I needed help so I made a decision to not go in the hospital this time since those doctors aren't offering me any help with medication now. This new hospital had a doctor that I like who would give me medications. She contacted my psychiatrist about what she wanted give me. Everything was a go, and she gave me two mood stabilizers and sleeping medication. I attended group therapy from 9:00-3:00 on M-F, and 8:30-12:00 on weekends. I was in the program for two weeks. Now I am finished with the group and am feeling much better. I think the meds are helping. I believe Jesus guided me to that hospital for help.

"Jesus, right now I am going to trust that You are going to give me wisdom to discern what kind of support You are going to provide next to continue my inner healing. You have put people in my life to help guide me into Your will. Probably the most important thing I can do is to spend time with You, Jesus. I need to sit and meditate on Your love for me, especially during these transition times. I need to pray and trust that You will open my spirit to discern Your will in my life. Lastly, I need to do what I believe is Your will for my life no matter what it is."

*"May the God of hope fill you with all joy and peace as you
trust in him, so that you may overflow with hope by
the power of the Holy Spirit."*
Romans 15:13

Chapter 35

Learning to Manage Thoughts and Emotions

Managing Emotions is Really Hard

*C*nflicts in my relationship with people, real or imagined, cause my emotions to plummet to a point of despair and sometimes wanting to commit suicide. I need hospitalization at that time. For some reason the trigger is caused when I think that someone rejects me or doesn't love me (real or perceived). When I look back at my thinking, I can see how distorted it was. These people weren't rejecting me at all, but they wanted to help. Secondly, these people were really expressing their love to me! I continued to criticize myself; no wonder my emotions sank to the bottom. I couldn't see these truths while depressed with out of control negative emotions. This spells disaster. In order to stay out of hospital, I desperately need to learn to manage these thoughts and emotions.

Changing what I'm thinking and feeling is no easy task. I'm a thinker and a woman of words. My mind excels at thinking—normal and now distorted this last two years. Teaching my mind to think in a healthy manner seems just about impossible. I do see how desperate my situation is with my thoughts and emotions running amuck. It is definitely time to continue to humble myself and embrace changes that will help my thought life. It is vitally important for me to learn to manage emotions.

Putting Off and Putting On

I have been practicing Putting Off and Putting On all day long every day. I try to be aware of my negative thoughts, and replace them with positive thoughts. Thank God for meditation. This is a skill that helps me get learn to release all the painful thoughts. I have been practicing meditation for just about a year. Meditation has been my foundation for emotional stability, yet I still have serious problems. Before my emotions get out of control, I need to get control of my thought life by distracting myself. I need to humble myself by thinking and saying kind words to myself. I need to listen to peaceful music and look at beautiful scenic mountains. I like to sit in a solitary place, close my eyes, and take several deep breaths. I then focus on my deep breathing and I try to settle my distressed mind by picturing myself sitting beside a mountain creek. Thoughts drift into my mind and try to take over. As soon as I become aware these thoughts, I gently release them to float down stream like a leaf. Emotions also bubble up and try to take over. I gently release them to drift on down the creek like a leaf too. It is vitally important to not get down on myself for having thoughts and emotions. That is how the brain works. Unconditional love is vitally important for success. I need to accept myself with unconditional love. I need to apply Putting Off and Putting On all day long so I can get practice releasing negative thoughts and emotions, so I can unconditionally love myself with compassionate thoughts. What I need to do is learn how to manage the thoughts and emotions so I won't end up in the hospital again. This motivates me to practice Putting Off and Putting On.

Embracing the Big Picture

Looking at the big picture of a situation that really upsets me is just about impossible. Yes, there is evidence that supports my negative feelings. However there's evidence that contradicts how I feel and even think. Am I stupid or what??? I criticize myself to the extreme when someone tries to help me see the whole picture. I condemn them for passing judgment on me, and trying to change me even though they are really expressing their love to me.

This is a difficult skill for me to embrace. I am way over sensitive to constructive comments. They feel like rejection. When I am in my emotional mind, the rejection or perceived rejection spells disaster. That is really a time that I need to embrace humility and accept constructive comments from people. Humility!!!

"O God, You love me through Your Spirit and through Your people. Help me to humble myself and ACCEPT Your help when I am feeling such intense emotional pain! Sometimes Your loving support includes Your

people coming to my side to help. Help me to be able to listen to them and to stop rejecting constructive criticism. It only hurts me."

Living with healthy thoughts is hard when dealing with severe depression. I have to humble myself so I can be open to ideas that seemingly contradict what I am feeling. Humility for me at this time can be expressed by setting aside my emotions for a moment to be open to God's point of view. This is the beginning of embracing wisdom by looking at the big picture. There are always two sides to a coin. I need to humble myself and be open to listening and accepting both sides of the emotional situation, my side and the person God has put in my life at that time's side.

"Lord, I have a really hard time embracing the big picture. I think my negative emotions are so justified that there is no other view. O Lord, help me to be humble so I can see my situation as You see it. Make my mind open to seeing the big picture, either through Your thoughts that You place in my mind, or through the loving people that You put into my life."

Now comes the hard part. It is my wonderful committed husband that tenderly and loving tries to help me see the other side of an emotional situation. I don't receive from him very well when I am emotional. When I am in my right mind, I can see that he is really lovingly trying to support me. I need to be open to what he tells me when I'm so emotional so I can see the big picture.

Coping Thoughts

When I'm having a hard time, reminding myself of my strengths and gifts that God has imparted in me really helps lift up my mood. Good coping thoughts soothe my emotions and are vitally important to managing my emotions. Coping thoughts have been a life saver that has helped turn my emotions upward. Here is an example of a coping thought: "Thoughts and emotions don't control my life, I do." This thought gives me the idea that I don't have to give into my negative thoughts and emotions. A good way to soothe my emotions is to embrace coping thoughts. Here is a list of coping thoughts that I am using that help diffuse some of the strong emotions:

- "Jesus, You love me even when I'm emotional."
- "I can accept my emotions right now."
- "I am a really nice person."

- "I can take all the time I need to *let go* and relax."
- "I've already been through other painful situations and survived."
- "This too shall come to pass. Remember, emotions are like waves!"

In reality, the application of most counseling skills in my life is usually combined with other skills to help bring peace during an emotional time. One skill I apply is to imagine myself sitting beside a creek meditating while I try to let the thoughts and emotions drift downstream like leaves in a creek. Another skill I apply is to tell myself, "I can take all the time I need to *let go* and *relax*."

Coping thoughts are powerful since they give me a sense that I can ride out the emotions victoriously. When left to my own thoughts in an emotional time, rumination dominates my mind. That is why coping thoughts are powerful because they can stop the rumination and help me to think positive thoughts. However, it takes great effort. Changing thoughts and emotions takes tremendous patience and endurance. The result of consistently practicing the skills is inner peace and happiness.

Balancing Thoughts and Emotions

This is such an important skill because when I am hurting and emotional, I pay attention to my side of what is really happening. I am blinded to the whole picture. This sounds familiar, doesn't it? I have a challenge to overcome. I need to balance out my thoughts and feelings. I need to be open to the evidence that supports both sides of an emotional event.

Balancing thoughts and emotions reminds me of a seesaw in a park. When I'm really depressed, it is like I'm on a seesaw sitting alone on one end. I'm weighed down on the ground with depressing thoughts and negative feelings. The other side of the seesaw is high in the air and it represents the thoughts and feelings that can bring my emotional mind into balance. How on earth do I bring balance to what I'm experiencing? There are two ways to bring the emotional turmoil into balance. One way is to listen intently to another person who can get on the other end of the seesaw. That person explains the other side of the problem I'm dealing with. When I embrace this evidence, then I allow the person to get on the other end of the seesaw and balance me out. Now I'm usually alone when I'm in an emotional state so the other way to balance out my thoughts and emotions is to get off the seesaw. This represents letting go of the depressing thoughts and distorted thinking and try to think of some evidence that will bring balance to this stressful time. When I think of some evidence, I embrace the truth and lift up the seesaw so it is balanced. Lifting the seesaw requires tremendous effort just like embracing balancing thoughts does.

Below are some examples of balanced thoughts:

- Self-criticism versus loving myself
- "No one cares about me" versus "remember specific people who love me"
- "I'm a failure" versus "using unconditional love and think of my positive attributes"

Balancing my thoughts and feelings is a difficult skill to apply when I am having a really hard time. It is okay to struggle implementing it. I need to accept myself all the time. To balance out my thoughts and feelings the first thing I need to do is begin to *let go* of my negative feelings as much as I can. I need to accept all the thoughts that can balance out my emotions. Listening to all the evidence helps me to conquer the intense emotions. I want to love myself and have a good self-image so when I struggle I don't beat myself up. When I finally conquer the strong emotions, I need to greatly reward myself as well!

I am in a difficult season in my life. Managing thoughts and emotions is necessary for me to ride out the cascade of emotions gracefully. The thing that I need to realize is that managing thoughts and emotions is really hard when I'm depressed. I need to love on myself when I'm having a hard time. Depression is not sin. It is sickness. Applying the skill to manage thoughts and emotions will hopefully help me to not go into crisis and need hospitalization. The skills require me to humble myself when I am depressed so I will be open to positive thinking.

"COME TO ME when you are weak and weary. Rest snugly in My everlasting arms. I do not despise your weakness, My child. Actually, it draws Me closer to you, because weakness stirs up My compassion – My yearning to help. Accept yourself in your weariness, knowing that I understand how difficult your journey has been." (Young, 2004, p. 235).

Chapter 36

How to Gain Control of My Emotions

ᘯ.ᘰ

Learning to Take Care of Myself When I'm In Crisis

*C*onflicts in my relationships with people, real or imagined, seem to cause me to plummet into depression and get into a crisis very quickly. These conflicts are emotional triggers and I need to learn how to deal with them or I will end up in a crisis again.

First of all, whatever I do I have to be careful that I'm not stuffing the emotional pain like I have done all my life. I have to decide whether to let out the *welcome mat* to the emotion and experience inner healing or try to get out of the painful moment. The key here is whether the emotion is really a crisis or not. A crisis is when I can't do anything with the emotion because my emotions are sitting on the throne of my life! I can't think rationally because I'm in too much emotional pain. I'm either too sad or too angry. This is the time to gain control of the cascading emotions by learning skills in how to deal with strong emotions. I really want to gain control of my emotions so I won't go in to crisis and end up back in the hospital.

Managing Extreme Emotions

I practice managing my emotions when I'm feeling better so when the emotions are extreme so I won't get into trouble. Instead of focusing on the emotional situation, I get in a solitary place and focus on deep breathing and begin remembering one of my favorite camping places, and picture myself sitting by a creek in my mind. The Oconaluftee River I picture in my mind is in The Great Smoky Mountain National Park. This helps me to stop thinking about my intense emotional pain I'm in and it helps me to relax. I love remembering my favorite places in the Smokies such as Smokemont Campground and walking the Appalachian Trail with my daughters. This is where God spoke to me about REST several years ago. When thoughts and emotions bombard me, like they usually do when I am in crisis, I really try hard to embrace the beauty of the Smoky Mountains. Sometimes the pain is so intense that I have to look at some pictures on my living room wall of the Smoky Mountains, wrap myself with my Smoky Mountain blanket, or go on the computer to look at Smoky Mountain pictures to help calm me. I want my mind and my heart to embrace this beautiful memory. My main focus is trying to turn my mind from being dominated by negative emotions to a point when peace starts to descend on my trouble mind. What a nice reward. However, this is a really hard skill to implement while in crisis. I am motivated to practice managing my emotions many times during the day when I'm not in crisis, so I will have lots of experience if another crisis comes.

Distract with Activities

I am learning to distract myself with activities when I am trying to get my emotions under control. I distract myself when I am in an emotional crisis. Distract means to do something that takes my mind off the negative emotion I am feeling. I am not going to stuff the emotion but I am going to push it aside and hopefully at a later time I can resolve the emotional issue.

One idea I implemented was to make flash cards listing my distract ideas. My wonderful husband suggested I write down every idea that comes to mind so I will have lots of choices to distract myself when I am so very emotional. I will list some of the activities that I do to distract myself.

1. Watch the *Radical Acceptance* video from the dbtselfhelp.com. (Dietz, 2003, Instant Mindfulness). This video helps me to accept myself when I'm severely depressed. This is a chance to really practice loving myself.
2. Listen to soothing music and think about positive moments.
3. Look at National Park pictures on the internet. (I like to remember camping times.)
4. Exercise and stretch my muscles.
5. Walk in the neighborhood or on a nature trail in a park.

6. Go outside and watch the clouds, listen to the birds sing, and watch the squirrels.
7. Play solitaire or work on a jigsaw puzzle.
8. Go to the coffee shop and get some flavored decaf coffee.
9. Write in my journal.
10. Text or call a friend. (This is effective because I'm a social person.)

Reward Myself

Rewarding myself is a most important step for me to implement. My hospital doctor asked if I rewarded myself for overcoming an emotional crisis. No I don't, and I don't even realize when I have overcome a crisis. Here is another opportunity to live in the moment. When I am in an emotional crisis, I need to pay attention when the crisis ends so I can reward myself. Hopefully rewarding myself will help me overcome a crisis next time.

This idea doesn't come naturally to me. Rewarding myself for overcoming a tough time is a real challenge. I usually beat myself up for getting depressed rather than loving on myself with a reward when I overcome it. Some of the rewards I have are getting a slushy or putting a bouquet of flowers on my kitchen counter. I might call one of my closest friends who has been with me throughout this very difficult season. We might go out to lunch or go on a walk in the park. I just need to hang in there during a serious emotional time so I can look forward to the reward.

Some Real Life Examples of Distracting Myself

A very helpful way to make distract skills effective is to practice the skills regularly when I am feeling well. I want to be comfortable with the skills so when I experience a tough time I will be able to implement the skills. For instance, walking in a park is one of my skills. I like to go to the park every Saturday morning to spend time with God and walk as I soak up the outdoors! Sometimes I buy a hot cup of coffee to sip on when I'm driving home.

I love music. I can listen to it when I am feeling well as it brings comfort. This is when I find different songs that are uplifting and gather these songs in one place. When I'm in an emotional crisis, I just sit in my favorite chair with my blanket around my symbolizing Jesus' arms around me and listen to this heartwarming music. I might cry to release some of the pain I'm feeling. Remember, it's not a sign of weakness to cry but a way to release emotional pain. When I get feeling better I need to reward myself for gaining the victory in a painful situation.

One important way I can overcome a crisis is to have someone I respect come along side to help me with the distract list. It is wonderful to not be alone when in crisis. Usually when I'm in crisis, I can't focus enough to comprehend what all is happening. A friend might be able to help. I have to mention that any friend that helps in crisis is very special. Shower them with thanks by writing a thank you card or buy them lunch.

A crisis is tough to go through, and as I look back in this last year, I remember being in crisis at least a dozen times. One time I walked the neighborhood with my husband. It didn't help at all! My husband was great but I couldn't stop ruminating. My husband even took me to an appointment with my counselor. At the end of the session my counselor called ahead to the hospital and told my husband to take me there. I had so many distractions that I had hoped would keep me out of the hospital but no... They didn't work. I went into the hospital for the eighth time that year. Sigh... As I look back on the situation, I realize that I tried to distract myself too late. I had already been in tears and ruminating for several hours before implementing my distract list. I tried to hide my pain from my family but crisis was written all over my face. I think a much earlier intervention would have been better.

Grieving Over the Changes in My Family Relationships

I just went through a really hard time. I woke up early like usual and spent time with the Lord. As I sat there I felt some sadness trying to bubble up from inside. I had two options and that was welcome the emotions or distract myself. I chose to welcome the emotions because the emotions weren't intense. I was not in crisis. I asked the Lord to help me not suppress my emotions but instead release them. I began to realize that I was sad and grieving over the changes in the relationships with my family members this last year. I am no longer in charge of the events that happen. I used to be quite a strong leader but now I mentally can't handle it. My family doesn't call me for loving support like they used to. They are walking on egg shells around me because of the fear of being a trigger for my depression. The list goes on and on.

I cried for an hour and a half in the early morning while sitting in God's Presence. Then I got ready for church. While at church I touched base with several friends then sat down in my chair. One good friend sat next to me and shared a story from her life. She also listened to me. I'm so grateful for friends. When worship started I didn't feel like singing at all. That is unusual for me because I usually love worshipping God. After worship was over I went out in the foyer and sat on a chair. I got a couple of tissues in case I wanted to cry. I just couldn't sit through a sermon at that time. After church I met a new Christian friend that I had talked to on the phone earlier in the week. It was a thrill.

After arriving home I began to realize that the emotions were getting out of control. I got upset with my husband in front of my youngest daughter. She was visibly distressed. It was time to use the distract skills. First thing I did was to take a nap. The next thing I did after my nap was to call my friend. We talked for a while then later that afternoon my husband and I went to my daughter's house to play my favorite board game and have dinner! After being there for several hours and having a lovely time I felt much better.

"Thank you, Lord, for helping me grieve over the damage in my family relationships because of the depression. Also I so thank You for helping get me out of emotional state by distracting myself. Lord, Your love for me is amazing and I thank You for helping me love myself. I so desperately need You."

An example of loving myself today was when I was in emotional pain, and I was open to the Lord bringing healing rather than suppressing the pain. I opened myself up to God's healing power by releasing the emotions. When the emotions started to get out of control, I was open to distracting myself to let the emotions subside. I now feel better. Stacey, you did a great job!

Lack of Motivation

Today I made it to water aerobics which was a miracle. The title of my life the last two weeks has been Lack of Motivation. All I want to do is sleep. I get eight hours sleep at night and five hours sleep during the day. I believe medication side effects might be the problem. I just don't feel like doing anything. There is nothing I can do about my meds but I need some kind of help. O brother, I am so discouraged and I don't even want to try to get help.

Right after water aerobics all I could do was cry and withdraw. I was not motivated to do anything even though my house needed some attention. All I can do is look around and get depressed. As my mind started to really get depressed, I used the distract skill of calling my friends. At first I called my counselor which was very helpful. I also called a good friend of mine. She encouraged me to make a gratitude list. I did, and boy do I have a lot to be thankful for. My husband came home early from work and the kids are gone. We are going to have a date night! Thank You, Jesus, for helping me to distract myself with phone calls and date nights!

It is a week later and I'm wide awake! My medication was adjusted. I believe I experienced a miracle. I'm still going to my Internal Medicine doctor. She gave me some powdered magnesium. I was taking one teaspoon the upped it to two teaspoons. Wow, the sleepiness is gone now! I'm happy! I can now hike the Depression Trail and watch for what God is going to do next. I feel like I'm at a high elevation waiting to see some beautiful scenery around the corner. Yes, the depression is gone for now!

The Rejection Button—Oh NO!

Rejection is usually the trigger for my major depressive episodes that leads to hospitalization. This time my emotional response has been the best response in a couple years. My friend who pushed my rejection button did it with a comment. After we ended the phone conversation I cried really hard. I needed to settled down enough to talk to my husband. He told me that I didn't need to accept what she said. I don't want to accept this negative comment because I know that Jesus loves me just the way I am. He is healing me from the depression with a gentle hand. I am focusing on those positive thoughts. I am not giving in to the rejection from my friend.

Shortly after that I called my counselor. He counselor called back and we talked. I am SO GRATEFUL to have a counselor who calls me in a timely manner, even on evenings and weekends. The next thing I did was work with my husband to sort pictures so he could scan them into the computer to email them to my adult daughter. I was very open to distracting myself this time, and it paid off. I'm doing better! I don't feel sad now and it is two hours later. I asked my husband if I could do something to **reward** myself—maybe some flowers or a slushy! We bought a cherry slushy. Yum!

Am I Actually Feeling Better? I Think So!

After dealing with the rejection from my friend, I believe that I had more of a normal response. Yes, I cried for a couple hours, but I didn't plummet into a state of despair. I am getting better. I have been feeling better for over a month. I attribute the change to my new medication that was started at my last hospital stay two months ago. My counselor gave me an "At a Girl" at my last counseling appointment. He commented that I have really worked hard this last year to apply the DBT skills. He has seen me apply them multiple times in each session, and he can tell by my conversations that I have internalized the skills. Halleluiah, the depression is starting to lift! The distract skills have been essential to my recovery. I usually put all my attention on the pain I'm feeling. Distract skills help get my mind off the pain and on to thinking healthier thoughts. Another reason I'm feeling better is that my doctor of internal medicine, who is also a natural pathologist, is helping me get physically healthy to get me over the depression. Adding magnesium to my diet seems to be helping me to feel better! Now I'm not tired all the time. I have some energy to do things and I feel better emotionally.

Learning how to gain control of my emotions has been a very important step to embrace. The distract skills have been essential to my recovery. My husband has been very supportive as I apply the distract skills. Sometimes he comes up with new ideas that we can implement. I have to give credit to the Lord for making it possible to implement the distract skills when I am in a difficult emotional state. Gaining control of my emotions is nothing short of a miracle. I never thought it would be possible to control my emotions again.

Chapter 37

Learning to Survive an Emotional Crisis

Reasons to Fight the Good Fight

*h*e truth comes out; I have been in a crisis so many times this last two years as I deal with severe depression and Borderline Personality Disorder. (All the doctors at the teaching hospital diagnosed me with Borderline Personality Disorder.) At any rate, I have ended up in the hospital ten times, attended group therapy for eight months, and had individual therapy the whole time. Sigh... Now I am learning how to ride out the crisis and stay home. It is hard to apply skills to help overcome a crisis, but there are many reasons to try really hard.

1. Avoiding a visit to the hospital can save a lot of money!
2. I love my family so much that I want to be healthy for them. It is easier on my husband when I am trying to overcome the emotions, rather than giving up and cascading into suicidal thinking.
3. I need to rewire my brain through the application of skills to help me think in a healthy manner.

Looking at the reasons to stay emotionally healthy are great motivators to overcome an emotional crisis. I have spent time while I am doing well to study what actually is a crisis. I want to know when I need to deal with the pain or when I need to distract myself. I don't want to avoid emotional healing when I am hurting but during a crisis it is time to implement some techniques to distract myself. I found a definition of crisis on the DBT website. (Dietz, L. 2003, Crisis Survival Video Part 1.)

What Is a Crisis?

1. A stressful event, or a traumatic moment
2. Short term
3. You want it resolved NOW!

Two Main Problems

1. Solve the problem if you can
2. Survive it

When Do I Need These Crisis Survival Skills?

1. Needs to be a crisis
2. Can't resolve it now
3. Can't afford to make it worse

There are many skills available to try when learning crisis skills. As I look over the material I believe that it would be better if I laid out this chapter in outline style. When in a crisis, it is best to have an easy reference. This outline contains skills that are focused on affirming myself and building myself up. I have worked on distracting myself when descending into a crisis. That has been helpful too. Marsha Linehan developed a list of Crisis Survival Skills in Dialectical Behavior Therapy (DBT) that are extremely helpful (Linehan, 1993, 1).

1. **Affirm Myself by Using Positive Self-Talk**

   a. Affirmations
      - "Even though I have this depression, I deeply and completely accept myself."
      - "Even though I cannot perform right now, I deeply and completely accept myself."
      - "Even though I feel emotional, I am a good person."
      - "No matter what I feel right now, I am okay."
      - "I have worth because I struggle to survive."
      - "My mere existence proves my worth. Jesus loves me deeply."
      - "I am lovable and capable."

2. Mindfulness—Seek to be emotionally balanced

    a. Watch the *Radical Acceptance* Video from dbtselfhelp.com (Dietz, 2003, Instant Mindfulness).

    b. Meditation (Resting the mind by releasing thoughts and embracing inner peace. This is a prime time to make myself available to experience Jesus' unconditional love.)

    c. Do not condemn myself, instead love myself unconditionally.

    d. "I am a good person. My worth is not dependent on my mood."

    e. "It is okay to have emotions. Just make sure I am managing them."

    f. "Jesus always loves me no matter what emotions I have."

3. Write about the Emotions—This a great time to capture the healing on paper.

    a. Write in my journal

    b. Write in my book

4. Seek Input—Receive input to help balance out the emotions

    a. Read my journal and this book (Writing has been very therapeutic, and reading over the victories I have already experienced reinforces the lessons God is teaching me.)

    b. Read my devotional book, *Jesus Calling* (Young, 2004). Meditate on the message.

    c. Contact my doctors or counselors and receive what they have to say

5. Internet resource (dbtselfhelp.com). Read the lessons and watch the mindfulness videos.

6. Read and Meditate on Reasons to Live

    a. Jesus loves me.

        • Jesus is helping me to experience His amazing love so it's not just head knowledge but it is heart knowledge.

        • I crawl into Jesus' lap and He holds me and tells me He loves me!

- I hold Jesus' hands while He looks into my eyes, and tells me that He loves me over and over and over again!
- Jesus sits beside me and wraps His arm around my shoulders!
- Jesus lies beside me in bed and wraps His arm around me!
- Jesus loves me just the way I am now, even with the cascading emotions.
- Jesus has a plan for my life both now and in the future.
- There is nothing I can do *or think* that will separate me from the love of God!
- God loves me so much and wants me to trust that He is really in control of my life even though it doesn't always *feel* like it.

b. I am growing in loving myself unconditionally.
- I am growing in loving myself unconditionally even with cascading emotions. Do I love myself when I feel depressed? Most of the time, "No!"

"O Lord, I need You to transform my critical spirit to a spirit that loves myself when depressed."

- I am learning to love myself even if I can't *perform* or *do* things I believe I should. Do I love myself when I can't *perform*? Not always. I usually get frustrated and feel *less* of a person. God loves me all the time, even when I can't *perform*. I just need to accept all my short comings.
- I am growing in my ability to love myself even when I am experiencing distorted thinking. Here are some cognitive distortions I am working on.

Jumping to Conclusions – Right now, I seem to be going through a phase when I perceive that people are rejecting/avoiding me by not returning phone calls or emails. Even though I feel emotional pain I should think the best of them. I need to release these people to live their own independent lives. I can change my thinking and love myself. This is a time to let Jesus love on me.

Labeling – Sometimes I think I am an *emotional basket case* or an *emotional wreck*. I need to realize it is not helpful to label myself negatively because it will cause me to become more discouraged and give up.

Overgeneralization – I refuse to believe that since one negative thing occurred, this doesn't mean everything else happening right now is not necessarily bad or negative. I am only a human being and like others, I welcome both good and bad experiences.

Focusing on the Negative – If I am focused on my depression, the feelings of hopelessness and frustration with my poor memory make the depression worse. This is an opportunity to **choose** to recognize some positive aspects of my life. I have a loving family: my husband is so loving and supportive, my girls are doing very well, my physical health is good. I have great medical care. I should stop focusing on the negative and cry out to God to help me to think about the positive things in my life.

Magnifying Negatives – I will not blow a bad event out of proportion. Instead, I realize things happen, and lots of times they are resolved just fine and end up not being catastrophic. I will be patient with myself and the situation I'm facing.

Shoulds – The main *should* I experience is "I should clean my house." Even though I'm sick, I tell myself that I should clean it up anyway. I beat myself up emotionally for having a messy house. I feel like a bad mother and terrible person. I feel like a total failure. STOP! I do not need to put pressure on myself or chastise myself like that. These two things set me up for failure. Cleaning should not be on the *should* list. I NEED HELP! After two years of severe depression, my husband hired a friend who cleans our house once a month. I am motivated to do some light cleaning. It's not because I *should* clean, but I want to clean. I have a desire to bless my family. This is a miracle!

c. I love my family
  • I love my husband deeply and want to tell him, show him, and encourage him.
  • I love all five of my girls, and want to tell them and show them frequently.
  • I want to have a positive influence on the girl's lives.

- I want to inspire the girls to grow in their faith in Jesus Christ.
d. I believe God is using me to advance His Kingdom
    - I inspire people to have faith in Jesus.
    - I inspire people to have a deeper awareness of Jesus' amazing unconditional love!
    - I inspire people to have spiritual growth so their faith becomes deeper.
    - I inspire people to become more compassionate.
    - I inspire people so they can gain victory over their depression.

This chapter has been the pivotal resource for me to overcome cascading emotions into suicidal ideation. Once again, I want to endorse Marsha Linehan's Dialectical Behavior Therapy (DBT) (Linehan, 1993, 1). She has many more Crisis Survival Skills in her book. She also has a very helpful list of distracting skills. I have applied DBT to my life over the last two years and it has helped me so much to become emotionally stable once again. I have been told that applying new behavior skills actually helps rewire the brain. I believe that has happened! Learning how to survive an emotional crisis is a worthy undertaking. Is that why I'm happy most of the time now?

Part 5

Recovery Is Possible!

Chapter 38

Embracing Self-Compassion

*"For you created my inmost being;
you knit me together in my mother's womb.
I praise you because I am fearfully and wonderfully made;
your works are wonderful, I know that full well."*
Psalm 139:13-14

Being Gentle with My Weakness

*a*m truly on a trail of humility to learn to see myself as my Lord sees me. I have served the Lord for thirty-five years but the last ten years I have been overcome with depression. The last couple years depression has led to the prideful thinking of suicide. God's love and my wonderful family are what have kept me alive. My self-esteem was so low, but God says I am fearfully and wonderfully made. How can I embrace this truth? It is time to see myself in the same way that God sees me. He loves me unconditionally and with compassion. So if I am going to truly imitate the truth of God's Word, than I am going to love myself unconditionally and with compassion too. I want to apply gentleness towards my weakness because this is God's way. Even as I meditate on Jesus' gentleness and compassion for me, the healing tears are released. I want to I focus on Jesus intimate love. This is where my healing takes place.

*"For great is your love toward me;
you have delivered me from the depths of the grave."*
Psalm 86:13
*"The LORD is gracious and righteous;
our God is full of compassion.
The LORD protects the simplehearted;*

when I was in great need, he saved me."
Psalm 116:5-6

Showing compassion to myself is a reoccurring topic that evades my ability as I walk the Depression Trail. A year ago my counselor perceived that I didn't love myself. I had no understanding of what loving myself with compassion and with gentleness even meant. Sure, I understood the words but had no idea how to apply them. Just recently when I was in the psych hospital, the patients and staff perceived that I had low self-esteem. Sigh... This has been truly a long journey learning to express love to myself. I don't know how to love myself, let alone be compassionate.

My childhood years were difficult because I received very little affirmation. I developed what I thought were good coping skills: performance orientation and people pleasing behavior which really helped my self-image. I could respect myself for what I did so I did everything perfectly. I became an overachiever and eventually burned out. I had several emotional breakdowns throughout the years and suffered years of depression. I am so performance oriented, which has become a curse since I can't perform now. Now I condemn myself continually. I need God to change me on the inside to have compassion towards myself.

I am in a new season of my life when I can't *do* much because of the depression. I lost my teaching job over a year ago. I can't serve in the church much without getting so overwhelmed that I start to cry. I'm having a hard time keeping up with cleaning my house. I have ended up in the psych hospital ten times in just over a year. I'm not *doing* anything that I can get any accolades. When I suffer from the severe depression, I can NOT perform so my self-image plummets to nothing. Now I feel like I'm a total failure and am unlovable.

I have many negative thoughts. I beat myself up for my inability to perform all the time which makes me feel worse. Here are samples of the thinking I succumb too. "I'm an emotional wreck." "I can't do anything productive." "I'm lazy." "I am a failure." "Because I'm depressed, I'm unlovable." I am way over sensitive to people's comments and get hurt too easily. These kinds of self-defeating thoughts swirl through my mind and end up as chronic depression and possibly suicidal thoughts. Sigh... I need Jesus to change my critical thinking so I can love myself.

A concept was shared with me "being gentle with my weakness." I can't imagine how difficult it is to be gentle with myself when my weakness is severe depression. I am learning that God loves me the same whether I'm happy or in deep despair. God is gentle with me even when

I am seriously depressed. God's love doesn't change. He loves me even when I am in deep depression.

An important concept to focus on is the fact that self-love is really a spiritual achievement. Working on overcoming a low self-image is worthy of my time. I need to love myself so I can fulfill God's plan for my life. He loves me so I should love myself.

Learning to love myself begins with a quiet time while focusing on my intimate God who loves me deeply. God has so much compassion that it is incomprehensible to me right now. Spending time with God helps me to focus on His love for me rather than my emotion pain. I am also focusing on *being* rather than *doing* what I think I should do. Remember, my *doing mode of mind* acted out when I performed for attention. This is something ingrained in me from childhood. I want to embrace the truth that Jesus loves me unconditionally no matter what I'm thinking or what mood I'm in. Nothing that I think is a surprise to Him. He is there to love on me and encourage me to love myself with compassion.

Last year when my counselor had perceived that I didn't love myself, I honestly didn't know what he was talking about. Throughout my Christian adult years the concept of Jesus' love for me has been my focus and has become a reality this last year. I now know that Jesus loves me when I'm happy as well as when I'm in despair. He loves me even when I'm at my lowest point of being suicidal and rejecting Him! He loves me even when I can't perform or when I don't love myself. My own love for myself is conditional. My conditional love rejects me when I can't perform. Rejecting myself is very painful. I want to learn to love myself unconditionally and with compassion like the way the Lord loves me.

"Lord, I know You love me unconditionally. Lord, You have so much compassion and acceptance of me even in my dark depression. Your love for me is amazing, no matter what I am going through. Lord, I come before You and ask for You to give me grace to love myself unconditionally too. I want to be compassionate and forgiving of myself. Help me to focus on the goodness that You have given me. Since I'm Your creation and a creation that You deeply love, show me how to love myself."

Wondering How to Love Myself

Learning to love myself with compassion is difficult since it is such an abstract concept. Receiving love from God, my family, and my friends is a good start. But honestly, loving myself is a concept that escapes my understanding so I can't experience it. I understand the concept of God's love but really I don't really know what loving myself means or feels like.

"Who shall separate us from the love of Christ?
Shall trouble or hardship or persecution or famine
or nakedness or danger or sword?"
Romans 8:35

My counselor told me that I don't know how to nurture myself. Isn't this called loving myself? He said nurture is a skill that you learn from your family while growing up, especially from your mother. I didn't feel loved by my mother. This seems to have crippled me emotionally. I need to learn how to nurture myself.

I have begun learning the abstract concept of loving myself with compassion by sitting in God's Presence and meditating. I spend time with God hoping that He will miraculously change me on the inside so I can really experience His humble grace to love myself. Here is a guideline that I use to help focus on God and focus on loving myself.

1. I find a place to sit before the Lord, and try to quiet my mind and focus on the verse *"Quietness and Trust are my Strength"* (Isaiah 30:15, personalized.) I try to quiet my mind from all the thoughts that bombard me by saying the word Jesus repeatedly with each breath. I also let the extraneous thoughts drift by like fallen leaves drifting by in a stream. Sometimes I focus on my breath. This is a time to sit in God's Presence.
2. I focus on the word *trust* and think on the idea that God can miraculously change me on the inside so I can love myself compassionately. He can heal my past, help me love myself for who I am now, and help me become the woman He created me to be.
3. I focus on the following list of *being* qualities. That is how God sees me. He loves me for who I am. As I sit in God's Presence, I read these positive attributes and pray to God that He will help me embrace them. I then think and meditate about each attribute and try to absorb the concept of each one. My desire is that God will change my brain and heart so I can be positive and love myself with compassion.

   a. I am teachable
   b. I am transparent

238

   c. I am authentic and real
   d. I am a grateful person
   e. I am an encourager of people
   f. I am friendly
   g. I am courageous
   h. I am creative
   i. I am self-directed
   j. I am persistent

As I look over this list, I realize that God did make me special. I'm not a loser. I have a good heart and tremendous love for all the people God has made. All I have to do is humble myself and embrace these positive qualities to help realize that Jesus has given me valuable qualities. I am going to try to *let go* of my negative thoughts and embrace God's wonderful love.

4. Throughout the day I encourage myself to replace negative thinking with positive thoughts. When I think or say a negative thought such as when I drop something, "That sure was clumsy!" I stop and change the negative words to positive ones. "This is okay, Stacey, just clean it up." This is an important exercise that helps me to stop beating myself up and changing my mind to focusing on loving myself all day. When I really get frustrated with myself, I have to sit down and meditate on God while I focus on quieting my mind. This exercise can restore me to peace, and help me to not beat myself up. I then think positive thoughts about myself.

"All of you, clothe yourselves with humility toward one another, because, "God opposes the proud but gives grace to the humble." Humble yourselves, therefore, under God's mighty hand, that he may lift you up in due time. Cast all your anxiety on him because he cares for you."
1 Peter 5:5-7

I know that this part of the Depression Trail I am walking is difficult. But I can see that God is giving me grace to overcome the low self-esteem. He loves me unconditionally and with compassion even during the emotional turmoil. I really want to imitate God by loving myself unconditionally and with compassion. Seeing myself through God's eyes helps me to love myself with compassion even though I may feel unlovable. God loves me deeply no matter how much I feel unlovable during the severe the depression I go through. I know that learning to love myself this way is a process that takes time. God doesn't get mad when I have negative thoughts or act out the depression. Instead, He encourages me to overcome and release the emotions to Him. I correct the wrong I may have done, and try to encourage myself rather than criticize myself. Learning to overcome my critical attitude toward myself and learning to experience loving myself with compassion seems to be a long process for me.

I know that building an intimate relationship with Lord is the only way to overcome severe depression. God's love during these intimate times is changing me from the inside—out. I know that He loves me when I am depressed. This inspires me to love myself too! Realizing who I am in God's eyes has helped me to realize that I don't have to perform for His love.

Halleluiah, I am *fearfully and wonderfully made.* As I meditate on this verse, I realize that it really contains words of self-love. This verse acknowledges that God did an awesome job creating me. Since God sees me as *fearfully and wonderfully made,* I want to spend time in His Presence and see myself in the way God sees me. I need Jesus to help change me on the inside so I can realize how special I really am.

Loving People with Compassion

"But he said to me, "My grace is sufficient for you,
for my power is made perfect in weakness.""
2 Corinthians 12:9

"As a father has compassion on his children,
so the LORD has compassion on those who fear him."
Psalm 103:13

One of the amazing things I am starting to experience, even during my weakness of severe depression, is God's amazing compassion. My weakness stirs up God's compassion to love on me. He has loved on me in so many ways, directly from Him and through many people. He loves me so much and I have felt it internally. However, I know that what I have been through is not only for my benefit, but the time is coming when I can love on people who are suffering. One of the fruits of overcoming severe depression is that I am now filled with so much compassion for God's hurting people. I have noticed that these people are not afraid to talk to me. I believe it is because I have been in their place and received

God's love. Now I really want to help people experience God's compassionate love.

"I will be glad and rejoice in your love,
for you saw my affliction and knew the anguish of my soul.
You have not handed me over to the enemy
but have set my feet in a spacious place.
Be merciful to me, O LORD, for I am in distress;
my eyes grow weak with sorrow, my soul and my body with grief.
My life is consumed by anguish and my years by groaning;
my strength fails because of my affliction, and my bones grow weak.
But I trust in you, O LORD; I say, "You are my God."
Let your face shine on your servant; save me in your unfailing love."
Psalm 31:7-10, 14, and 16

Chapter 39

Happiness and Joy Once Again!

"Is any one of you in trouble? He should pray.
Is anyone happy? Let him sing songs of praise."
James 5:13-14

Embracing Moments of Happiness

*h*is last week has proven to be a miracle week. I am actually happy! I'm not used to this wonderful feeling. It is foreign to me! Of course my *doing mode of mind* wants to know why I feel happy. I give the credit to God for guiding me to embrace His unconditional love, the various caring doctors, and the DBT counselors. I am on new psychiatric medication and am continuing to practice DBT skills, which is helping immensely. My family lovingly supports me too. My *being mode of mind* just wants to bask in Jesus' Presence so I can experience more happiness. It is such a good feeling after so many years of depression.

My relationship with my family is now on a road toward healing. The depression has been so difficult for them to handle. I will pray for God to heal our relationships. I want to have the energy to clean the house. It needs some TLC (Tender Loving Care) after being neglected the last couple years. I am just tackling it a little bit at a time. Now it is time to continue to praise the Lord and spend some quiet time with God. I want to meditate and experience His Presence.

The challenge is to not fall back into depression by giving into critical thinking. It is a hard habit to break. I still need to love and accept myself. I need to look at Jesus' unconditional love as an example. I need to break the habit of judging everyone, everything, and myself. Judging is such a destructive habit that that leads to depression. Self-acceptance is the solution. I need to accept myself all the time, even on the days when I have a relapse of depression.

Experiencing a Time of Refreshing Joy!

God is truly amazing. After one week of happiness I had a time of joy during a luncheon outing with my friends. There were four of us and one was taking chemo for cancer and I was recovering from severe depression. One had experienced depression and the other was a retired social worker. We shared our experiences with each other. The amazing thing is that we really didn't know each other that well, but we shared from the depth of our lives. One lady shared with tears about her near death experience with an infection. Her story deeply touched me. We shared so many stories with each other. The amazing thing is that we laughed so much. I have not laughed that much in years. This was definitely a gift from God! Imagine a person suffering from severe depression and a person in year two of chemo treatment laughing! It was a miracle! The four of us laughed so much that the hostess came in our alcove and told us she was going to turn in her time card and come join us! Joy is contagious!

"Those who sow in tears will reap with songs of joy."
Psalms 126:5

Loving God's People

I know that the joy that was birthed from enduring the difficult times strengthened me. I know all that God brought me through isn't just for myself. He wants me to take what I learned and share it with others. In doing this, it will bring joy to someone else. I shared what God is doing in my life while I was in group therapy. I had such a strong desire to tell people what experiencing God's grace feels like. I am so thankful for experiencing God's healing touch in my life that I want to tell others. I really have an intense desire to share God's incredible love to all the people He loves.

Chapter 40

Peace, a Blessing from God

*"Daughter, your faith has healed you.
Go in peace and be freed from your suffering."*
Mark 5:34

Feeling God's Refreshing Peace

e ace is so refreshing to experience after years of suffering from depression! I am relieved and immensely grateful to have times of peace once again. For me the peace came at a great price. Since depression dominated my life, peace was almost absent unless I made an effort to sit in Jesus' Presence and meditate several times during the day. I had to practice quieting my mind of negative thinking and embrace Jesus' love for me even though my feelings were incredibly sad deep down at the root of my being. I hoped that if I sat in Jesus' Presence while quieting my mind that He would change me from the inside—out and that's what He's doing! Now I feel peaceful more times than not!

*"You will go out in joy and be led forth in peace;
the mountains and hills will burst into song before you,
and all the trees of the field will clap their hands."*
Isaiah 55:12

Embracing Peace and Rewarding Myself

Inner peace doesn't come naturally to me. I deal with a low self-esteem which leads to negative thinking. Learning to embrace peace requires changing the way I think. I need to remember that sitting in God's Presence mysteriously brings peace to me. There is my starting place. Here are some skills I learned this last year to help me embrace peace. Notice the rewarding myself. It is so important.

1. The first skill is to meditate and rest in God's Presence. I focus on my breath and imagine a scenic place like the Oconalutee River in the Smoky Mountains. When a negative thought enters my mind, I let it go by picturing the thought as a falling leaf drifting down stream to disappear or a cloud drifting by in the sky. This discipline helps to develop my ability to be aware of what's happening in my mind, both positive and negative. When I experience negative thinking, I love on myself by changing the words to positive ones. This is how I feel peace once again. I then **reward** myself.

2. As I go about the day, I need to catch myself having negative thoughts. Most of the time I'm not aware of my negative thoughts. I suppose I've had them all my life. I have a wonderful husband that is aware of my bad thoughts. However, I didn't want his comments; I was stubborn. It is months later and now I am starting to become aware of my negative thoughts. I really had to work hard at this. Meditation has been the best skill to help me be aware of negative thinking. As I become more aware of my inner life and things that I think, it is time to **reward** myself.

3. When I go about my day and start thinking negative thoughts, I try to distract myself by changing something in my environment. As soon as I realize that I have a negative thought, I do something that will get my mind off it. Sometimes I listen to my favorite music, drink a cold drink or hot drink, and look at nature scenes. Basically I am opening the door to peace by distracting my mind from negative thinking. When I start thinking thoughts that make me peaceful, I **reward** myself!

4. Sometimes I have to deal directly with the negative thoughts so I can experience inner peace. In order to really do this, I first lean on my meditation experience which is very helpful to identify the negative thoughts. As soon as I think negatively I try to reword the thought to something that is positive. This is called reframing, and it's hard. I can come up with the positive words but can I really believe the words in my heart? I need to embrace the truth about myself. I know one time at church while talking to another lady, I called myself lazy. I quickly rephrased the words right in her presence. I told her that "I was having a difficult time cleaning my house." Now here's why I work on this skill so much; I have real-

245

ized negative thoughts usually lead to depression. I DON'T WANT
TO GO THERE ANY MORE! I am motivated to do anything I can do
to help combat depression. When I embrace the positive feelings
from reframing, then it's time to **reward** myself! It's wonderful
learning to think good thoughts – that lays the foundation to inner
peace.

5. Sometimes I really get in a funk and plummet into a deep pool of
depression. Is there a God of peace? It doesn't feel like it. In fact,
when I'm consumed with depression, I have a hard time hoping
that peace will ever come back. I remember that God loves me,
even depressed! The pit of depression is only temporary. I have
ridden this emotional roller coaster for years. I tell myself to stop
thinking about the bad emotional feelings and remember God's
wonderful Presence. Hope is foundational in getting over depression, and peace is a reward when overcoming the heaviness.
After calling on God, I remember that He loves me even when I'm
depressed. I bask in His Presence by meditating and embracing His
love for me. As I embrace God's Presence the depression lifts and
God's peace descends on me. As I experience God's peace, I will
reward myself for overcoming the depression.

6. **Reward** myself? This has been an important link to learning to overcome depression. I had a wise psychiatrist at the hospital ask me if
I rewarded myself when I overcame depression. I didn't know to,
but it made sense. There are many ways to reward myself: flowers,
slushy, flavored coffee, or call a friend. I give myself big teddy bear
hugs or give myself small treats. Rewarding myself gives me warm
fuzzies and helps me to want to continue overcoming depression
so I can experience peace.

Enjoying God's Peace in the Outdoors

Experiencing God's peace is a wonderful goal to have in my life. There
are many ways to embrace peace even in the different emotional states
I go through. Experiencing peace for me is directly linked to my experience with camping in *God's living room*, both when I was a child and now
that I am an adult. I really love to embrace peace while in the beautiful
outdoors of God's creation. The peace I experience is linked to sitting quietly before the Lord while imagining myself sitting in *God's living room*. I
practice meditation and focus on the sensations of the outdoors around
me: the singing birds, the sound of a rushing creek, the sunlight dancing

on the water, the refreshing smells from nature, and the wild flowers and majestic trees. I meditate and allow God to quiet my mind and emotions. I love nature and I believe that it is a gift from God to His people. Even now as I write, I am enjoying listening to the birds sing outside.

The beauty of having a love for nature is that I can admire nature while on a walk or when I drive. I glance at the wildflowers, blooming bushes, the numerous kinds of trees, and rock formations. While I was driving this summer, I remember glancing at a field of yellow wildflowers and was overcome by the beauty. Later that week, I remembered the yellow wildflowers in my mind several times, and felt a sense of awe at the beauty again. A feeling of peace descended upon me each time. Now I look for fields of yellow wildflowers when I drive. I am blessed that I can experience the peace that nature brings to me when I see them or imagine the scenery in my mind. Letting pictures of nature enter my mind seems to have as much a calming effect as being there.

Enjoying God's Peace Indoors

Nature is outside, but I'm inside most of the day. How can I experience peace indoors? Remembering pictures of nature only brings me peace temporarily. I want to experience peace more often. How can a depressed person experience peaceful times most of the day? The answer is meditation. This is a skill that has brought me so much closer to God so now I can experience inner peace even though I suffer from depression. This is amazing!

> *"The LORD gives strength to his people;*
> *the LORD blesses his people with peace."*
> Psalm 29:11

Meditation is a skill to not have preconceived ideas how it should be done. Expecting what will happen while meditating can bring discouragement. When I practice meditation, I first desire to be in God's Presence and REST. I don't pray while meditating; I do that at a separate time. My goal is to quiet my mind and REST so I can experience God's peace.

Settling my mind to meditate isn't always easy. Thoughts enter my mind and emotions bubble up and try to take over. Rumination comes natural when depressed so I have to be nice to myself for experiencing these distractions. What I'm experiencing is normal. However, I do two things to combat these distractions. One is to focus on my breath to settle my mind. The second thing I do is when the thoughts and emotions enter my mind is *let go* of them, than *replace* them with a picture of nature scene from my memory. It is work to focus on meditation when depressed but well worth the effort.

Meditation takes practice. It is so easy to get discouraged for not meeting expectations. Remember, letting go of expectations is a vitally important to experiencing inner peace. In fact, now that I think about it, I remember the phrase *"let go and let God"* is foundational to experiencing inner peace.

Self-Soothing with the Five Senses

A new skill that really helps me feel peaceful is self-soothing. Soothing myself reinforces the truth that I am deeply loved by God. It is also a practice that helps me to nurture myself. Sometimes I have thoughts that I'm unworthy of good feelings. Sigh... God loves me so much, and He wants me to love myself by applying the self-soothing skills. They help me avoid periods of depression. Here's a list of self-soothing skills that uses the five senses.

See—I love to look around me when on a walk and enjoy nature, or while indoors enjoy the wall hangings or pictures on the computer.

Hear—I love to listen to different kinds of music.

Smell—I love putting scents in the house, right now I'm enjoying the cinnamon candle. I use perfume.

Feel—I love to breathe in the fresh air on my daily walks or take hot bubble baths.

Taste—I enjoy seasoned food or a cup of herbal of tea or flavored coffee.

Self-soothing helps bring me out of depression so I can feel God's wonderful peace once again. When I'm depressed, I usually hate myself. This feeling is devastating, but if I put forth a little effort to love on myself through my five senses I feel a little better so I can put myself into God's hands. Remember that God loves me no matter whether I'm happy or depressed. When I feel down I should love on myself with my five senses while I sit in His Presence. God's peace is right around the corner. This is significant when dealing with depression. For some reason peace evades my mind when I'm depressed but stimulating my five senses is a good place to start embracing inner peace. Nurturing myself with my five senses draws me to the Lord. I combine meditation with self-soothing skills to help me embrace God's peace and love. Both of these skills bring me into full awareness to God's Presence. These skills help me to focus on the Lord and feel His love.

Rewarding Myself for Overcoming Negative Thoughts

Thinking negative thoughts is a habit that I need to break. It is difficult to change the way that I have thought over my entire life. When I turn negative thoughts to positive, I reward myself. This is such a great achievement, and I can experience happiness when I am having positive thoughts. My rewards vary depending on my mood. Creative awards are great benefit to overcoming depression. It doesn't have to cost money either. The important part is not the reward itself, but the effect of the reward on my mood. I want the reward to reinforce the feelings of peace and happiness in my life.

Embracing peace has been such a great experience and now I can feel God's peace way more than the depression. I still meditate and focus on the Lord. I am becoming more aware of my negative thoughts so now I can work to reword them with the truth so I can experience God's peace again. When depression knocks at my door, I distract myself so I can experience peace again. The good thing is that all my effort to live in God's peace has paid off. Peace is on the throne of my live most of the time now.

Chapter 41

Loving Those around Me

"Each one should use whatever gift he has received to serve others, faithfully administering God's grace in its various forms. If anyone speaks, he should do it as one speaking the very words of God. If anyone serves, he should do it with the strength God provides, so that in all things God may be praised through Jesus Christ. To him be the glory and the power for ever and ever. Amen."
1 Peter 4:10-11

Focusing on Loving My Family

*L*fe has been so difficult these last couple years. It has been a season of trying to cope with my emotions so I don't end up in the psych hospital again. Just a week ago my medication was adjusted again. This last medication change seems to be working! I feel better and really have a deep desire to express love to my family. I need to sit at Jesus' feet and cry out for the grace to love my family in a way that they feel loved. Even though I am starting to heal, my family suffered great emotional pain with my depression, so they need to see my unconditional love displayed to them over a long time. Now, it is time to walk in my healing by showing my love to my family.

The challenge for me is to get out of myself and focus on other people. I want to listen as they tell their stories, and share experiences in their lives. I can stay in their presence while they are conversing with me, and enter into the conversations by asking questions. This is a challenge for me. I have the tendency to withdraw and not say anything. When I do want to say something I shouldn't be so deep because it confuses them. They don't want to hear about the inner workings in my life. I need to practice not being so deep around people, even though that is where I live most of the time.

There are many ways I can show my love to the family. The first thing I do is wake up every morning and cleanup myself so I will look healthy for my family. School is back in session and my husband is working. We aren't together very much during the weekdays. This little time I have in the morning to serve my family is an opportunity to show my love to them. They have seen me very sick for a couple years, so this is my opportunity to show them I'm getting better.

The best way that I show love to my family is to fix their meals. In the morning I fix breakfast and pack lunches. I like to focus by sitting and conversing with my girls while they eat breakfast. This is definitely the best time to show them my love. I then focus on my husband and fix his coffee and breakfast. The schedule for the rest of the day varies greatly. In the evening activities fill the lives of my family, so we are not always together. I still need to figure out ways that I can show them my love during what sometimes feels like chaos. I believe that I need to focus on serving dinner every time the family is together. I have to push myself because fatigue settles in during the evenings. Evenings are definitely not my best time of day so it's really hard to reach out of myself in the evenings, but my family needs me to.

Expressing Love by Cleaning My House

> *For God did not give me a spirit of timidity*
> (lack of courage or self-assurance),
> but *a spirit of power* (capacity to do something),
> of *love* (feel tender affection)
> *and of self-discipline* (ability to motivate myself—
> the ability to do what is sensible).
> 2 Timothy 1:7, personalized

Why did I use this scripture for this section on cleaning the house? It is because of this difficult section of the Depression Trail I'm on—apathy. I love being a Christian because God's Spirit speaks into my heart and encourages me. This scripture speaks loads about being motivated to love my family by cleaning the house. God gave me a spirit of power so I can show my love to my family. He has given me self-discipline so I can be motivated to clean the house. For some reason the Depression Trail section I am walking on has been full of apathy and inability to do what I want to do like love on my family through cleaning.

Cleaning the house is a wonderful way I can show my love to my family, however it is difficult for me now. I haven't cleaned much in the last couple years. I have a tendency to be really hard on myself for not cleaning. I used to be really good at cleaning the house, but now I am just full of apathy. I am definitely out of the routine of cleaning. Several of my Fichus Trees died as a result of my neglect. It is a good thing my husband moved them out of house. They represented my neglect of my watering them. All the flat surfaces are cluttered with all kinds of stuff. I haven't dusted in a long time. I could go on and on about the neglect of the house, but that's not beneficial to getting better. This is an opportunity to try to think positive thoughts that would encourage myself vs. self-condemnation.

As I gaze at the clutter, I pray. How on earth can I tackle the mess and not feel overwhelmed? I asked my oldest daughter if she could help me get organized to clean the house. She made up a To Do List of cleaning that would take me around thirty minutes a day to clean each work day. I have a list of projects to tackle a little at a time. Hopefully cleaning the house a little each day and working on a project during the week will give me a sense of accomplishment.

One of my doctors asked me if I rewarded myself when I overcame depression. I caught the concept of rewarding myself and am applying it to cleaning my house. I purchased a cinnamon broom to make the house smell better. I bought some Celtic music to play while I clean. This helps me to focus on the blessing of life rather than the cluttered environment I'm working on. Cleaning has become a rewarding experience and a giant step in my healing.

Back to the Old Grind? Not Yet...

"O God, I'm so lethargic that I'm having a really hard time doing anything. I don't have the energy this week. I just want to quit again. I come to You and ask for the grace to clean my house by sticking with my daughter's cleaning list. It is light cleaning, and doing the cleaning should lift my mood."

It seems that the depression is haunting me again. The wind is out of my sail again. I have no desire to do anything except to sleep. When is this section of the Depression Trail going to end? For some reason I can't get into a healthy routine here on the home front. I believe that this is the time to seek God for the grace to have energy to do things outside of myself. I am going to go before the Lord during my meditation times to ask for grace to clean. I really want to love on my family by cooking and cleaning the house.

I am going to take each task one at a time, and reward myself. I hope this will help me to get in the habit of cleaning my house again. I want to love on my family in this way so they will receive my love in their hearts.

Fortunately, I told my psychiatrist about the apathy and the loss of wind in my sails. I have slept well at night and took five hour naps during the day! He changed one of my meds from morning to night time. I am starting to feel much better! No more naps, but I still have a hard time motivating myself to clean my house. I need to stop thinking about the work, and focus on how I can love my family with my actions.

Comforting Others

God has given me great comfort these last several years through many people and directly from His throne of grace. Now that I have experienced His comfort, it is now a wonderful opportunity to reach out and comfort others. Struggling with a major illness seems to be more common than I realized. I have found that my heart is full of so much compassion that I want to befriend hurting people. It appears that I can relate to people who struggle with both emotional and physical issues. So many people need to experience God's love and receive love from people who will comfort them with God's love. I want to be a servant of God and love on these hurting people. We are walking a common trail. I can just be myself and share God's love to these people. I never would have imagined myself walking this path on the Depression Trail with other people!

"O Lord, my heart is filled with tremendous love, more than I have experienced in my life time. I suppose this love comes from the love You, O Lord, and Your people showed me during my most desperate times. I have learned to love myself even during this deep depression. The low self-esteem was such a huge hurdle to overcome. This deep love has now changed my heart. I am more sensitive and compassionate towards people. Lord, help me to express this love to my family and all the people you put into my life."

Chapter 42

Thankfulness in This Present Moment

"Enter his gates with thanksgiving and his courts with praise;
give thanks to him and praise his name.
For the LORD is good and his love endures forever;
his faithfulness continues through all generations."
Psalm 100:4-5

God's Goodness in the Midst of Difficult Times

*h*ere are many things I can be thankful for but what I really want to focus on is being thankful in the present moment. This really helps me to fight depression. During the times of depression it is easy to focus on the negative things. Sometimes I even focus on things in the past that went wrong, or I think about the future when things might go wrong. Not good... I am learning to focus on what is happening right now in this moment. I have seen this skill in all my counseling sessions, and my Bible study group. Living in the present moment in prayer and with thankfulness has been a tremendous way to combat depression.

*"Be joyful **always**; pray **continually**; give thanks **in all circumstances**,*
for this is God's will for you in Christ Jesus."
1 Thessalonians 5:16-18

*"Sing and make music in your heart to the Lord, **always** giving*
thanks to God the Father for everything, in the name
of our Lord Jesus Christ."
Ephesians 5:19-20

I am so thankful for the grace and ability to sit in solitude with God and feel His peace descend upon me. During this time I experience visions of God's affectionate love. I need this so much right now. Throughout the years I have spent time in solitude with God while camping and while in my living room. God meets me any place that I choose to spend time with Him. Being close to God while waiting on Him and quieting my mind brings me to tremendous inner healing. Can I actually experience peace while depressed? I admit that experiencing the peace of God while depressed is a tremendous gift from God! I am so very thankful for His gift.

I want to thank the Lord for guiding me through the difficult recovery process. When I spend time with Him, I seem to be more sensitive to know which medical and life decisions to make. I can't imagine going through this season of depression without the wisdom of God guiding me.

I want to thank the Lord for being in control of everything in my life including family, friends, counselors, and psychiatrists, and other medical doctors. All these people have a great influence in my life right now. I want to discern God's will to know which ideas these people tell me are inspirations from Him. As I focus on God and embrace that He is in charge of everything, a spirit of thanksgiving begins to descend on me.

I feel thankful when I acknowledge that God is in absolute control of everything moment by moment. I try to be aware of His Presence and to trust that He is in control of everything all day long. Knowing that God is in control of my life helps me to release worries and frustrations. Giving God all the situations and responsibilities (I dump them in His lap) helps me to relax. This releases me to discern what is going on right now. I know that sometimes things appear to go wrong. Instead of focusing on the wrong which leads to depression, I focus on what is going right. This helps me to feel peaceful and thankful for everything that is happening in this present moment.

Today, I have been thankful for lots of things. Here are some specific things that I am thankful for: a refreshing night sleep, a meaningful quiet time with God, healthy food to eat, a refreshing walk in the morning while soaking in the beauty of the nature around me with the flowers and singing birds. I am thankful for God's grace to write, the opportunity to help a friend who also suffers from depression, receiving a phone call from a new friend, and a good counseling session. I have many other smaller things I'm thankful for such as a yummy mug of flavored decaf coffee and my two cuddling dogs. I try to live moment by moment and be thankful for everything around me.

Thankfulness is a great gift from God that helps me to overcome depression. It helps me to stop ruminating on negative thinking. I have to admit that at times when I am depressed; it is hard to be thankful. This is the time to do things that will help me to be happy. I apply the Distract skills such as go on a walk, listen to music, or take a bubble bath. I then focus on thanksgiving again. I love to spend quiet time in God's Presence and focus on the good things in my life. As I draw near to God and feel His unconditional love, I am overcome with thanksgiving.

Chapter 43

Demonstrations of God's Love

"Dear friends, let us love one another, for love comes from God.
Everyone who loves has been born of God and knows God.
Whoever does not love does not know God, because God is love.
This is how God showed his love among us: He sent his one and
only Son into the world that we might live through him. This is
love: not that we loved God, but that he loved us and sent his
Son as an atoning sacrifice for our sins. Dear friends, since God
so loved us, we also ought to love one another. No one has ever
seen God; but if we love one another, God lives in us and his love
is made complete in us."
1 John 4:7-12

An Expression of Gratitude for the Network of Support

*M*y journey in this season of depression started ten years ago, but I believe that the journey toward inner healing became more real after getting off psychiatric medication two years. That was the beginning of experiencing my whole range of emotions. My exuberant highs and extreme lows colored my life and affected all the people around me, especially my husband. ECT helped stabilize me enough so I could function and work on managing my emotions through the skills taught in DBT. However the most important part of my recovery is the growth in my relationship with the Lord. As I spend time with the Lord in quietness, this gave me the grace to trust that God is providing whatever is needed to help me on the next step on the journey toward emotional healing.

As I ride the huge waves of emotions, I find that I need so much support. I want to be independent like I once was, but that's not where I'm at right now. The Lord has given me a large network of people for support,

257

and I want to share my gratitude. So many people have spoken into my life and have helped me so many ways I wonder if it isn't God Himself reaching in my heart. May God strengthen all of you wonderful people greatly and bless you in your walk with our loving God.

The first person I want to express my appreciation for is my wonderful husband. He has exhibited so much of God's unconditional love to me that it has given me a deep realization that God's love is way beyond my greatest imagination! He has transported me to the hospital emergency room repeatedly without getting mad at me for the tremendous inconvenience. He frequently visited me when I was in the hospital. He has transported me to many treatments of ECT. He doesn't get mad when we get the hospital bills either. He just loves me and wants to take good care of me. He supports me nonjudgmentally when I have emotional meltdowns. I feel no condemnation from him, just His tender love. He is nonjudgmental attitude offers guidance to help me make decisions about my medical and spiritual support. He reaches out tenderly and strokes me to help my mind to settle into God's peace. He talks tenderly about me to the children. He is just an awesome example of God's deep love.

Now I want to express my appreciation to my five wonderful daughters. It has not been easy for all of you having a mother that suffers from major depression and borderline personality disorder. I home schooled three of you for twelve years. I was your mother, counselor, spiritual teacher, academic teacher, social organizer, as well as many other roles. I was everything in your lives for years, the *super mom*, but one day that changed. I got very sick and was unable to perform any of these motherly roles. My love for you had not diminished but my ability to express my love had. God supplied many people to take my place in your lives but this was a very difficult transition for all of you. Despite the tremendous hardship, you still loved me and gave me hugs. God has reached down in each of your lives and given you victory during the difficult time. You are now all thriving where God has planted you. My two younger girls probably don't remember the *super mom* era. They only remember the depression as an emotional rollercoaster, yet their love and acceptance for me is very evident of God's grace. My husband has stepped into their lives in a big way, and now these girls are two of the happiest girls I know. Their contentment is beyond comprehension. Thank you Jesus!

I want to express my gratitude for my most beloved neighbor. I knew her because my daughter and her daughter were best friends. Ten years ago when I had the breakdown she ministered to me in so many ways. One way she showed her love was by lining up meals for my family for over three months. She helped me get lined up with my psychiatrist who wasn't taking new patients! She contacted the high school our girls attended and they purchased many presents for under our Christmas tree! She befriended me and had me over to her house many times. She was such a gem!

The next person I want to express my appreciation for is my psychiatrist. I have seen him since the beginning of the breakdown ten years ago. At the beginning when I needed him, he wasn't taking any new patients, yet he accepted me anyway. Thank you very much! He has the best bedside manners of any doctor I know. Now that I have met many psychiatrists, I realize his tenderness and compassion are rare attributes among his peers in the field of psychiatry. He not only is very knowledgeable with psychiatric drugs, but he can effectively communicate what he knows to his patients. It is these qualities that have helped me to trust his judgment about my psychiatric care. I have the freedom to be real with him without feeling judged or condemned. He has filled out hours of paper work for social security benefits and the ECT. I am so grateful for his very supportive staff, the physician's assistant, the counselors, and the receptionists.

The next people I want to thank are the many hospital psychiatrists that helped me this last year. I want to thank the hospital psychiatrists for encouraging me to not go in the hospital again and directing me to do DBT. My ECT psychiatrist really encouraged me to do DBT. I want to thank the latest hospital psychiatrist. She encouraged me to not go in the hospital again too. Instead, she encouraged me to continue to embrace DBT. Imagine that! God spoke through three psychiatrists about DBT. I really believe that the Lord spoke through these doctors.

I want to express my gratitude to the staff where I had ECT. At first, I had eight treatments of ECT with the addition of medicine. The medication caused emotional havoc in my life and I ended up in the hospital again. Later, I started Maintenance ECT. I want to thank the ECT doctor for helping me experience my emotions again by helping me get off my psych meds. This opened up the door to embracing DBT. It was very helpful except for the effect on my short term memory issues. When the doctor spaced the ECT to ten days, the depression started coming back. Sigh... Not again. Is there anything that will get rid of the depression? Apparently not. Now I am off all psychiatric drugs and on Maintenance ECT. That only works when I have treatment a week apart. Right now I just finished my sixteenth treatment and I have many more treatments left for at least three more months. All the staff – the psychiatrists, the nurse practitioner, and all the nurses have been so nice and supporting. I am so grateful that they have shown so much kindness.

It is later and I am off ECT and I got suicidal again so now I have had a new doctor at the new psych hospital I was in. She along with the other doctors wanted me to apply the DBT skills to keep myself out of the hospital. She had me order a DBT workbook. She was so encouraging and really lifted my spirit. She put me on so new medication. It is working! I haven't been in crisis for over three weeks! This is huge!

Now I want to express my appreciation to my first counselor who supported and guided me for the eight years. She helped me through my most desperate times. I remember her telling in our first session that she saw me as a much worn out tapestry with Jesus faded picture woven in it. She informed me that I was experiencing a physical, emotional, and spiritual breakdown. I had lost my voice for three months from a sinus infection. I couldn't function at all emotionally. I could only retreat to my room to be alone and my bed was inviting me every moment of every day. I was so suicidal at that time that I had no connection to Jesus. My faith was void. Oh, this was a dark time in my life! She reached into my broken heart and with Jesus' help patched it back together. She directed me back to Jesus and encouraged me to journal. My journals during the first three years after the breakdown were full of love conversations with Jesus. My counselor read all my writing during her off time! She loved on me so much that I was drawn back to my Savior and back to being able to function again. I want to share one principle that she worked so hard to help me embrace; God loves me for who I *am*, not what I *do*. During that time I couldn't function by doing anything and my self-esteem was zero. I had learned to perform for love my whole life. She spent session after session helping me realize that I don't have to perform for Jesus' love. He loves me for who I am, even all broken down with depression. This was huge!

I had another counselor for a short while who guided me in the Exchanged Life Principle. She showed me insight into the lies I was hearing from Satan during my childhood, and helped me replace those lies with truth from God's Word. She shared scripture after scripture of who I am in Christ. I still need to embrace these truths. She definitely showed me God's unconditional love. Thank you.

I want to express my appreciation for my first DBT counselor. He is so compassionate and encouraging. He tenderly guides me with skills that help me learn to manage my emotions. It is definitely an uphill battle. He is available for phone support in between the weekly sessions when I have those emotional meltdowns. Sigh... He never seems to tire from my calls. He tells me that he is very encouraged with my progress. Most of the time, it is hard for me to see any progress. I suppose that is the depression masking the truth. Thank you for your unending loving support.

I have two wonderful DBT group therapists that are helping me learn to manage my emotions. They have been so supportive even between groups. One of them responds to my emails with great sensitivity and wisdom. She returns my desperate phone calls for additional help. Thank you very much.

My last DBT counselor moved away so now I am going to a new DBT counselor. She could tell that I have learned and am applying many DBT skills. The good news is that I'm not in crisis these days but she told me that if I go into crisis to give her a call. She is very knowledgeable about how to use DBT in my life. Thank you, Lord, for supplying my needs.

I have a new medical doctor who is treating the depression as if physical problems can cause problems emotionally. She has treated the yeast. She also wrote out prescriptions for yeast medicine, medicine for my adrenal glands, thyroid medication, and OTC medicine for my digestive system. I am now on a diet that hopefully will make me healthy. I have cut out the foods that cause inflammation such as dairy, wheat, artificial sugar, and pork. These changes have really helped me feel better and at this time I have lost forty pounds! Not only is this doctor helping me physically but she encourages me during my visits.

I have a wonderful chiropractor who adjusts my back to help me be in the best possible health so I can get over the depression. Thank you so much.

I have had tremendous support from God's ministers as well. The first person I want to thank is my old pastor's wife. She suffered from depression during an earlier season in her life and offered such comforting words that helped me accept that I wasn't alone in this journey. Thank you. My Associate Pastor struggled with depression years ago as well. He has supported my husband and me the last nine years with great wisdom and comfort. I am so grateful for a man reaching out and guiding my husband while he had to take on the household manager position when I first got sick. He has stuck to our sides all these years with tremendous patience, understanding, and wisdom. God also gave me a wonderful melancholy pastor. His heart is so pure and tender toward the Lord. He is on a path towards growing more intimate with God through times of solitude. God has given me insight through the words he shares directly with me, through his blogs on the computer, as well as through the messages from the pulpit on Sundays.

"O Lord, thank you for encouraging me through this man of God."

I have four sacred sisters I have known for over thirty years. They have been such great support as well. They love me deeply and faithfully pray for me. A couple of them call to check up on me then spread the word to the other ladies. They speak with wisdom from God Almighty and encourage me in this journey.

Now that is not all the support I have; God has provided many saints in the Body of Christ who have supported me as well. I cannot forget my dearest friend. Right after we joined Grace Church eight years ago, she approached me before the service. She asked me the same old question everyone asks, "How are you?" I said, "Fine." I really wasn't fine and she knew it. She then asked me, "How are you really?" Of course that question opened Pandora's Box and I started crying. She then asked me, "Do you have any friends?" I answered, "No." I had been feeling very lonely since we just joined this new church. She became my first friend at Grace Church and was not intimidated by my depression. She was available all the time for support, but more importantly then that, I was able to support her in her difficult walk with her health problems with Lupus and struggles with family life. Our friendship grew deeply through the years. I was filled with grief when God took her home a year ago. She is no longer suffering and is in Jesus' Presence all the time now!

God gave me a new best friend. She is a retired social worker therefore is not intimidated by the depth of emotions I now experience. When I am really struggling, she is available to help me. She meets me at the restaurant Tea Fusion with several friends once a week for fellowship. I need this time away from home to be with my friends. I am encouraged to hear what God is doing in their lives. One of my friends is a writer like me. Her poems show her deep love for God, and she has such a warm heart for God's people. She is so humble, and has such a good listening ear. Our childhood was similar, and our children are approximately the same age. We have encouraged each other in our walk with the Lord many times. I have another dear friend who visits with us at Tea Fusion. She is learning skills to win her struggle with her depression, and is such an encouragement to me. She shares insights from scripture that has helped her on her journey. One such verse is *"Your word is a lamp to my feet and a light to my path"* Psalm 119:105. Sometimes there is only enough light for the immediate step in front of you. The rest of the path requires faith. Thank you, my friend, for this insight.

One of my best friends is full of love and has tremendous wisdom. In fact, her love for the Lord is astounding and such an inspiration to me. The Lord has used her for guidance and encouragement. She helps people from the depth of love from her heart. She is full of wisdom and can help people in the difficult times in their lives, including me. She connects me to other believers in Christ who provide spiritual strength with compassion and mercy in the midst of my depression.

God with His rich provision has supplied even another friend for support! I am amazed at the tremendous love she has. My friend has suffered from depression so therefore is a great encouragement to me when I seem to descend into suicide depression. I don't have to travel this road alone anymore and end up in the hospital. She comes by the house and sits and visits with me when I probably shouldn't be alone. Her words of understanding and tremendous faith always encourage me to dig down and grasp my faith in Jesus and get back in the Lord's Presence.

There are other people in the Body of Christ who have crossed my path on this journey through depression for which I am grateful. My two home school friends taught my children right after I got sick, and before we transitioned them into the school system. Many wonderful women took care of my children after school hours since I couldn't take care of them. The great number of women from my church and the my friend's church, home school mothers, parents from the high school swim team, and many more who prepared meals for our family for over a three month period! The people in my 242 group (also known as a home group or cell group) have supported me all through the years with many prayers, meals, phone support, and visits. The parents of my children's friends have loved me too. The teachers and counselors at the public school have shown their love. The list goes on and on. God has poured out His amazing love to me through a vast network of support. Thank you Jesus!

"Lord, thank you for providing the Peaches Women's Group at church." This is a Bible Study group that helps us to focus on Jesus. I learned more mindfulness concepts that encouraged me to accept and really embrace the concept of mindfulness. I found out it is also a Christian concept. I now have many friends at church which is very good for a social person.

Expressing Gratitude to God for the Depression!

Now comes the greatest challenge for me, can I thank God for this depression, anxiety, and emotional turmoil? He has provided a network of tender loving people to support me. This I am grateful for, but can I be grateful for the depression itself? One of the manifestations of God's grace is thanksgiving.

It has been at least ten years of riding the emotional rollercoaster of depression. I was mad at God most of the time, but now that time has passed, I have become much closer to God. His tenderness and acceptance has caused the anger to dissipate. I now know that God loves me unconditionally and I'm learning to love myself unconditionally as well. This is an awesome concept—full of love and mercy. God's love brings a tremendous peace into my heart.

"Lord, as I think about the emotional turmoil and misery I have felt off and on through the years, it has been extremely hard to be grateful for it. At first I was very mad, but now it is beginning to get easier to thank You. As I sit in Your Presence and draw close to You, I realize that I am experiencing the tremendous depth of Your love for me. You have given me visions of when You expressed Your love to me by wrapping Your arms around me. You speak the words "I love you" deep in my spirit during my saddest times. These visions have never left my mind, even with the ECT effecting my memory. Lord, You loved me in the darkness and lifted my spirit and gave me hope."

"Thank You, Jesus, for what You have done in my life during these difficult times. I am definitely closer to You now. This proves to me that trials and tribulation can draw people closer to You. You are with me in the good times as well as the difficult times. Thank You for helping me to find Your grace during the difficult times. Thank You for giving me the grace to draw closer to You during times of discouragement when I had set backs and repeated hospitalizations. You gave me hope to trust You, even though it seemed like I was never going to get better. You helped me to spend time with You even though sometimes I had so much anger toward You. Your Presence diffused the anger and my love for You returned. You always reached out to me in the desperate times and brought healing to my inner being."

"You are truly awesome to me, Lord, and I really mean that! Thank you for reaching down from heaven and touching my heart during these really tough times. Thank you for being a REAL God! Your Presence is healing me moment by moment."

"Lord, You give me tremendous hope that helps me overcome discouragement and despair. This hope gives me a deep desire to keep up the fight to become emotionally healthy one day. Thank you Jesus."

"NOTHING CAN SEPARATE YOU from My Love. Let this divine assurance trickle through your mind and into your heart and soul. Whenever you start to feel fearful or anxious, repeat this unconditional promise: "Nothing can separate me from Your Love, Jesus"" (Young, 2004, p. 224).

Chapter 44

Loving Hurting People like Jesus Loves Me

"Who can take away suffering without entering into it? The great illusion of leadership is to think that others can be led out of the desert by someone who has never been there" (Nouwen).

We all have been wounded. Let us take that woundedness and allow God to use it for His balm of healing in the lives of all those who cross our path... our realm of influence... and point them to Christ!" (Byrne, 2011)

"Lord, I have been feeling so much better, and I have an intense desire to love Your hurting people You put in my life. I'm not a lone island unto myself, but You are healing me so I may share the message of Your merciful love and healing to others. There are many people who need this message, and I want to be the person sharing Your love with them. I am learning to be constantly aware of Your Presence even during the affliction of depression. Your Presence has become more real than I thought possible. You are loving me and healing me. Jesus, I love You so very much, and am blessed to be a recipient of Your intimate love to pass on to others."

I thought about passing on God's grace to others, I realize that I am a spiritual mentor, not a counselor. Fear gripped my heart momentarily. I don't have official training, but I have real life experience which is being expressed with compassion for others. I want to pass on the grace of God through the mercy He has shown me. I know that God poured out His grace for healing when I sat in His Presence. As I thought about the calling of God, I felt very insecure. The Lord reassured me that I am equipped to help people enter into healing by coming into God's Presence to the throne of Grace. I am a teacher and have taught children how to enter the throne room of grace. God has equipped me both as a teacher of academic subjects and as a spiritual teacher. God has graced me with the ability to help adults enter into God's Presence and feel the Healer's touch deep in their spirit. This is what I have a deep desire to do. I understand emotional pain as well as have experienced the touch of God's Healing love deep within my spirit.

Many people with emotional problems need an encounter with God's Spirit. They don't feel loved and some feel unlovable. *"O Lord, I can't imagine they pain they suffer. Jesus, You want me to share Your love to those people who are hurting."* I know, without a doubt, that Jesus wants me to reach out to these people. God has given me a wonderful message of love to share. I have experienced God's unconditional love while experiencing suicidal depression. God reached down from heaven and loved me during my most desperate times which lead to many psychiatric hospitalizations. Jesus loved me when I was desperate and became angry at Him. He lovingly forgives and unconditionally loves me.

"O God, I am deeply moved in my spirit by these memories. Your love is incomprehensible to the human mind, but Your intimate unconditional love is what eventually brought healing from the depression. You touched me in my heart and spirit. Thank You, Jesus!"

This passage from 2 Corinthians has been so comforting over the last two years that I want to put it in this book twice. God has given me hope for my future. He has given me a purpose for the depression in my life. God wants me to comfort others who are having trouble with the comfort He gave me. I do have a purpose for my life. Thank You, Jesus!

"Praise be to the God and Father of our Lord Jesus Christ, the Father of compassion and the God of all comfort, who comforts us in all our troubles, so that we can comfort those in any trouble with the comfort we ourselves have received from God. For just as the sufferings of Christ flow over into our lives, so also through Christ our comfort overflows. If we are distressed, it is for your comfort and salvation; if we are comforted, it is for your comfort, which produces in you patient endurance of the same sufferings we suffer. And our hope for you is firm, because we know that just as you share in our sufferings, so also you share in our comfort."

2 Corinthians 1:3-7

An Opportunity to Express My Compassion!

It has been over six months since I've written in this chapter. God is opening up an opportunity to comfort those in trouble with the comfort I have received from God. It is awesome! I feel so compassionate about helping because of all the depression and mood swings I have been through. God has put five people in my life. I am having a group in my home titled *"Abiding in Christ," A Group for Those in a Desperate Place.* God is using my gift of teaching and love for music to reach their heart. These gifts that God has developed in my life are not lost forever.

"O thank You, Jesus. Help me to encourage and inspire Your people to spend time with You. Only You, O Lord, can bring healing to their lives. Let me be an instrument to draw them You. Thank You, Jesus. I am yours, O Lord. Help me to walk through the doors of opportunity to reach Your people. I really want to touch people's lives with Your love. I want to lead them to Your Cross."

Chapter 45

Praising the God of Mercy!

Mercy Triumphs Once Again!

> *"I will praise the LORD, who counsels me;*
> *even at night my heart instructs me.*
> *I have set the LORD always before me.*
> *Because he is at my right hand,*
> *I will not be shaken.*
> *Therefore my heart is glad and my tongue rejoices;*
> *my body also will rest secure,*
> *because you will not abandon me to the grave,*
> *nor will you let your Holy One see decay.*
> *You have made known to me the path of life;*
> *you will fill me with joy in your presence,*
> *with eternal pleasures at your right hand."*
> Psalm 16:7-11

"*Lord, I praise You, Lord, for being so merciful to me. You have loved me with a forgiving love that is taking the depression away. As the depression leaves, You are giving me inner peace, happiness, and love for You and the people around me. Lord, You are most certainly the God that heals, but You do it in Your way and in Your timing. Lord, walking on this Depression Trail has caused my heart to be filled with so much compassion. Gone is the critical judgmental spirit, Lord. You have changed the way I think in a big way. Jesus, You are awesome; I thank You for transforming my heart.*"

l l I want to do is praise Jesus. His mercy is incredible. His compassion is limitless, and He loves me even though at times that I am filled with so much distress that I get filled with anger at Him. I hate to admit, but I even tried to deny God's very existence. The truth is that I can't deny my God who has patiently endured me through all my crazy moods over the years. I love Him so much! He is healing me after ten long years of suffering from depression. I am feeling His peace deep in my heart, and His love surrounds me like a blanket. He fills me with His warmth in my heart. God's love is very real, especially when I have the intense mood swings. He still loves me. God's love is not contingent on my emotional state. He loves me no matter how I am feeling, even when I'm mad at Him. This is amazing! It is God's merciful love that is bringing healing to my mind.

Experiencing God's Mercy during a Relapse!

I hate to admit it but I have relapses into depression. This gives me an opportunity to embrace the Lord's mercy. Remember, The Lord forgives me all of the times I give up and deny His very existence. He forbears with me when I am in despair. He is moved with compassion and loves me to the depth of my being.

My heart is bubbling over with gratitude, and I am happy most of the time. Going from severe depression to inner peace and happiness is a miraculous change.

"Thank You, Jesus, for healing me. I ask You, my Lord, heal me in such a way that the depression will be gone forever."

As I write that prayer, I realize that any depression that I might feel could be a reminder of Jesus' love for me. This is powerful! The depression that I have suffered from has brought me closer to Jesus. Any moments of relapse into depression are reminders of God's unconditional love! Every time I was at the bottom condemning myself Jesus was showering His love on me.

"Jesus, You have empowered me to learn many life lessons this last two years. Even when the emotional pain was unbearable, You taught me skills to quiet my mind so I can experience Your love and peace once again. You, O God, delivered me from the depression and made me well. Thank You so much!"

My life has been transformed. The depression was severe, but God's love triumphed. I spent hours in God's Presence with the intense desire for God's peace to encompass my heart. God helped me discern His will concerning major decisions in my life. There were important medical decisions to make; I wanted to have some idea what He was doing. I wanted to know what God's will was concerning the types of treatments the psychiatrists had for me. I had some apprehension, but to overcome the fear I spent more time sitting in God's Presence. As I experienced His intimate love, the fear dissipated and peace entered my soul. The treatments with psychiatric drugs and Electroconvulsive Therapy (ECT) are serious steps to undergo. As I waited on God, He guided my husband and me to make the right choice for what He was doing in my life at that time. I had to apply what I was taught in my group therapy and individual counseling. It took the power of God to help me apply what I learned in my counseling sessions. This is no small matter considering depression makes me not want to do anything. *"You are awesome Lord. You, O Lord, are healing me!"*

One of the most dramatic changes in my life is that I am like Mary from the Bible who sat at Jesus' feet. Before, I was a Martha who went around *doing many good things*. A good friend at church observed that I am like Mary. This is a huge change! Now I sit in Jesus' Presence for hours every day. I love Him so much. I am so grateful!

"O Lord, You are so merciful. You had compassion and forbearance with me during my emotional upheavals this last ten years. I have received your mercy, and it has changed my life forever. Please, Lord, give me grace when I have relapses. I know that You still love me. I'm not only Your child, but I am Your good friend."

"As I come into Your Presence, O Lord, You continue to change me on the inside. You are healing me because of Your great mercies. Thank You so much, Lord. Let me always proclaim Your goodness to the people You bring into my life. Thank You so much for delivering me from the depression! Let this healing last the rest of my life time. You not only healed me, but You completely transformed my thinking and way of life. I no longer need to perform for acceptance, and I have embraced resting in Your Presence while absorbing Your love and mercy. This is huge! I have been transformed from the inside—out. You changed me from a stress filled life to having deep inner peace. You have been so merciful to me. You heard my cry for help, and Your life changing mercy was granted to me! THANK YOU!"

"Praise be to the LORD,
for he has heard my cry for mercy.
The LORD is my strength and my shield;
my heart trusts in him, and I am helped.
My heart leaps for joy
and I will give thanks to him in song."
Psalm 28:6-7

Glossary

CB radio	A Citizens' band radio, a short-wave radio used to communicate individuals. In the 70's they were widespread among truckers.
Cognitive Behavior Therapy	(CBT) a form of psychotherapy that emphasizes the important role of thinking in how we feel and what we do. It is a treatment that focuses on patterns of thinking that are maladaptive and the beliefs that underlie such thinking.
Cursillo	A ministry of the Roman Catholic Church. A Cursillo is a 3-day retreat. The weekend includes fifteen talks, some given by priests and some by lay people.
ECT	Electroconvulsive Therapy, shock therapy used to treat severe depression
God's Living Room	The great outdoors where nature resides, the wilderness
Grace	The free unmerited love and favor of God
God's Presence	Drawing near to God through meditation is an excellent way to experience God's Presence. During this quiet time, God's Presence pours down from heaven to fill us with His peace and joy deep in our spirit.
Mindfulness	Living in the present moment with a nonjudgmental attitude.
Mindfulness Meditation	Sitting quietly while focusing on clearing the mind of thoughts and emotions.

	Meditation is a great way to draw close to the Lord.
p.r.n.	Take the prescription as needed
Rumination	A way of responding to distress that involves repeatedly thinking on the symptoms, causes, and consequences of distress.
Solitude	A time spent alone with God while quieting the mind with the intent to draw close to the Lord.
Snag	A tree or a part of a tree that protrudes above the ground

Bibliography

Barton, R. (2004). *Invitation to Solitude and Silence*, Downers Grove IL: InterVarsity Press.

Byrne, Nancy, (2011). *Woundedness*, (www.takeeverythoughtcaptive. blogspot.com, Craving Soul).

Dietz, L. (2003, November 14). Dialectical Behavior Therapy. Retrieved from (www.dbtselfhelp.com).

Emotions Anonymous, (2001), *Shame* [Brochure]. St. Paul, MN.

Kabat-Zinn, J. (2007). *Guided Meditation Practices for The Mindful Way through Depression*. New York, NY: Guilford Publications, Inc.

Linehan, M. (1993). *Skills training manual for treating borderline personality disorder*. New York, NY: The Guilford Press.

Nouwen, H. (1979) *Wounded Healer, Ministry in a Contemporary Society*. New York, NY: An Image Books, Doubleday.

Ruskin, J. (1925) *Quoted by L. B Cowman's Streams in the desert*. Los Angeles, CA: Cowman Publications.

Tada, J. (1976). *Joni, an unforgettable story*. Michigan: Zondervan.

Williams, Mark , Teasdale, Zindel, Kabat-Zinn. (2007) *The Mindful Way through Depression.* New York, NY: The Guildford Press.

Young, S. (2004). *Jesus calling*. Nashville, TN: Thomas Nelson, Inc.

CPSIA information can be obtained
at www.ICGtesting.com
Printed in the USA
LVOW11s2110130817
544853LV00001B/84/P

9 781622 304714